MODERNIZATION

MODERN

MYRON WEINER

EDITOR

IZATION

THE DYNAMICS
OF GROWTH

BASIC BOOKS, INC.

PUBLISHERS

New York / London

Preface

These essays were originally prepared as lectures for Forum, an educational radio program sponsored by the Voice of America for broadcast throughout the world. They represent the efforts of twenty-five American scholars to present their reflections on the most challenging problem of the twentieth century—how modernization occurs and how it can be accelerated.

Though we all use it, the term "modernization" is an elusive one. In the nineteenth and early twentieth centuries, "modernization" was generally used to refer to the growth of rationality and secularism and to a process by which men broke away from the constraints of tyrannical regimes as well as the constraints of superstition. Today the term "modernization" is often used simply as another word for economic growth or as a more palatable synonym for still another elusive concept, "westernization." Because the term is so loosely used, it is tempting to drop it entirely and to speak more precisely of changes occurring in individual attitudes, in social behavior, in economics, and in politics. But scholars persist in using the term not only because it is a part of popular speech, but also because they recognize that these many changes are related to one another—that many countries in the developing world are today experiencing a comprehensive process of change which Europe and America once experienced and which is more than the sum of many small changes.

What are these changes, how are they related, how do we study them, how can these changes be hastened? These are among some of the most difficult questions facing both social scientists and policy-makers. As coordinator of this lecture series, I have tried to select some of the most important aspects of modernization in an effort to provide the listener—and the reader—with a comprehensive view and to invite as participants some of the country's leading social scientists studying modernization. The scholars who have prepared these lectures have wrestled with these questions; many have combined their scholarly interest in modernization with an active role as consultants to governments and foundations concerned with accelerating the modernization process.

Obviously these talks have not been able to treat all aspects of modernization, and, given the need for brevity and simplicity, the contributors have only been able to make limited incursions into subjects on which they and others have written at greater length. For those who want to study further, other writings on modernization by the contributors are listed in the respective capsule biographies in the section entitled "The Authors."

I wish to take this opportunity to express my appreciation to Theodore Wertime, director of Forum, who made this series possible, and to Nancy Weber and Helaine Levi for their editorial assistance.

MYRON WEINER

Cambridge, Mass.
February 1966

The Authors

C. Arnold Anderson is Director of the Comparative Education Center and Professor of Education and Sociology at the University of Chicago. He holds a B.A., M.A., and Ph.D. from the University of Minnesota. He was an instructor at Harvard in the early 1930's, was appointed assistant professor at Iowa State, and was a professor at the University of Kentucky before coming to Chicago. He has also been a visiting professor at Harvard, at the University of California at Berkeley, and at Uppsala in Sweden. He has written extensively on social mobility and social change and on comparative education and in recent years has focused on educational problems in the developing areas. He is the co-editor of *Education and Economic Development*.

Leonard Binder is Professor and chairman of the Department of Political Science at the University of Chicago. A graduate of Harvard University, where he was a John Harvard Fellow, he spent several years in Oriental studies at Princeton and Oxford before returning to Harvard for his Ph.D. in Political Science. After four years of teaching at the University of California at Los Angeles, Professor Binder joined the University of Chicago, where he continues his research, writing, and teaching on the Middle East. He is the author of *Religion and Politics in Pakistan, Iran: Political Development in a Changing Society*, and *The Ideological Revolution in the Middle East*. He has recently been engaged in research on Egypt and Lebanon.

Cyril Edwin Black is Duke Professor of Russian History at Princeton University. Professor Black spent his boyhood in Turkey and Bulgaria, attending the American College in Bulgaria before re-

turning to the United States to take his B.A. at Duke University
and his M.A. and Ph.D. at Harvard. He has since been at Princeton where he has established his reputation as one of the leading
scholars of Russian and East European history. Professor Black
has served as a member of American and United Nations Missions
concerned with Eastern and Southern Europe. He has authored
and edited *Communism and Revolution, Rewriting Russian History, Transformation of Russian Society, Russia on the Eve of
War and Revolution,* and *Twentieth-Century Europe.*

RALPH BRAIBANTI is Professor of Political Science and chairman of the
Committee on Commonwealth Studies at Duke University. After
receiving his Ph.D. from Syracuse University, he served as adviser to the Civil Administrator of the Ryukyu Islands. In recent
years, he served as the chief adviser to the Civil Service Academy
of Pakistan and has been a consultant to the Governmental
Affairs Institute, the National War College, and the Agency for
International Development. He joined Duke University in 1953.
Professor Braibanti's writings reflect his long experience in administration in developing societies. He is co-author and co-editor of
*Tradition, Values and Socio-Economic Development, Administra-
tion and Economic Development in India, and Asian Bureaucratic
Systems Emergent from the British Imperial Tradition* and is au-
thor of *Research on the Bureaucracy of Pakistan.*

MARC GALANTER is Assistant Professor in the Social Sciences at the
University of Chicago. He graduated from Chicago with a B.A. in
the social sciences and went on to secure his M.A. in philosophy
and Doctor of Jurisprudence at the Law School, where he was
associate editor of the *Law Review.* He began teaching at the
Chicago Law School, but was drawn into Stanford University's
International Legal Studies Program as assistant director. He subsequently returned to Chicago, where he now specializes in comparative law. Professor Galanter has been a visiting scholar in
England and India and has organized a conference on South Asian
law. He has published a number of articles on legal systems and
social change in India.

ALEXANDER GERSCHENKRON is Walter S. Barker Professor of Economics
at Harvard University. He was born in Russia and completed his
Ph.D. in economic history at the University of Vienna, Austria.

After coming to the United States, he joined the Department of Economics at the University of California in 1938. He subsequently became a staff member of the Board of Governors of the Federal Reserve System and then chief of its Foreign Affairs section. He has lectured at George Washington University and been a visiting professor at the University of California. He joined the Harvard faculty in 1948. His scholarly studies include *Bread and Democracy in Germany, A Dollar Index of Soviet Machinery Output, Economic Relations with the USSR,* and *Economic Backwardness in Historical Perspective.*

NORTON GINSBURG is Professor of Geography at the University of Chicago. Holder of the B.A., M.A., and Ph.D. degrees from that university, he also attended the U. S. Navy Japanese Language School at the University of Colorado during the war and ultimately served in China both for the Navy and for the Department of State. Professor Ginsburg has been a member of the Joint Committee on Contemporary China and the Committee on Urbanization of the Social Science Research Council during his active career. He has pioneered in the study of the geographical aspects of economic development, including work on regional planning and urbanization. Secretary of the Association of American Geographers, he also has edited the Association's *Annals.* He is author and editor of a number of books including *Malaya, Essays on Geography and Economic Development, Atlas of Economic Development,* and *The Pattern of Asia.*

ALEX INKELES is Professor of Sociology at Harvard University and Director of Studies on Social and Cultural Aspects of Development at Harvard's Center for International Affairs. He combines an interest and expertise in the sociology of Soviet society as well as in the developing areas. He holds a B.A. and M.A. from Cornell University and a Ph.D. from Columbia University and has studied at the Washington School for Psychiatry as well as at the Boston Psychoanalytic Institute. As an outgrowth of an intensive program of interviewing refugees from the Soviet Union, Professor Inkeles published several well-known studies: *Public Opinion in Soviet Russia, Soviet Citizen,* and *Soviet Society.* He has spent a year at the Center for Advanced Study in the Behavioral Sciences at Palo Alto and is a member of the American Academy of Arts and Sciences and chairman of the section on Social Psychology of the American Sociological Society.

RICHARD D. LAMBERT is Professor in the Sociology Department and in the South Asia Regional Studies Department of the University of Pennsylvania. A graduate of the University of Indiana, he was awarded his M.A. and Ph.D. by the University of Pennsylvania. He has spent his entire career teaching at the University of Pennsylvania, except for two years when he served as resident director of the American Institute of Indian Studies at Poona. He is the associate editor of *Annals*, a publication of the American Academy of Political and Social Science and has been chairman of the Committee on South Asia and a member of the Board of Directors of the Association for Asian Studies. He was Director of a UNESCO project on *The Role of Savings and Wealth in Southern Asia and the West* and was Director of a study of Indian students at the University of Pennsylvania, which resulted in the publication of *Indian Students on an American Campus*. He has conducted research in India since 1949, and his scholarly writings on India include *Workers, Factories and Social Change in India* and *Resources for South Asian Area Studies in the United States* (editor).

JOSEPH LAPALOMBARA is Professor of Political Science at Yale University. He holds a B.A. and M.A. from the University of Illinois and an M.A. and Ph.D. from Princeton. He has taught at Oregon State University and at Michigan State University, where he was chairman of the Department of Political Science from 1958 to 1963. He is well known for his research in comparative bureaucracies and for his work on Italian politics. He is the author of *Guide to Michigan Politics, The Italian Labor Movement: Problems and Prospects,* and *Interest Groups in Italian Politics;* co-editor of *Elezioni e Comportamento Politico in Italia* and *Political Parties and Political Development;* and editor of *Bureaucracy and Political Development.* Professor LaPalombara has lived and conducted research in Western Europe and traveled extensively in Asia. He has also spent a year as a Fellow at the Center for Advanced Study in the Behavioral Sciences at Palo Alto.

DAVID C. MCCLELLAND is Professor of Psychology and chairman of the Department of Social Relations at Harvard University. He received his B.A. from Wesleyan University, his M.A. from the University of Missouri, and his Ph.D. from Yale. Professor McClelland taught first at Connecticut College for Women; joined the faculty of Wesleyan University, became chairman of its Psychology Department; and was appointed to Harvard in 1956.

He has been Deputy Director of the Behavioral Science Division of the Ford Foundation and has served as chairman of the Fulbright Advisory Panel on Psychology. He has also been associated with programs of the Social Science Research Council and the National Institute of Mental Health. Professor McClelland is well known for his pioneering experimental research on the "need to achieve." He is the author or co-author of *The Achieving Society, The Achievement Motive, Personality, Roots of Consciousness,* and *Motives in Fantasy, Action and Society* and editor of *Studies in Motivation* and *Talent and Society.* He is a fellow of the American Academy of Sciences and has had long association with the American Friends Service Committee in its overseas work.

MAX F. MILLIKAN is Professor of Economics and director of the Center for International Studies at M.I.T. He holds his B.S. and doctorate degrees from Yale University. Professor Millikan is well known for his work in the fields of economic and political development and for the many studies he has written focusing on the problems of American foreign policy toward the developing areas, particularly in the field of development assistance. He is President of the World Peace Foundation and has served on several Presidential committees on foreign aid. He is the author of *Investment Criteria and Economic Growth,* co-editor of *The Emerging Nations: Their Growth and United States Policy,* and co-author of *A Proposal: Key to an Effective Foreign Policy.* He is a frequent adviser to a number of government agencies and foundations concerned with development problems.

LUCIAN W. PYE is Professor of Political Science and a senior staff member of the Center for International Studies at M.I.T. He completed his B.A. at Carlton College and his M.A. and Ph.D. at Yale University and subsequently spent several years as a research associate at the Center of International Studies at Princeton before joining M.I.T. He is known for his theoretical work in the field of political development as well as for his studies of Southeast Asia. He is currently studying political behavior patterns in Communist China. Professor Pye is chairman of the Social Science Research Council's Committee on Comparative Politics. He is the author of *Politics, Personality and National-Building* and *Guerrilla Communism in Malaya,* co-author of *The Politics of the*

Developing Areas, and editor of *Political Culture and Political Development* and *Communications and Political Development.*

PAUL N. ROSENSTEIN-RODAN is Professor of Economics at the Massachusetts Institute of Technology. He was educated at the University of Vienna, where he completed his Ph.D. in 1925. He began teaching at Vienna, but, after a year as a Rockefeller Fellow in Italy, was invited to the University of London where he remained from 1930 to 1947 as a professor of economics and head of the Department of Political Economy. In 1947 he came to the United States to become assistant director of the Economics Department of the International Bank for Reconstruction and Development in Washington. He subsequently joined the Department of Economics and the Center for International Studies at M.I.T., where he has been the director of research and advisory programs both in Italy and in India. He is a member of the Panel of Nine of the Alliance for Progress, a consultant to several organizations of the United Nations, and a Fellow of the American Academy of Arts and Sciences. His published works include *Capital Formation and Economic Development* and *Pricing and Fiscal Policies.*

EDWARD SHILS is Professor of Sociology and Social Thought in the Committee on Social Thought at the University of Chicago and a Fellow of King's College, Cambridge. He has a B.A. from the University of Pennsylvania and an M.A. from Cambridge University. He is known as the translator of works by Max Weber and Karl Mannheim and as a prominent contributor to social theory. He is co-editor of *Toward a General Theory of Action* and *Theories of Society* and the author of *The Torment of Secrecy: The Background and Consequence of American Security Policies.* In recent years, he has been very much concerned with political development in the newly independent nations and in the role of intellectuals and education in development. He is the author of *The Intellectual between Tradition and Modernity: The Indian Situation* and *Political Development in the New States.* He is chairman of the Committee for the Comparative Study of New Nations of the University of Chicago and editor of *Minerva: A Review of Science, Learning and Policy.*

MILTON SINGER is Paul Klapper Professor of the Social Sciences in the College and Professor of Anthropology of the University of Chicago. He holds a B.A. and M.A. from the University of Texas and a Ph.D. from the University of Chicago. Professor Singer has been at Chicago since his appointment as Instructor in 1941, a career punctuated by appointments at the University of Puerto Rico, the University of California at Berkeley, and the Center for Advanced Study in the Behavioral Sciences in Palo Alto and frequent trips to South Asia. He has written extensively on the comparative study of civilization, on the relationship of cultural anthropology to psychology, on the philosophy of the social sciences, and on the theory of culture and culture change and has pioneered in the development of South Asian studies at the University of Chicago. He is co-author of *Shame and Guilt: A Psychoanalytic and a Cultural Study,* co-editor of the series *Comparative Studies of Cultures and Civilizations,* and editor of and contributor to *Traditional India: Structure and Change* and *Krishna: Myths, Rites and Attitudes.*

NEIL J. SMELSER is Professor of Sociology at the University of California at Berkeley. He was an undergraduate at Harvard University and a member of its Society of Fellows. A Rhodes scholarship took him to Oxford University, from which he returned to Harvard for his Ph.D. He participates actively in the American Sociological Association and is the former editor of its journal, *The American Sociological Review.* His major writings focus on the relationship between sociology and economics. He is the co-author with Talcott Parsons of *Economy and Society* and the author of *Social Change in the Industrial Revolution, The Sociology of Economic Life,* and *Theory of Collective Behavior.* He is also co-editor of *Personality and Social Systems.*

ITHIEL DE SOLA POOL is Professor of Political Science and Chairman of the Department of Political Science at the Massachusetts Institute of Technology and director of research on simulation of the communication system of the Communist states at its Center for International Studies. He holds a B.A., M.A., and Ph.D from the University of Chicago. He served first as a research associate at Chicago, taught at Hobart and William Smith Colleges, then moved to Stanford as director of a communications research project at the Hoover Institute. He joined the faculty of M.I.T. in 1953, where he has been distinguished by his research on the ways in which people think, communicate, and make political choices in the United States and in other countries. He is co-author of the prize-winning study, *American Business and Public Policy: The*

Politics of Foreign Trade, The People Look at Educational Television, and *Candidates, Issues and Strategies: A Computer Simulation of the 1960 Election Campaign.* He is a frequent consultant to governmental agencies and private organizations.

JOSEPH J. SPENGLER, James B. Duke Professor of Economics at Duke University, is well known for his studies in the history of economic thought and for his work in demography and economic development theory. His B.A., M.A., and Ph.D. degrees are from Ohio State University. He has been Vice-President of the American Association for the Advancement of Science and of the Economic History Association and President of the Population Association, the Southern Economic Association, and the American Economic Association. He is the editor and co-author of *Natural Resources and Economic Growth* and co-editor and co-author of *Essays on Economic Thought: Aristotle to Marshall* and of *Tradition, Values and Socio-Economic Development in India.*

EUGENE STALEY, Development Economist, is Professor of Education in the Stanford International Development Education Center, Stanford University. Concurrently, he serves as Senior International Economist of Stanford Research Institute. He has worked in many newly developing countries—among them India, Egypt, Thailand, Colombia, and Peru—and as a consultant on industrial development and human-resources planning for such agencies as the United Nations, the World Bank, the Ford Foundation, and the United States Agency for International Development. During the first half of 1965, he was a Senior Specialist in Residence at the Institute of Advanced Projects, East-West Center, University of Hawaii. He is the author of numerous books and articles, including *The Future of Underdeveloped Countries: Political Implications of Economic Development* and, jointly with Richard Morse, *Modern Small Industry for Newly Developing Countries.*

MYRON WEINER is Professor of Political Science and senior staff member of the Center for International Studies at M.I.T. He was awarded his B.A. by the City College of New York and his M.A. and Ph.D. by Princeton University. He taught at Princeton University and at the University of Chicago before joining the M.I.T. faculty. Professor Weiner has written extensively on political organization and political participation, particularly in South Asia, where he has done extensive field research since 1953. He is the author of *Party Politics in India, The Politics of Scarcity,* and *Political Change in South Asia;* co-author of *The Politics of the Developing Areas;* editor of *Indian Voting Behavior* and of the Rand McNally series on Political Change; and co-editor of *Political Parties and Political Development.* He is now completing a book entitled *Party Building in a New Nation: The Indian National Congress.* Professor Weiner has served as the assistant editor of the *Journal of Asian Studies* and has been a consultant to the Ford Foundation Calcutta Metropolitan Planning Organization, the U. S. Department of State, the United States Information Agency, and the Rand Corporation. He is a member of the editorial board of the *American Political Science Review* and is on the board of directors of the Association for Asian Studies.

STANISLAW H. WELLISZ is Professor of Economics at Columbia University. Holding a B.A. and Ph.D. from Harvard University, Professor Wellisz also studied at Cambridge, England. He began teaching at Williams College and continued at the University of Chicago, where he became a professor of Economics before joining Columbia University. He has held a Ford Foundation visiting professorship at Warsaw University in Poland and has been a member of the Harvard University advisory groups to the governments of Liberia and Pakistan and the Ford Foundation advisory team to the Calcutta Metropolitan Planning Organization. He is the author of *The Economics of the Soviet Bloc* and has written extensively on economic development problems of the developing areas and on economic planning.

CLIFTON R. WHARTON, JR., is Director of the American Universities Research Program of the Agricultural Development Council. Dr. Wharton holds a Harvard B.A., an M.A. from the School of Advanced International Studies of Johns Hopkins, and M.A. and Ph.D. degrees in economics from the University of Chicago. For many years, he was on the staff of the American International Association for Economic and Social Development. From 1958 to 1964 he was stationed in Southeast Asia for the Council where he taught at the University of Malaya and was responsible for the Council's program in Vietnam, Thailand, Cambodia, and Malaysia. He has written extensively on problems of economic development with a special concern for agricultural development.

ROBERT C. WOOD is Undersecretary of the U. S. Department of Housing and Urban Development, currently on leave from his post as Professor of Political Science at M.I.T. He received his B.A. summa cum laude from Princeton University and his M.A. and Ph.D. in Public Administration from Harvard. He was associate director of the Legislative Reference Bureau of the State of Florida for two years before joining the Office of Management and Organization of the Bureau of the Budget in Washington. In 1957, Professor Wood joined M.I.T. He is an associate of the M.I.T.–Harvard Joint Center for Urban Studies and is concerned with the research process in natural science and engineering as it bears on questions of public investment in and support of science. Consultant to the City of Boston and to the White House, he is the author of several books on American suburbia and on urban politics, including *Suburbia: Its People and Their Politics, 1400 Governments: The Political Economy of the New York Metropolitan Region,* and is co-author of *Schoolmen and Politics.*

HOWARD WRIGGINS is a research associate at the Washington Center of Foreign Policy Research on leave from the Policy Planning Council of the Department of State. Possessing an M.A. and Ph.D. from Yale University, where he was a Sterling Fellow, he also studied at Dartmouth College (B.A.), the École Libre des Sciences Politiques in Paris, and the University of Chicago. He was first immersed in foreign affairs as a relief administrator for the American Friends Service Committee, then entered academic pursuits by way of the Yale University Institute of International Studies. He has taught at Vassar College, George Washington University and the School of Advanced International Studies of John Hopkins University in Washington and has been chief of the Foreign Affairs Division of the Legislative Reference Service of the Library of Congress. In 1961 he joined the Policy Planning Council of the Department of State. He is author of *Ceylon: Dilemmas of a New Nation* and is now completing a book tentatively titled, *Politics in Afro-Asia: Strategies for Political Survival.*

Contents

MODERNIZATION

Introduction

Myron Weiner

Taken together, these essays represent an attempt by social scientists to look at the modernization process in its totality. In these introductory remarks, I should like to turn our attention to two features of these essays: to what extent do today's social scientists agree in defining and in analyzing the modernization process, and what conflicting theories of modernization are now propounded?

Ever since Adam Smith inquired into the causes of economic growth, intellectuals have sought to explain why some societies have become modernized more rapidly than others. The emergence in recent years of dozens of newly independent countries with elites committed to modernizing their societies and economies has provided a new impetus to studying the modernization process. Not only have the numbers of scholars increased but also their approach differs considerably from that of most of the nineteenth- and early twentieth-century historians and social theorists of modernization.

Firstly, today's scholars attempt to be more rigorously empirical. There is a concern for formulating hypotheses in such a way that they can be subjected to empirical verification or refutation. Few social scientists would claim that they have scientifically proved their generalizations, for often the economic data, the experimental studies, and the survey research with which many work are inconclusive; but the point is that social scientists do seek to make their hypotheses precise and testable.

Secondly, while earlier studies focused on western Europe and the United States as areas in which modernization first occurred, contemporary research is increasingly universalistic and comparative. Countries outside western Europe where the modernization process is well advanced, particularly Turkey, Japan, and the Soviet Union, are being studied, and attention is increasingly being given to cultures in much earlier phases of development. The study of the modernization process as it occurs does, of course, have some distinct disadvantages, for often we do not know whether a particular process is in fact facilitating or retarding modernization—at least, until the outcomes can be foreseen; but on the other hand, it is now possible to study at first hand attitudes, motivations, and relationships that can often only be inferred from historical evidence.

Thirdly, the new scholarship on modernization is increasingly specialized as each discipline within the social sciences approaches the modernization process from its own expert point of view. Thus, scholars are now capable of analyzing aspects of modernization in a more systematic fashion, such as how urbanization occurs, how social structures change, and how educational systems are transformed, as well as how industrialization takes place.

Finally, social scientists are concerned not only with how modernization takes place but also with how it can be accelerated. One consequence is that governments, both in the developed and in the developing areas, are turning to social scientists for information and for policy guidance.

In short, by becoming more empirical, universalistic, and specialized in their concern for using knowledge to accelerate modernization, social scientists are themselves reflecting the spirit of the modern societies in which they live.

On Defining Modernization

Each of the social science disciplines has focused on different elements of the modernization process. Economists see modernization primarily in terms of man's application of technologies to the control of nature's resources in order to bring about a marked increase in the growth of output per head of population. Sociologists and social anthropologists have been primarily concerned with the process of differentiation that characterizes modern societies. They have explored the way in which new structures arise to assume new functions or to take on functions once performed by other structures, and they give attention to the differentiations occurring within social structures as new occupations emerge, new complex educational institutions develop, and new types of communities appear. Sociologists also study some of the disruptive features of the modernization process: rising tensions, mental illnesses, violence, divorce, juvenile delinquency, and racial, religious, and class conflict.

Political scientists, also, have been concerned with some of the disruptive features of modernization, but they have focused particularly on the problems of nation and government building as modernization occurs. They have been concerned with the ways in which governments increase their capacity to innovate and to adapt to change—to make policies for the society. Since these capabilities assume that the populace shares a national identification and views the political system as legitimate, political scientists have given attention to the circumstances under which such attitudes develop. They have also been considering the ways in which governmental elites respond to the efforts of new participants in politics to share power and to make demands upon those who wield power. In other words, political scientists concerned with development are interested not only in who exercises power and how—familiar concerns for all political scientists—but also in how governments increase their capacity to innovate change, respond to demands for change, and cope with social conflict.

None of these interpretations, even when stated more precisely, leads us very far toward a generic definition of modernity, for the simple reason that none is sufficiently general to encompass a "modern" economy, society, and polity. Some scholars suggest, therefore, that the starting point of any definition of modernization is not in the character of the society, but in the character of individuals. Thus Cyril Black, from his vantage point as a historian, suggests in his essay that modern societies are characterized by the growth of new knowledge and that this presumes the existence of men with an increasing capacity to understand the secrets of nature and to apply this new knowledge to human affairs. David McClelland, from a psychological viewpoint, underlines self-reliance and an achievement orientation as essential qualities of modern men. Both Arnold Anderson and Edward Shils, writing about education, stress the development of skills and a spirit of creativity. In short, all these definitions emphasize new ways of thinking which make it possible for men to create modern industry, modern society, and modern government.

In an effort to provide an empirical basis for defining modern man, Alex Inkeles conducted a survey of people in six nations and concludes that there are certain attitudes shared by men in modern societies, irrespective of cultural differences. Among these modern attitudes, Inkeles lists a disposition to accept new ideas and try new methods; a readiness to express opinions; a time sense that makes men more interested in the present and future than in the past; a better sense of punctuality; a greater concern for planning, organization, and efficiency; a tendency to see the world as calculable; a faith in science and technology; and, finally, a belief in distributive justice.

On the importance of skills and creativity as an *enduring* feature of modern societies, there is remarkable agreement among most of the contributors to this volume. Almost no one would disagree with Robert Wood when he suggests that the decisive element in modern man's capacity to solve his problems of urbanization and social disorganization and to achieve distributive justice may lie in the range and quality of scientific knowledge and technical skills. The $15 billion a year spent by the United States government for research and development is one measure of the importance given to this dimension of modernization.

How Modernization Occurs: Two Views

How do men develop modern skills and attitudes? How does a society, an economy, and a polity become modern? And which comes first: modern men or modern institutions? It is easy enough to suggest that modern men and modern institutions are related, but *how* are they related? This question, with the divergent answers that scholars give, raises some of the most difficult and fundamental issues in the social sciences today. Our diagnosis of the capacity of particular systems to modernize, our prognosis as to whether or not they will develop, and our prescriptions as to what steps should be taken to hasten modernization are affected by our answers to this basic query.

Some scholars have suggested that the existence of *certain* modern attitudes is a *precondition* to development. David McClelland, for example, boldly argues that effective entrepreneurship presumes the existence of a way of thinking that leads men to behave in a particularly energetic way—a "mental virus" which psychologists call "need achievement." Other scholars have gone further in suggesting that there must be an even wider range of modern values if modernization is to occur. Thus, it has been suggested that family particularism is an obstacle to modern entrepreneurial behavior; so are fatalism, laziness, a preference for leisure over work, consumption over thrift, and so on. But if certain values are an impediment to modernization, how does any society modernize its values? Where did modern values come from in the first place?

Some scholars have turned for an answer to the writings of Max Weber, who suggested that certain traditional societies had within them the seeds of modernity. He held that the development of commerce, the emergence of politically autonomous urban centers in the late medieval world, and above all the Protestant Reformation laid the foundation for modernization in the West. Weber further suggested that the value system of Calvinism contained the "mental virus" (to use McClelland's vivid phrase) that made modern entrepreneurship possible.

This position has been opposed on at least two grounds. Alexander Gerschenkron, an economic historian, suggests in his essay that Calvinism facilitated development, but that many different value systems seem to exist in modernizing societies. To support his argument, one might note that Catholicism has apparently not impeded the extraordinary high rate of economic growth of many Latin American countries through the nineteen-fifties; nor does an analysis of religious beliefs throw any light on why Indians and Chinese have been so much more productive outside their home societies than within. Gerschenkron warns against converting historical facts (the role of Calvinism is one example among many) into logical prerequisites, which implies the untenable concept of historical necessity. He suggests instead a principle of "substitutability." Credit creation by banks or a public tax system may be a substitute for the use of previously accumulated wealth or for private frugality. The state may invest when private entrepreneurs do not. Moreover, values most of us would describe as "traditional" may hasten development, depending on the social context and the use to which these values are put. After all, even family particularism need not be an obstacle to modernization, as recent scholarship on the development of family enterprises in modern Japan suggests. Furthermore, Marwari, Jain, and Parsi entrepreneurs in India, though committed to family particularisms, have impressive records of successful entrepreneurship.

A second reservation to the Weberian view is expressed by anthropologists who warn against the notion that traditional societies are static or are necessarily homogeneous in their values. Milton Singer, Bernard Cohn, and M. N. Srinivas, in a joint discussion, suggest that even Hinduism, described by Max Weber as an impediment to modernization in India, has not proved to be an obstacle. They point out that one can find a variety of value systems within Hinduism (there are considerable variations, for example, in the values of Brahmans and the mercantile bania castes) and that religious beliefs and practices may themselves undergo major changes. Religion, too, can be modernized, not simply secularized, and, while it may not be the lubricant for modernization, it need not be an obstacle either. In short, recent studies of the relationship of religion and modernization suggest, as Singer points out, "that the relation of 'ascetic Protestantism' to early industrialism, far from being a lonely exception, may turn out to be one of the many cases of mutual interaction and adaptation between religious and social change."

In this connection, a number of scholars have suggested that we distinguish between *tradition* and *traditionalism*. Tradition refers to the beliefs and practices handed down from the past; as we reinterpret our past, our traditions change. In contrast, traditionalism glorifies past beliefs and practices as immutable. Traditionalists see tradition as static; they urge that men do things only as they have been done before. This distinction between tradition and traditionalism calls attention to a fundamental issue in development: how do people see their past? Are the values and practices of the past to be preserved or adapted? Here we see the difference between nineteenth-century China and Meiji Japan. While the Japanese sought to reinterpret their past so as to make it congruent with their efforts to modernize, many Chinese leaders were hostile to innovations that violated previous practices. When people are attached to the past in such a way that they will not adopt new practices that modify past behavior, we are confronted with an ideology of traditionalism. Traditionalism, by virtue of its hostility to innovation, is clearly antithetical to the development of modernization; traditions, which are constantly subject to reinterpretation and modification, constitute no such barrier.

Parenthetically, we might note a third view put forth by some scholars, who argue that the effort to justify changes within the context of tradition is itself dysfunctional to change and that a policy of rejecting one's traditions is a more efficacious way of creating in individuals a readiness to change. Revolutionary regimes often take this view and thereby discard the past in an effort to create new values rapidly. We shall say more on this strategy later, but suffice it to mention here that the elites of most modernizing societies find that a policy of putting new wine in old bottles eases the acceptance of change.

If the variations among traditions do not lead us very far in explaining why some societies become modern and others do not, what, then, are the instruments for modernizing man's values and attitudes? Among those most frequently pointed to have been education, communications, ideology, and especially nationalism, charismatic leadership, and coercive governmental authority.

Turning first to education as the prime instrument—a liberal instrument, if you will—in creating modern men, Edward Shils and Arnold Anderson indicate the role education plays in inculcating a sense of national loyalty and in creating skills and attitudes essential for technological innovation. But Anderson notes by way of qualification that education itself is not adequate, that the social environment for education is critical, and that there are a variety of ways in which men may learn new skills and attitudes other than through formal education. Moreover, the emphasis on university education in many societies may be a waste of resources, for it may lead to an increase in the number of students with degrees without an increase in the number of people with modern skills and attitudes.

Ithiel Pool, an authority on communications, suggests that the development of mass communications, including the telephone, radio, television, and motion picture in rural areas, is an important means of spreading modern attitudes. According to Pool, the diffusion of modern ideas—the much-discussed "demonstration effect"—is facilitated through the mass media, since "the media create knowledge of desirable things faster than these things themselves can be produced." The danger, he warns, is that the media may only increase frustration unless they are part of a program of sustained economic development.

The role of ideology as an instrument for changing mass behavior and attitudes is explored by Leonard Binder. After reviewing contemporary development ideologies in the Middle East, Africa, and Southern Asia, he concludes that these ideologies often serve as a unifying influence in bridging social cleavages within plural societies and as a device of the elite for changing the behavior of masses of people. Nationalism, for example, has often been described as a lubricant for changing men's values and work patterns. Instilled with a sense of passionate loyalty, men may die, or at least work harder, for their country. But Binder warns us not to confuse the symbols of modernity with the substance: elites may have an ideology that appears to be modern, but are they acting in ways that facilitate development? Moreover, is it not possible that some contemporary development ideologies may actually be significant barriers to the adoption of public policies that would hasten development?

A similar theme is pursued in my own essay on political participation and development. There I suggest that while charisma and coercive authority may play a role in legitimizing national authority and in maintaining a national framework (though even then, in the absence of attitudinal research, how are we to know that attitudes have in fact been transformed?), the same elements have also often turned out to be impediments to development. Nationalism, under the aegis of an authoritarian regime, may lead a country into suicidal expansion abroad rather than development at home; charisma (and how fragile charismatic leaders have often proved to be!) may be used as an instrument for personal glorification rather than national development; and an authoritarian regime may strengthen feelings of submission and obedience rather than independence and self-reliance. Moreover, in the absence of empirical information, how are we to assess the effectiveness of developmental ideologies, charismatic leadership, or coercive authority in actually demonstrating modern values and attitudes? All too often we naïvely accept the aspirational claims of those who wave revolutionary banners without the critical examination that we give to the achievements of more moderate regimes.

An Alternative Model

Although there are differences among social scientists as to *how* values and attitudes can be changed, it is possible to speak of one school of thought that believes that attitudinal and value changes are prerequisites to creating a modern society, economy, and political system. Other social scientists take issue with this rather fundamental assumption. As an alternative model, they suggest that the appropriate attitudes and, more importantly, the appropriate behavior will be forthcoming, once *opportunities* and *incentives* are provided. This position finds support among many economists and some political scientists.

The most forceful exposition of this view comes from the economists who point to the existence of institutional impediments to productive activities in many developing or premodern systems—land tenure systems that deny peasants the gain from increasing productivity, taxes that slow the flow of goods from one portion of the country to another, and elaborate bureaucratic regulations that retard the rate of investment. It is not values, writes Stanislaw Wellisz, an economist, that impede profitable economic activity, since people often described as indolent in one environment may prove to be effective entrepreneurs in another—overseas Chinese or Indians, for example. Richard Lambert, a sociologist, points out that, cultural differences notwithstanding, developing economies seem capable of recruiting a labor force for a wide variety of economic activities. And Alexander Gerschenkron explicitly takes issue with those who argue that innovating personalities or a milieu in which the dominant values are favorable to entrepreneurship are prerequisites for development. He suggests that development has often occurred in the absence of these "preconditions."

Many economists conclude that it is the institutional framework of development as it provides both opportunities and incentives which makes development possible. This position, which can be traced back to the writings of Adam Smith, has received strong support in recent years from sophisticated, liberal economists, who are increasingly impressed with the power of new economic tools to make predictions on the basis of admittedly simplified assumptions as to how men behave. For example, it has been widely argued that many traditional peasants engaged in nonmonetized subsistence agriculture have a low level of aspiration, value leisure over profit, and do not respond to economic incentives. But Clifton Wharton, an agricultural economist, cites several studies to demonstrate that traditional peasants are also responsive to higher prices and profits. He concludes that inputs in seeds, fertilizers, and water, land reforms that make it possible for peasants to reap profits from additional effort, higher, more stable prices for agricultural commodities and a reduction in risk may be the most effective means of modernizing agriculture. In short, one need not transform the values and attitudes of peasants to make agriculture more productive.

Underlying these notions of opportunities and incentives is, of course, a model of man moved by economic self-interest. Needless to say, no economists claim that all men are motivated in this way in all circumstances; they recognize that men are moved by a complexity of motives and values. The economic-man model only suggests that in most societies there are enough people motivated by the desire for personal economic gain to make an economy grow if the obstacles to the achievement of private gain are eliminated or reduced. In short, those who postulate the economic-man model are suggesting that their model explains and predicts economic behavior more satisfactorily than do other psychological models of admittedly greater sophistication and complexity.

Recently, one economist has turned to psychological theory to provide support for the proposition that value changes may follow, not precede, behavioral changes and are therefore not a prerequisite for modern economic or political behavior. Albert Hirschman[1] cites the experimental work done on cognitive dissonance theory, which hypothesizes that when there is an inconsistency between the behavior of men and their values, it is often the values that change. This implies, argues Hirschman, that once you impel men to behave in ways that speed growth—because either incentives have been provided or war impels them to invest or work to defend their country—then values and attitudes will change.

It is on this assumption that Staley, Spengler, Millikan, Rosenstein-Rodan, Wellisz, and Wharton, as economists, all consider the environment for investment. Wellisz, for example, explicitly calls attention to many of the institutional blockages to development in many underdeveloped countries, and Staley, discussing the role of the state, emphasizes the need of governments to make greater use of market mechanisms and incentives. In short, these

---

[1] Albert Hirschman, "Obstacles to Development: A Classification and a Quasi-Vanishing Act," *Economic Development and Cultural Change* (July 1965).

velopment program and for social overhead investments; a psychologist, for rewriting the textbooks for school children; a political scientist, for the expansion of local government or the creation of a national party with local cadres; a communications expert, for the establishment of a radio or television network; a lawyer, for the reform of the legal code; and a specialist in public administration, for the reorganization of the bureaucracy. They may all be right, but can a government—especially a weak government—do all this? Paradoxically, the very governments that face the most formidable tasks are generally the ones with the lowest capabilities for a balanced, comprehensive development program. To which recommendations should a policy maker give priority? How should he allocate his scarce resources? In the concluding essay of this volume, Lucian Pye urges policy makers to make hard choices and personally opts for paying more attention to agricultural development and population control. But, whatever the choices, he insists that governmental elites must assign priorities.

Until that happy day comes when scholars have developed the intellectual tools for assigning weights to these many recommendations, political leaders will have to trust to their own judgment and instincts to decide what is the appropriate strategy for their own society. The important point to stress here is that societies differ so vastly that the priorities of one may not be those of another. In some societies, so few people may be motivated toward development that an elite may decide to emphasize education, communication, and other devices for restructuring motivations and attitudes on a large scale. In others, structural impediments may be so great that men with positive attitudes and motives are not given the opportunity to improve themselves or their society. In short, the skill of the governmental elite in grasping the nature of the problems in its own society and in skillfully choosing the most effective strategy for using its limited resources may be the paramount factor affecting development.

I

PERSPECTIVES
AND CONDITIONS

Chapter 1

Change as a Condition of Modern Life

Cyril Edwin Black

I

The revolutionary change in man's way of life in modern times, which for several centuries was confined principally to the Western peoples, has in our lifetime come to affect all of mankind. For the first time in history, a universal pattern of modernity is emerging from the wide diversity of traditional values and institutions, and peoples of all nations are confronted with the challenge of defining their attitudes toward fundamental changes that are world-wide in scope. This definition of attitudes is more than an academic exercise. The achievements of man in the modern age provide unprecedented opportunities for human welfare and fulfillment, but they have also placed in the hands of man instruments of universal destruction. If only for their own preservation, men must seek a correct understanding of the modern age and support the values and institutions best suited to the interests and welfare of all mankind.

The origins of the modern age may be seen in the phenomenal growth of knowledge that can be traced to the revival of Greek science in western Europe in the twelfth century. At first slowly, and with a rapid quickening of pace after the fifteenth century, man has met with increasing success in understanding the secrets of nature and applying this new knowledge to human affairs. In the twentieth century, this expansion has been so rapid that accepted systems of knowledge in specialized fields have been overturned within a single generation. This process of intellectual growth is continuing without any slackening of pace, and changes in our understanding in the years ahead may well be greater than those that we have seen in our own lifetime.

One of the most important consequences of the application of this new knowledge to human affairs has been the increased integration of policy making. In the private realm, systems of transportation, communication, business, and education have tended to become larger and more centralized. Most communications at the national level have become unified, and many are now organized on a world-wide basis. Similarly in the public realm, governments have increasingly tended to accumulate functions formerly performed by the province, district, tribe, or family. Even the most tyrannical of governments in earlier times did not have the degree of control over individuals that is now normally exercised by governments in advanced societies. As life has become more complex, the legal system has also grown to the point where almost all human activities come in contact with the law in one form or another. This integration of policy making has brought peoples within states into an unprecedentedly closer relationship and has resulted in a great complexity of social organization.

The effects of the new knowledge have been particularly noticeable in the economic sphere. Technical improvements have made possible a mechanization of labor that has resulted in mass production, the rapid growth in per capita productivity, and an increasing division of labor. A greater quantity of goods has been produced during the past century than in the entire preceding period of human history. The contrast today between the level of living in relatively modern countries and that in traditional societies is very marked, indeed. In the advanced countries, per capita income per person may be as high as $2,500 or $3,000, whereas in countries still using traditional methods, it may be as low as $50 to $100.

Equally important are the changes that have taken place in the social realm. Traditional societies are typically closed and rigid in their structure. The members of such societies are primarily peasants living in relatively isolated villages, poor and illiterate, and having little contact with the central political authorities. The way of life of the peasants may remain virtually unchanged for centuries. Modern knowledge and the technology it has created have had an immense impact on this traditional way of life. In a modern society, two-thirds or more of the population lives in cities, and literacy is virtually universal. Health is also greatly improved. Cosmopolitan criteria of personal association replace the restraints imposed by race, creed, family, and caste. The former divisions between peasants, townspeople, and aristocrats have given way to a more homogeneous society in which one's position depends more on individual achievement than on inherited status.

This complex and interrelated series of changes in man's way of life is generally known as "modernization." The Western peoples have been undergoing this process for some five centuries, and peoples in the least-developed regions for less than a century. Modernization is part of the universal experience, and in many respects it is one that holds great hope for the welfare of mankind. Yet it has also been in many respects a destructive process. It has destroyed traditional patterns of life which through the centuries had evolved many humane values. It has led to the overthrow of empires and states in a series of local and world wars which have been among the most destructive in history. It has undermined a pattern of rural and family life that brought great satisfaction to the individual and has led to a population explosion that threatens to outstrip food production in many countries. In exchange for the old, it has created a mass society where privacy, individualism, and quality tend to be submerged by standards of taste and administrative processes in which the expediency of public affairs is frequently the determining factor.

II

A central feature of the modern age has been the world-wide diffusion of modern institutions from western Europe, where they originated, to the rest of the world. The European settlements in North and South America and in Oceania brought to the New World political forms that were already relatively modern and established adaptations of European systems of government. A different pattern is represented by such countries as Russia, Japan, Turkey, and China. Countries that did not participate significantly in the original development of modern ideas had inherited from the past a tradition of strong governments. When faced with the competition of the more modern Western states in the eighteenth and nineteenth centuries, these countries at first accepted modern reforms for primarily defensive reasons. Only in the latter part of the nineteenth century did they undertake modernization in a more thoroughgoing fashion.

The remaining societies of the world, which were ushered into the modern era as colonies of more modern societies, are in an earlier phase of development and are still in the process of seeking their own formulas of political modernization.

In some, such as Egypt and India, peoples with a well-established political heritage have been subjected to the rule of more modern societies and have interacted successfully with them. The less-developed societies of Africa, on the other hand, have borrowed from more modern societies not only political institutions, but their language and elements of their culture as well.

The relative domestic stability of the countries that modernized first was due in no small part to the fact that they developed in a world in which they had few rivals and eventually became the most influential centers of political power and in many respects the avowed models for all other societies. By contrast, those that came under the influence of modern ideas and institutions later not only had to undertake the process under conditions of greater strife and instability, but were also under the urgent pressure of seeing before them models so much more advanced that the desired goal seemed almost unattainable. The juxtaposition of societies differing widely in degree of modernity cannot but exert a disruptive influence on less modern societies, although the extent of this disruption depends on the circumstances under which modernization is introduced. In any event, where the jet plane and the oxcart exist side by side, the strains of modernization are immeasurably greater than where the development of the various aspects of a society have been more gradual and balanced.

Nevertheless, the countries that started late on the road to modernity have enjoyed distinct advantages. Imperialism is frequently seen only as a source of political oppression; but in fact it has served to diffuse the benefits of modernity at a cost that is, relatively speaking, quite modest. As a consequence of imperialism, many of the achievements of the advanced countries have been made available in their most highly developed form, relieving less modern societies of the costly experimentation that was originally required to create them.

At the same time, the more advanced countries were generally not eager to see a thoroughgoing modernization that would inevitably lead to the independence of the colonies and the loss of such benefits as were gained from the unequal relationship. Moreover, thoroughgoing modernization is a revolutionary process, and the advanced countries had neither the personnel nor the material means to undertake such a revolution in the colonies. Thus, the pace of modernization has generally been restrained in the colonies, and they have frequently been impelled to seek independence while still in a relatively early stage of modernization. In this they have been aided by the extent to which a balance of power and influence has been maintained among the more modern societies, giving the late-comers a freedom of action out of proportion to their strength.

In the long run, the world-wide diffusion of modern institutions has had the effect of encouraging contradictory trends toward both nationalism and interdependence. On the one hand, it has encouraged the development of a growing number of independent nations, and this has correspondingly aggravated the difficulties of maintaining international order. While all the countries of the world tend increasingly to perform the common functions characteristic of modernity—such as the promotion of knowledge, political integration, economic development, and social mobilization—the means by which they perform these functions depend to a great extent on the traditional institutions of each country. Thus, the countries that developed feudal institutions in their traditional phase, such as those of western Europe, have tended to evolve representative political institutions in the modern era. Those that traditionally had autocratic institutions seem to function better in modern times with centralized political controls.

Most countries have not yet developed sufficiently to permit a judgment as to how their political institutions are likely to evolve under modern conditions. It seems most likely, however, that for the foreseeable future the forms of modern government, as distinct from the functions that they perform, will be scarcely less diverse than their traditional systems. Like language, traditional forms of political behavior seem able to survive a considerable variety of adaptations. Not only do the new nations preserve much of their traditional distinctiveness, but they are also increasingly involved, in certain significant respects, with domestic problems at the expense of international interests. The requirements of modernity have led to the need for society-wide controls in the social and economic realms in order to establish a reasonable degree of order, consensus, and institutional uniformity in a period of rapid change, and the main burden of this responsibility has fallen on the national state. The state has therefore become most jealous of its prerogatives and has been reluctant to dilute its sovereignty with international concerns.

In contrast to this nationalist trend, it is significant that many forces have tended to make societies interdependent—forces such as improvements of means of communication, the universality of modern ideas and institutions, the expansion of the area within which goods and services are exchanged, the migration of many millions of people from one society to another, the emergence of international associations of functional groups, the economic specialization of regions and even of whole societies. The full development of modern ideas and institutions requires a range of resources and skills such as is rarely found within the limits of a single politically organized society. There are a few societies that are able, by virtue of their territorial extent and the variety of their resources and skills, to modernize in relative isolation from their neighbors. These are the exception, however, and the powerful forces tending simultaneously to strengthen and to undermine political authority have frequently resulted in an acute sense of insecurity that has been shared by all countries.

III

Modernization affects not only the domestic development of societies but also the relations among them. It has changed the power relationships among societies by rapidly strengthening the position of some at the expense of others. The process within each of the individual societies has also been profoundly affected by the point in time at which modernization has been undertaken and by the pressures exerted by the world-wide influence of the early modernizers.

At the same time, societies have become more interdependent, and the conduct of their relations has been transformed. While many of the traditional forms of international relations have survived—alliances and war, conquest and colonization, cultural diffusion and propaganda—these forms have been infused with new meanings. Moreover, increasing interdependence has led to the development of more orderly procedures for regulating relations among societies, such as diplomatic practices, conferences, and international law.

In many respects, the most dramatic aspect of this process has been its effect on the relative position of the societies that were the first to modernize. They were transformed from outposts of traditionally powerful empires to the greatest centers of influence that the world had thus far known. As the initiators of modernization, they were also cast in the role of its missionaries; and as aggressors, they carried modern ideas and institutions to the ends of the earth. At the height of their influence (1900–1920), the societies of western Europe held no less than a half-billion non-Europeans under their rule. This relationship of rulers to ruled engendered continuing strife, and modern practices were frequently rejected when imposed by the sword. It also fostered the phenomenon of anti-European modernizers, who simultaneously borrowed European practices and fought European rule. Nevertheless, in the long run, the more modern societies also served as the tutors of other societies, bringing them the benefits of modernization as well as its inescapable problems. In this respect, imperialism may be regarded as a modernizing force. When, as a result of this process, the colonies reached the stage of being able to reject both the political control and the tutelage of the more modern societies, the world-wide influence of the latter gradually declined.

This transformation in the relations of peoples was accompanied by the growing sense of insecurity that can be traced to the tensions resulting from the simultaneous development of nationalism and interdependence. Indeed, this sense of insecurity has been such a pervading force that one may venture to interpret the various forms of imperialism, alliance relationships, wars, and experiments in political integration that have characterized international relations in modern times as a search for security that is significantly more urgent than in earlier times. Seen in this light, for instance, the imperialism that reached its climax in the last decades of the nineteenth century may be regarded as an attempt on the part of more modern societies to enhance their security by extending their sovereignty over less modern societies in order to gain control over their resources and skills.

It is clear that neither investments, trade, nor surplus population necessarily followed the flag and that the various groups favoring imperialism in modern societies were motivated by a variety of considerations. At the same time, in a sufficient number of instances, imperialist states gained advantages they would not otherwise have had from their overseas possessions so that there seemed to be good reason to regard empires as a reasonable guarantee of security. Moreover, as the benefits to be drawn from foreign holdings could not always be calculated in advance, there was a strong inclination on the part of imperialist states to seize territories in order to prevent rivals from acquiring them. In addition, the maintenance of an empire often necessitated the acquisition of strategic positions for the purpose of protecting the more valuable or distant possessions. A few modern states were able to extend their rule over less modern peoples living in contiguous territories and to incorporate them into the metropolitan society instead of ruling them as colonies.

This expansion over the territories of less modern societies came to an end about 1900, not because of a revolt on the part of the latter, which did not come until a generation or two later, but because there was no more land to conquer. In their search for security, modern societies now sought through alliance systems that which they failed to achieve through imperialism. The alliance relationships that had hitherto been regarded as secondary bulwarks of security, to be sacrificed if necessary when territorial gains were at stake, now became issues of the first importance. These relationships were regarded as so vital that it was considered justifiable to risk general war to protect an ally, however small, if the alternative might be the weakening of the alliance system. Under these circumstances, international conflicts were endemic, and indeed World War I came about as a result of just such a crisis.

World War I resulted from the inability of the European political system to adjust to the contradictory pressures of nationalism and interdependence. The peace settlement in 1919, moreover, did nothing to resolve this fundamental problem. Quite the contrary, the war greatly stimulated all the forces that tended toward the strengthening of nationalism, statism, and economic self-sufficiency and weakened the institutions and beliefs that worked for the reconciliation of differences among societies. Thus, cultural nationalism and economic autarchy became the order of the day and militated against all proposals at the peace conference and later to strengthen arrangements designed to institutionalize the international pressures of modernization. The unprecedented economic depression was greatly intensified as a result of economic nationalism, which also obstructed all efforts to relieve the crisis through international measures. The profoundly disturbing consequences of the depression, nevertheless, brought to a head three programs of action that were soon to come into conflict in World War II: the first aimed at an integration of large parts of the world under the Axis powers, the second favored the establishment of a world socialist state under Soviet auspices, and the third advocated a pluralistic international system within a loose framework of international political and economic arrangements under the leadership of the Western democracies.

With the defeat of the Axis powers in World War II, the Western and the Soviet programs of modernization became rivals for influence throughout the world for a period of almost twenty years. This rivalry was intensified by the acceleration, as a result of the war, of a process under way for a generation or more: the national independence of the many less modern societies that had been under foreign rule. The two world wars not only gave these societies unprecedented opportunities for throwing off foreign rule but also fostered a more rapid modernization, due to the inability of the metropolitan countries to maintain the services they had provided in time of peace. In the years after World War II, the urgency of problems of modernization was generally heightened; and as the costs of international war became prohibitive, the ability of the great powers to manipulate and gain influence over domestic modernizing revolutions was increasingly accepted as the principal means of altering the international balance of power. At the same time, the rather rigid polarization that had characterized world politics in the decade or two following World War II gradually dissolved into a more fluid series of relationships. In these circumstances, the developing countries have been able to seek assistance from a number of sources and have been increasingly free to adapt and combine a variety of foreign models in their search for modern institutions suited to their traditional heritages.

In the mid-nineteen-sixties, no more than fifteen or twenty of the countries of the world may be regarded as "advanced," in the sense of having gone a long way toward utilizing the possibilities for betterment that modern knowledge has made available. The great majority of the peoples of the world in one hundred or more countries still face the long and difficult task of adapting their institutions to modern functions and of co-operating toward the establishment of an international order that will make the world safe for modernization. The United Nations has assumed a central role in this process, and within that organization it is to the advanced countries that the peoples of the world must look for guidance and assistance.

Chapter 2

The Impulse
to Modernization

David C. McClelland

Why do some nations "take off" into rapid economic and social growth, while others stand still or decline? The question has
always fascinated historians. Why did the Greek city-states, and
particularly Athens, begin expanding in the sixth century B.C., until a couple of centuries later they had spread their culture unfor-
gettably across the origins of Western civilization? Why did the
landlubberly Romans, defeated again and again in their naval
battles with the Carthaginians in the fourth century B.C., persist in
finding the money to build new fleets until they finally won? The
Romans were in an expansionist phase that not even costly defeats
could stop. Or, to move to more modern times, why did one part
of North America, first settled by the English, develop rapidly
economically, and another part, settled initially by the Spaniards,
who thought they had a richer piece of real estate, develop slowly
until recently? Why did Japan take off economically in the nineteenth century, but not China? The comparisons can be multiplied endlessly, but the questions are always the same: What impulse produces economic growth and modernization? What is it
like, and where has it come from?

Psychologists have made an unexpected contribution to this ancient mystery—unexpected in the sense that they were not working directly on this problem when they made the discovery that ultimately shed some light on the process of economic growth. They were working in the laboratory to isolate what might be called, for the sake of convenience, a certain type of "mental virus," that is to say, a certain way of thinking that was relatively rare but which, when it occurred in an individual, tended to make him behave in a peculiarly energetic way. Following the course of this discovery for a moment will help us understand in more detail what the impulse to modernization is and where it comes from.

The mental virus received the odd name of n Ach (short for "need for Achievement") because it was identified in a sample of a person's thoughts by whether the thoughts had to do with "doing something well" or "doing something better" than it had been done before: more efficiently, more quickly, with less labor, with a better result, and so on. For instance, individuals may be asked to tell a story to get samples of their spontaneous thoughts: Individual A tells a story about "a young man who is studying for an exam but finds it hard to concentrate because he keeps thinking about his girl." Individual B tells a story about "a young man who is determined to get a high grade on the examination because he wants to go on to professional school. He is studying hard late at night, is worried that he won't do well enough, and so forth." Individual B clearly has more n Ach thoughts than Individual A and gets a higher score. He is more infected by this particular mental virus. The methods of detecting the virus—the presence of such thoughts—are quite accurate and objective. They can even be applied by machine to samples of thoughts from individuals or from the mass media or other forms of popular literature.

It was when samples of popular literature were coded for the presence of n Ach over long periods of time that the relation of this mental virus to economic growth began to be apparent. For example, it was found that the n Ach content of early Greek literature (seventh to sixth century B.C.) was much higher than for later Greek literature (from the fifth century B.C. on) and that the n Ach content of English popular literature in the sixteenth century was much higher than in similar Spanish literature at the same time. Could it be that n Ach was the mental virus that made the early Greeks economically so much more successful than the later Greeks and the English in North America so much more economically successful than the Spanish? More striking results followed: the n Ach content in England of folk ballads, sea captains' letters, and popular plays was coded every quarter-century roughly from 1400 to 1800, from the Tudor kings to the Industrial Revolution. At the same time, a rough index of *rate* of economic growth was computed from coal imported at London. Twice, a rise in n Ach in popular thought was followed about fifty years later by a rapid rise in the rate of economic growth—once around 1525 and again around 1725–1750—and twice declines in n Ach were followed by periods of relative economic stagnation.

It began to look as if n Ach might be a part of the impulse to economic growth—an identifiable, measurable part. Nowhere did this become more apparent than in a couple of more ambitious studies, described in my book *The Achieving Society*,[1] in which a nation's "infection level" with the n Ach virus was estimated by coding the imaginative stories the country used to teach its third- and fourth-grade children to read. These estimates of n Ach infection levels turned out to be significantly correlated with subsequent rates of economic growth, taking either a 1929 or a 1950 base line. That is, a country that was high in n Ach level in its children's texts around 1925 was more likely to develop rapidly from 1929 to 1950 than one that was low in n Ach in 1925. The same result was obtained when 1950 n Ach levels were related to rates of economic development in the late nineteen-fifties for a sample of some forty countries. Nations higher in n Ach developed faster.

But suppose for the moment that the psychologists have found a way to measure a part of the impulse to do better, to grow economically; just exactly how does the process operate? There has been much theorizing on the subject, but the simplest way to understand and summarize it is to take an actual community and see the impulse at work in concrete ways. Several years

[1] David C. McClelland, *The Achieving Society* (Princeton, N. J.: O. Van Nostrand Company, 1961).

ago, it was decided that if the *n* Ach virus was important for economic growth, one ought to try to infect a community with it to see if it would produce the effects so often described retrospectively after a take-off has begun. One could run a controlled experiment, so to speak, in which one community is infected and a comparable one is not, to see if in fact it is a crucial factor in the take-off process. The experimental community chosen was Kakinada, a town of about 100,000 population in Andhra Pradesh, India, on the Bay of Bengal. Previous research had established that businessmen are the best "hosts" for this virus: they are most likely to harbor some *n* Ach already and most likely to benefit concretely from being infected with more of it. So the businessmen of Kakinada were invited to participate in this experiment, which involved a 350-mile trip to Hyderabad, the capital city, to attend a ten-day self-development course at the Small Industries Extension Training Institute designed to increase their *n* Ach and otherwise give them insight into themselves and their work. In all, fifty-two in four groups trained at intervals during 1964.

It would be impossible to describe in any detail the nature of the course. It will have to suffice to say that it was voluntary, residential, intensive, and made use of every scrap of information we had collected about the nature and functioning of *n* Ach in seventeen years of research: that is, the participants learned how to think easily in terms of *n* Ach, to act in lifelike games like a person with high *n* Ach, to reconcile *n* Ach with their self-image and conflicting cultural values, to form a self-perpetuating interest group (The Kakinada Entrepreneurs Association) that would keep the idea alive, and so on.

What is more germane here is the outcome of the course: on the whole, it was fairly successful in implanting the *n* Ach virus in these businessmen. Based on studies here and elsewhere in India, we have estimated that in any given two-year period about one-third of such a group of businessmen will show signs of *unusual* or *innovative* business activity—for example, start a new product line, do something that results in a big salary raise, or take a course in accounting. After our courses, two-thirds of the businessmen of Kakinada showed such signs of unusual entrepreneurial activity. In other words, the courses had *doubled* the normal or spontaneous rate of innovative activity for India. We obtained the same result following some courses in Bombay.

But the statistics hide the interesting part. What did individual businessmen do? Let us consider some cases.

1. Many of the men paid more attention to business after the course. Some of them had inherited family businesses, like cycle shops, that gave a fair return if entrusted to assistants while the owner relaxed and enjoyed life. A change in n Ach stimulated their attendance at work. They came early, stayed late, paid attention to customers, and found their businesses improving. The view of a businessman as someone driven to work hard by a desire for profits simply had not occurred to many of these businessmen. They had enough money to be comfortable. Why exert themselves? After the course they did, not to make money as such, but because they were determined to do a better job, to make a better showing for themselves, for Kakinada, and for India. Note that a "love of work or industriousness" was not inculcated nor an interest in profit as such. They did not "love" work or money any more afterward than before; they worked longer hours because that seemed the appropriate way for them to do a better job and get more satisfaction out of life.

2. Other men started innovating. Endless discussions can take place as to what constitutes a "real" innovation; but in simple business terms, it means doing something new or different for a particular time and situation. What is an innovation for Kakinada is not an innovation for Bombay. Most of the innovations were extensions of work the man was already doing. A photographer decided to go into lens grinding because spectacles could not be ground locally; a dealer in grains investigated various types of dal mills to find the one that could be used most profitably for the local market; a cycle-shop owner decided to manufacture cycle stands locally; efforts were being made to discover how the Japanese formed the indigenous palmyra fiber into brushes so that the latter could be made locally instead of simply exporting the raw material. One of the leaders of the group egged the others on by pointing out he had been put out of the castor-oil business because someone in Bombay had developed a technique for producing a purer product. These men were intensively active in search-

ing for new ways of doing old things, or at least doing locally what could now be done only at great expense and delay by sending away to the big urban centers. The innovation that people with high *n* Ach engage in is not real artistic creativity; it is more simply motivated by the desire to find a *better* way of getting a job done.

3. Several men began investing money differently. Most conspicuous was the manager of a local bank who says that before the course he lent money solely in terms of the security provided. Usually this meant putting up land as collateral, which meant in turn that money could be lent only to the wealthy landowners who (*a*) did not need loans and (*b*) were generally not entrepreneurially active anyway and would need to borrow only for some extraordinary expense like a wedding. As a result, his bank did not lend much money and was rather a static affair. After the course, he decided he should lend not only in terms of the security provided but also in terms of the quality of the man requesting the loan and the quality of the project for which he wanted the money. Accepting these two new "revolutionary" loan criteria led him to accept some greater risks than he would have taken by the old standard of absolute security; but so far they had paid off handsomely, not only in greater activity in the commercial loan department but in more deposits, for example. His bank had become a force for promoting change in the town; he had been offered a better job in Calcutta, but had decided to stay to continue helping the community to develop. He had found a great new pride in what he was doing for Kakinada. Note how a small shift in attitude toward doing a better job had a tremendous economic impact locally, when it occurred in a man in a position to make important decisions.

Another type of banker, a traditional moneylender, came to me and asked, "Why should I invest in industry for this town, when I know I can lend out money at 2 per cent a month with absolute security? I might lose my money in industry. Also I have to wait a long time before I get any return at all." Why, indeed, should he invest in business? I should like to hear anyone give an *economic* answer to his question that would persuade him to give up earning 24 per cent a year, payable immediately at 2 per cent a month, with absolute security, in favor of a long-term investment in industry that *might* start paying off in three to five years at perhaps 10 to 15 per cent a year *at best*. Yet this is the basic problem in Kakinada. There are many wealthy families in the community, so there is no lack of capital to finance new ventures. Yet there are simply no financial reasons why the money should be used for development purposes. The prevailing attitude is that money is to be stored and turned into gold for the most part. My answer to this particular moneylender was already implicit in his question. I told him he was going to invest in developing businesses "because he couldn't help it; now that he had been infected with *n* Ach he would simply never respect himself again if he sat around and did nothing, which bored him anyway." In other words, he got an irrational answer, and he is beginning to behave irrationally (in strictly economic terms) by investing in such enterprises as a small papermaking concern that was initiated at one of the courses when he provided the money for an inventor (who had discovered a new papermaking process) and a manager to go into business together.

4. A few started entirely new enterprises. The owner of a small radio shop decided to set up a paint and varnish factory, which appears to be a large and growing concern. He raised the money, hired a chemist who knew the business, acquired a plant, and began operation and sales all within a few months. He exemplified all the characteristics found in the laboratory to be associated with high *n* Ach. He took a calculated risk only after he had carefully researched the situation as to the profits that might be expected in selling various products. He took active personal responsibility for seeing the project through and was doing something new and different that others were not doing. In all this, he was gaining achievement satisfaction—carrying out, by himself, a slightly risky venture that not everyone could handle and assessing concretely his progress in terms of sales and profits. Furthermore, he also started a branch radio shop in which he installed a woman as manager—quite a startling innovation in his town. This illustrates nicely how the restless desire for constant improvement may break up strong social traditions in the search for new ways of doing things better. Here, in part, is why businessmen have

tended to be unpopular from Plato's time to the present: they often break with tradition when infected with n Ach.

In short, a minor economic revolution appears to be in the making in Kakinada which, if the n Ach virus remains firmly implanted, may in time produce a take-off into rapid economic development. Note particularly that what came from the outside was not material aid or technical instruction—all of which the businessmen of Kakinada have or can obtain from the government—but an idea, the motive, the spark, the impulse, that seems to be necessary to set such a process in motion. But note also how far-reaching its effects can be, because these businessmen control most of the institutions that matter in the town: the banks, the cinemas, the shops, the foundries, the mills. Their actions and decisions will vitally affect employment income, levels of demand, the prices farmers get for some of their crops—all aspects of the community's economic life.

But n Ach is by no means all there is to modernization. It is only one key ingredient. To balance the picture a little, it is worth describing one other input, not so well researched as yet, but almost certainly as important. N Ach by itself is an individual virtue; it does not automatically lead one into socially useful activities or projects. In the absence of conscience, it could lead to success in crime, for example. Yet in the Kakinada study it was apparent from the outset that the men wanted to do something not just for themselves but for Kakinada, for India, and possibly even for the whole world of stagnant communities like theirs. It was only as their "conversion" took on this larger social significance that it really gripped them. Furthermore, they wanted to join together actively: to plan an industrial estate, for example, for the town. Anyone familiar with India knows how limited is this type of co-operative action across caste lines; yet these men were strongly moved by the desire to do something in unison for the common good.

This theme of concern for the common good was also found more often in the children's textbooks (referred to earlier) used by those countries that subsequently developed more rapidly. That is, their stories more frequently described people being influenced by the wishes and needs of others. In the stories for children from more slowly developing countries, on the other hand, there were more references to traditions or habitual ways of doing things. A person in the story did something because it had always been done that way, not because of the needs of some other character. It was almost as if some countries realized that in order to get people thinking about modernization, they had to replace their normal traditionalism with a concern for the welfare of others who might even be strangers to them. Furthermore, it is probably in this way that one may most easily explain the correlations that have been found between investments in health and education and subsequent rates of economic growth. Why should investments in health speed economic growth? Rationally, one might expect they would slow it down by decreasing infant mortality and therefore increasing the population faster than the active portion of the populace could produce food. Yet careful study of the history of some thirty to forty developed countries shows that in nearly every case a minimum public health standard was achieved before the country could break through to a rapid rate of economic growth. One explanation may be that public health care directly reflects man's concern for his fellow man, and this, in turn, is that other key psychological ingredient essential for modernization. Similarly, investments in education, even at the secondary-school level (to say nothing of primary school), do not accelerate rates of economic growth immediately, but they do in the long pull—that is, some twenty years later, when the secondary-school graduates are at the height of their powers. Again, it cannot be immediate economic gain or even n Ach that leads people to start stressing education for their young. It must be this other ingredient, which might be called the "concern for the common welfare of all." Eventually, such a concern pays off economically.

In short, the impulse to modernization in ideal psychological terms seems to consist in part of a personal virtue—n Ach—and in part of a social virtue—interest in the welfare of the generalized other fellow. But where does such an impulse come from? To judge mostly from our knowledge of n Ach, which is more detailed, it is not a racial or environmental characteristic, since clearly a given culture can be infected with the virus at one moment in history and not at another. It does not derive from military conquest. In fact, the reverse seems more often to have been the case: the conquered seem more often to have developed n Ach, perhaps because power was denied them. It does not result from the spread of education, technology, or economic growth; at least, not in a simple way. Here is one example of behavior, which every development economist can illustrate a hundred times over. The government of India decided to help the fishermen of Kakinada by providing them with nylon fishing nets, which were a clear technological improvement. For instance, they required less mending and did not break or tangle easily. The idea was that the fishermen would catch more fish, make more money, and buy more consumer goods, leading the businessmen of Kakinada to expand their businesses, and so on. The fishermen caught more fish, to be sure; but two unexpected things happened. Some stopped fishing as soon as they had caught as much as they were used to catching (they worked less); and others made more money, which they spent on bootleg liquor (the state is dry). This is probably not the end of the story, but over and over again technological innovation has been shown *not* to produce attitude change. Better fishing nets did not increase the n Ach of the fishermen: their desire to do better, to save, to invest. All through the Industrial Revolution on the northern shore of the Mediterranean, the inhabitants on the southern shore simply failed to get really interested in all the technological innovations taking place up north, even though they had plenty of exposure to them. At that time, the Arabs were not much interested in the machine culture the Europeans were developing. On the other hand, improved motives clearly lead to rapid adoption of technological changes, just as our radio-shop owner, after the n Ach course, decided to import technicians who could make paint and varnish.

But where do the motive changes come from, if not from obvious happenings "out there" in the environment? If opportunities do not create the impulse to take advantage of them, what does? Sometimes n Ach levels are clearly the result of local history. For example, lower-class Negro Americans are generally low in n Ach, a fact that seems clearly to be the result of the near-slave status of such groups, particularly in the South, for we know that dependent peoples are usually rewarded for being obedient and responsible rather than self-reliant and achievement-oriented. On the other hand, what is to account for the fact that in Nigeria the Ibo and Yoruba are both highly infected with the n Ach virus, while the Hausa are hardly infected at all? Only careful local historical analysis could give the reasons, which are often based on different migratory patterns.

However, one generalization can be made. Zealous, reformist religious groups—or at least the children of the first generation— are nearly always highly infected with n Ach. The best-documented case is that of the early days of the Protestant Reformation in the West, which produced an n Ach-infected business behavior like that of the Kakinada businessmen just described. But there had been other religious minorities, like the Parsis or the Jains in India, the Jews in many countries, the Zen-oriented Samurai in Japan, or the overseas Indians in East Africa or Asia, that have shown extraordinarily high business success and presumably high n Ach. What is characteristic of all these communities is an intense, religiously based feeling that they are *superior* to other people living around them and that in one sense or another they hold the key to salvation, perhaps not only for themselves but for all mankind. Thus the two psychological elements essential to economic success are there: the desire to prove oneself better than others and the need to promote the common good—at least of their minority group, which is often somewhat persecuted. The Communists have managed to create these psychological convictions strongly in their adherents in the present century, and it is therefore not surprising to find that the n Ach infection level rose in Russian and mainland Chinese literature after their Communist revolutions. It is a curious paradox that the Communists have managed to produce rapid economic growth in a country like Russia, not, as they believe, because of socialism, but because of their fanatical belief in its superiority. That is, here, as elsewhere, a conviction in one's superiority has spread the n Ach virus, which is more directly responsible for accelerating the rate of economic growth than the socialist type of economic organization.

Must we, then, encourage people to embrace rigid, doctrinaire, minority convictions so that they may feel superior and develop n Ach? Fortunately, science has provided us with an alternative that is less dangerous to the peace of the world and probably more effective. By direct training, we can apparently infect the people who need it with both n Ach and a sense of public responsibility, just as we did in Kakinada. Science has provided at least some of the information needed by a people who wish, by taking thought, to increase the strength of their own impulse to modernize.

Chapter 3

The Future
of Modernization

Robert C. Wood

Before people adopt "modernization" as a national goal, common prudence suggests that they inquire about the nature of their final destiny. Too often nations commit themselves to the process of modernization, expecting that once the sacrifices and special efforts involved in industrialization and development are over, their future will be free of problems. More than a tinge of utopia is implicit in many a five-year plan. Leaders and public alike tend to assume that the quest for modernity follows the path of a rainbow, with a pot of gold at the end.

The plain fact is, of course, that no nation possessing a large industrial base, a high standard of living, and a sophisticated technology is without its troubles. The United States, the countries of western Europe, and Japan are all caught up with the complex issues of human and public affairs that arise at advanced stages of development.

It is important for all countries to understand the implications of modernization and to recognize that a commitment to change is essentially an unending one. Most particularly, it is important to try to understand the character of life that a modern society exhibits. Such understanding and anticipation of the future are an important guarantee against disillusionment and frustration for nations on their way up.

One way to foresee the course of modernization is to investigate the conditions of life in today's so-called "advanced" societies and then project the immediate future. Obviously, in limited space one can sketch the present character of these societies only in the broadest terms. Obviously, too, no projection is completely realistic: for so rapid is the process of change at the frontiers of development, so continual the flow of innovations in science and technology, economics, and social and political organization, that no one can define the path of advanced modernization precisely, even for the coming decade. Nevertheless, the exercise of summarizing outstanding present conditions and then projecting does serve to pinpoint major challenges that lie ahead.

Modern Nations Today: Statistical Well-Being

A starting point for probing the future of modernization is recognition of the problems that advanced societies have solved. Clearly their basic accomplishment is technological mastery over natural resources: a capability for harnessing energy sources and using materials to provide physical well-being for the majority of their populations.

The United States, for example, with 6 per cent of the world's land area and 5 per cent of its population, now produces 30 per cent of the globe's output of oil, 25 per cent of its steel, 35 per cent of total electric power, and 48 per cent of all automobiles. The production of these and other necessities produces sophisticated research and industrial processes and results in sustained high productivity. Today the American worker produces seven times as much as his counterpart in 1850. By 1975, he will be producing twelve times as much. So the Gross National Product per person in the United States is today $2,786, twice as much as that of the second ranking nation.

Western Europe represents even more impressive economic miracles. From 1948 to 1960 its GNP grew from $175 billion to

$318 billion and is projected to reach $600 billion by 1975. This is an annual compound rate of increase exceeding that of the United States, and in instances such as West Germany, twice as rapid. The production of steel, ships, and houses has more than doubled in the last twelve years. Aluminum and oil production have increased fourfold; the output of natural gas and production of automobiles has grown even faster.

The years immediately ahead promise more of the same. The United States' population in the present decade will increase a full 15 per cent, and grow from 190 million in 1965 to 210 million by 1970 to 235 million by 1975. Yet the volume of goods and services will rise even more rapidly. Five years from now, the American Gross National Product is expected to touch $750 billion, representing a 25 per cent increase in the standard of living since 1960, taking into account the additions in population. Concurrently, the average work week will continue to decline, dipping below thirty-seven hours a week in the United States and below forty hours in western Europe. Along with these changes in work weeks, radical shifts in consumer spending are under way, so that outlays for recreational activities and equipment are double those of ten years ago. In the United States, close to $40 billion a year is spent on recreation.

PAY-OFFS FOR THE INDIVIDUAL

This continuous impressive outpouring of material products, the ever-increasing reliance on nonhuman energy resources, and increased productivity, mean greater material abundance: more food, more clothing, better homes. But the trends imply other distinctive qualities in the life of the average citizen.

For one thing, the child of a modern nation can look forward to a longer and healthier life. Diseases such as polio and diphtheria are now effectively eliminated; epidemic diseases are rare; new drugs control high blood pressure, diabetes, mental disease, and allergies. On the average, the baby born in 1960 can expect to live to the age of seventy, compared to the life expectancy of forty-seven for those born in 1900 and sixty in 1930. The same additions apply in Europe, where infant mortality has been reduced by a factor of six, child mortality by ten. Even in relatively slow-growth nations, such as Spain between 1900 and 1960, the life span has almost doubled.

Moreover, in modern nations individuals have much greater opportunities to acquire skills and develop talents not cultivated elsewhere. Literacy, for all intents and purposes, is universal, and an increasing percentage of young people spend a longer time in school. United States expenditures for education now exceed $32 billion, three times the expenditures of 1950 and seven times those of 1940. In Europe, progress toward advanced education for all has not proceeded so rapidly. Nevertheless, by 1970 practically all European countries will have adequate elementary schools, and great progress can be expected in secondary and university expansions.

Healthier, more skilled, and knowledgeable people, supported by and operating a sophisticated technology that produces with increasing efficiency, enjoy circumstances of expanded personal convenience. The average American now lives in a five- or six-room house that costs over $14,000 to build. The family is surrounded by home appliances that are designed for almost every conceivable household use: washing and drying machines, refrigerators, mixing bowls, shoe-shining equipment, broilers, polishers, furnaces, and air conditioners. Except for making the beds, every household chore can now be carried out with the help of a machine. And the future promises even more miracles through technology: ultrasonically operated garbage disposals and dishwashers, and windows that close automatically when rain falls.

With more production, more income, and more jobs come more choices in the way persons in modern countries spend their time, work, and play. More than 10 per cent of American workers change jobs every year—8 million of a labor force of about 75 million—and two-thirds of these move to a completely different industry and a completely different occupational group. More than 7 per cent of all male workers make a change of residence each year, and more than half of these move to another state or region. Change in place of work and home is a common occurrence in a modern nation.

THE CORNUCOPIA OF TECHNOLOGY

Underlying the exponential growth in material resources, freedom from disease, increase in education, personal convenience, and career choice is a steadily changing base of science and technology. The modern society builds its stockpile of resources and expands its supply of usable materials in ways undreamed of a generation ago. What sustains the apparent insatiable material appetite for a large number of people is not the abundance of land, water, minerals, and chemicals their country may possess. The critical element is the range and quality of the scientific knowledge and technical skills ready to unlock new sources of energy and extract new materials from the earth's crust and the atmosphere. The future of every modern nation relies on the substantial scientific enterprise—the organization of highly skilled scientists and engineers in a research and development process—that constantly alters materials available to a people and expands the base of a *usable* resource.

In the United States, the national government alone invests $15 billion a year in research—60 per cent of the total the nation spends annually for new products and innovation. Each year, the fruits of progress ripen, replacing old resources or expensive ones and increasing productivity. Microwave stations perform more cheaply the old function of cross-country cables. Skin banks, artery banks, blood banks, mechanical hearts, mechanical kidneys, support and sustain the human body. Insecticides, fungicides, chemical fertilizers, new varieties of seeds, and new breeds of livestock multiply the yield of lands. Electronic controls, computers, synthetic materials, and plastics undergird new industry.

In short, the problems a modern nation has largely left behind are those of mastering nature to secure the necessities of physical existence. The capacity to command the energy and matter required to sustain life exceeds the increase in population. Thus the amount of resources available to each person steadily increases.

THE CHALLENGE OF MODERNIZATION:
LIVING WITH CONTINUAL CHANGE

Yet, solving the problem of abundance generates further riddles. Vexing issues of public and private behavior arise: how to ensure that the steadily expanding supply of material is most effectively used, and how to cope with the task of accepting new science, new technology, and innovation as a way of life. The fundamental and continuing condition of modernization is the capability of a people to adjust to changed circumstances not once or twice in a lifetime, but every year. This process of adjustment requires social and political institutions, processes and ways of behavior, that permit a constant introduction of new products, new processes, new careers, and new standards of conduct, into a society without too great a disruption in personal lives and careers. The development of these institutions, processes, and life styles— as every modern nation has discovered—is not a simple matter.

A number of surface signs attest to this constant tension of adjustment in absorbing innovation while maintaining a sense of individual and national direction.

One is the continual pressure of obsolescence in occupations, professions, and industries that lose their utility in the space of a few short years. During the last generation, the United States and western Europe have witnessed an absolute decline in the number of people in agriculture, and the forced evacuation of farm families through occupational displacement. They have seen the relative decline of manufacturing and productive enterprises, and a lessening demand for semiskilled and unskilled workers. Currently the requirements for clerical and salesworkers, scientists, engineers, and technicians has risen rapidly, as has the demand for so-called service occupations: workers in finance, insurance, wholesale and retail distribution, transportation, and utilities.

Transitions among these occupations are not easy, unless the individual brings to the task a broad-based education and a considerable feeling of personal confidence. To many American or European workers innovations that increase national productivity are personal disasters. When coal is replaced by atomic power as a basic source of energy, miners find that their services are no longer required. Railroad workers lose their jobs when the volume of air traffic expands. Factory mechanics find that they are no longer needed when automation replaces men on assembly lines. In a very real sense, an individual in a modern society discovers that human energy and diligence are no longer very valuable commodities. Willingness to work, when not associated with possession of a skill, no longer guarantees a job. There is, in short, "no room at the bottom" in a modern society. Only those whose talents fit the needs of the moment seem capable of prosperity and advancement.

The sharp, sudden dislocations that affect groups of workers and families and blight personal careers are often accompanied by uncertainty as to how the new material well-being shall be directed by the majority. Critics of modern life have come to emphasize the so-called materialisms of advanced cultures: the conspicuous display of prosperity in long vacations, fancy cars, high living, and a reliance on gadgets. To many philosophers, matters of the spirit, religion, and moral purpose are lost sight of in a consumption-oriented economy. Modern nations have been held to be inferior in the attention they pay to culture, customs, manners, and the human element in their societies. They are called deficient in national purpose and sense of communality. Their citizens are said to know how to live comfortably, but not well.

ROOT PROBLEMS: THE TASKS OF A MODERN SOCIETY

Yet, basically these criticisms of sudden dislocations and excessive preoccupation with getting and spending are not the genuine problems of a modern culture. Indeed systematic explorations reveal that the desires for security and material well-being are common elements in human nature. Modernity simply brings these characteristics to the fore. The unsolved task of modern life is not the deterioration of a nation's character by virtue of becoming "soft"; rather, it is the task of coping with life on a vastly expanded size and scale and of dealing with great complexity in social, economic, and political patterns.

Put another way, developing nations are often said to have a task of stimulating entrepreneurship; advanced societies often have the need to provide a countervailing force to the aggressive, atomistic, and individualistic actions set loose by the drive for productivity. They require new arrangements—or more precisely, systems—to assure intercourse, encounters, and a sense of mutual concern among their members.

In this context, four needs particularly stand out. How does a modern nation shape cities—reconcile itself to becoming an urban culture, rather than a rural one? Second, how does a modern nation provide support for the individual personality in a world in which ties of family, friendship, neighborhood, and community rapidly decline? Third, how does a modern nation assure that all its members participate in the new abundance? Finally, how does a modern nation maintain its innovative processes—its energy and drive and its capacity for continuing to want and to accept change?

City Building

The steady flow of people from country to city is the most striking physical manifestation of modernization. One out of six western Europeans lives today in a city of a half-million people. In the Netherlands, portions of England, and the Ruhr, parts of cities run together in giant "megalopoli." The same trends are discernible in Japan, where Tokyo regained its prewar population of 11 million from a 1945 low of 3 million in less than a decade and now spreads steadily into the countryside. In the United States, urban areas increase in population at the rate of 3 million each year. By 1975, four out of every five Americans are expected to be living in urban areas. The European pattern of interurban blending is also apparent in the United States: thirty-nine major metropolises now merge almost imperceptibly into one another. The acceleration of the widespread use of the automobile and the continued construction of single-family residences heralds the arrival of "the spread city," replacing the more congested cities of the past.

This continuing process of urban development raises a host of problems. Some are simply those of finance and engineering: how to secure the investment for continued construction necessary to house the urban population; how to provide public utilities, water, and sanitary facilities; how to build roads, subway lines, and commuter railroads. More basic ones hinge on the form and size of modern urban areas. Questions of planning for the effective use of space, assigning appropriate functions to old central cities and to new suburbs, grow increasingly persistent.

Here, Europe has clearly led the way. In rebuilding its cities after World War II, conscious plans, imaginative use of public power, and the carefully calculated intermeshing of transportation facilities, homes, and places of work characterize the rebuilt urban complexes of the Low Countries, Scandinavia, Germany, and England. Only slowly have the United States and Japan arrived at a position where consistent and workable public policies guiding the process of city building are appearing. But every modern nation now grapples with the job of checking massive urban concentration, whether in Tokyo, Paris, London, or New York. And every modern nation has begun the process of building entirely new communities to provide for the regional dispersal of its people.

Identity in an Urban World

As urbanization proceeds apace, a second problem appears. Millions of immigrants from farms and small towns no longer required in agricultural pursuits pour into the cities unprepared for the urban way of life. City living, dependent as it is on the specialization of jobs and the development of large business and governmental organizations, tends to be depersonalized living. The daily process of commuting from home to job, the sheer number of individuals active in small spaces, and the complex set of facilities and services required for organized urban existence all tend to undercut ties of neighborhood, friendship, and family which are so strong in small towns and rural life. Symbolic rituals and folk experiences decline, and a sense of personal identity becomes more difficult. So life today becomes increasingly a lonely existence to many residents, untutored in coping with its complexity and lacking the social skills for adjustment.

A wave of social commentary has interpreted these conditions of modern urban living as a result of overorganization: the rise of the gigantic corporations and bureaucracies that direct each aspect of an individual's life. Yet these analyses seem misdirected in two ways. First, they overlook the decline of autonomous, hierarchical, tightly directed institutions: the replacement of the business firm and government agency by interdependent systems of relationships that shape human activity more in terms of voluntary co-option than authoritative fiat and decree. Modern nations are less likely to be organizational societies than they are persuasive societies. Second, these complex new systems for the competent participant are not destructive of individual choice. On the contrary, they provide more choices, more options, fewer working hours, shorter work weeks, and more time for leisure than ever before. In a very real sense, men and women are freed from the daily routines and grinding labor that characterized poverty-stricken farm areas.

It is probably nearer the truth to say that the difficulty of many people in modern circumstances is not that they are overdirected or overcontrolled, but rather that they lack the resources to find meaningful personal lives. Institutions, customs, habits, and clearly identified appropriate roles and styles are hard to find. Consequently, all the awesome stresses, strains, and pressures of the urban world come to play on the individual personality structure. These must be coped with, handled, and absorbed by whatever defenses the individual psyche may possess. Clear guidelines of professional and organizational behavior tend to disappear.

Increasingly, modern people become preoccupied with job and immediate family circles and find it difficult to engage in meaningful encounters with other classes and groups. It is probably symptomatic of these pressures that the United States' most prevalent disabling ailment is mental illness. Half the beds in nonfederal hospitals are occupied by mental patients. In 1960, more than three-quarters of a million patients were in institutions, suffering from some type of mental illness.

The Nonparticipants

If all members of a modern society find adjustment a continuing and exacting exercise, some are unable to adapt at all to the special roles that fit the needs of the technologically based economy. The constant shift in the composition of the job market and the emphasis on new skills become overwhelming—not in a psychological sense so much as in terms of innate physical and mental capabilities.

Alongside the challenge to ease the tension of change for the majority, every modern nation faces the need to provide employment, purpose, and meaning for a hard-core minority of so-called "marginal men." In the United States, almost one-fifth of the population falls in this category—displaced workers and the increasing proportion of old people. Our attention turns to the ways and means for making sure that all people share in the general well-being: special educational programs, neighborhood centers, and new systems to prepare rural immigrants for urban life.

Maintaining Abundance

Finally, as population grows, expectations reach higher, life becomes more complicated, and the need arises for a continuing flood of innovations, research, and development to provide a firm base for an expanding economy. Productivity rates for the most advanced societies tend to become sluggish, and the capacity so to direct innovation becomes more difficult. In the natural sciences and engineering, which now include a vast community of three million Americans alone, the process of making, communicating, and applying innovation is an increasingly complex affair. Major questions of the appropriate level of finance and of the right methods for the organization and management of scientific enterprise rise in importance. For instance, how much should society invest in fundamental physics compared to frontier research in biology? Should we explore the ocean floor or outer space, and, if so, with how much money and man power? What are the best techniques for sustained scientific collaboration among government, business, and university? And how rapidly can we expand our new knowledge in social science in order to design the great urban complexes so that we pay more attention to human needs, improve the learning capacity of the disprivileged, and provide psychological supports to the lonely? All these questions are high on the agenda of advancing nations today.

Thus, the future of modernization is not without its problems. How to live in the cities, how to offer rich, full, individual lives in complex circumstances, how to assure that all participate in a society of ample resources, and how to push that society ahead in the future are persisting and perplexing questions.

But it is important to re-emphasize that these are not the issues that many commentators have identified in their criticisms of modernity. Modern society does not oppress the individual by great organizations so much as it perplexes him in the array of choices it spreads before him. Modern society does not emphasize materialism and sensate experience at the expense of the reflective, the critical, and the contemplative. In the use of expanded leisure time in most modern societies, philosophy, music, and the arts grow as rapidly as mass sports and spectacles. There is no documentation to prove that there is more violence or disorder in modern life than in earlier eras or that the modern character is less moral, less strong, and less ethically oriented.

The genuine issue of modern life is the capacity to mix quality and quantity: to handle new masses of people and new and complex systems of social, economic, and political behavior purposefully with respect for the individual.

Here answers seem not impossible. Today our capabilities in architecture, in planning, and in social organization for building attractive, orderly, pleasant, and helpful cities are greater than ever before; so are our knowledge and techniques for providing specialized vocational education to restructure the capabilities of the men and women now in danger of being left out of this society. Our capacities to direct science and technology for the peaceful uses of mankind likewise expand. As they grow, most modern nations move in the direction of new public investments, attention to amenities, and concern with the human condition that should powerfully counteract the difficulties in their social orders. As they increase the effectiveness of these programs, as they redouble their efforts to understand the machine and put it to human purposes, and as they invest more in the facilities for training and knowledge, the future of modernity is bright. The call of adventure in the quest for quality can be as exciting and rewarding as any in the history of mankind.

II

THE
MODERNIZATION
OF SOCIETY
AND
CULTURE

Chapter 4

The Modernization
of Religious Beliefs

Milton Singer

INTRODUCTION

The dominant note usually struck in discussions of the relation of
religion to modernization is that Asian religion is a major obstacle
to modernization because it is a bulwark of traditionalism and a re-
pository of beliefs and values incompatible with modern science,
technology, and the ideology of progress. The most famous expo-
nent of this view was the German sociologist Max Weber, who
concluded from his impressively learned studies of the sociology
of world religions that

> for the various popular religions of Asia, in contrast to ascetic
> Protestantism, the world remained a great enchanted garden in
> which the practical way to orient oneself, or to find security in
> this world or the next, was to revere or coerce spirits and seek
> salvation through ritualistic, idolatrous, or sacramental procedures.
> No path led from the magical religiosity of the non-intellectual
> classes of Asia to a rational methodical control of life. Nor did any
> path lead to that methodical control from the world accommoda-
> tion of Confucianism, from the world-rejection of Buddhism, from

the world-conquest of Islam, or from the messianic expectations
and economic pariah law of Judaism.[1]

This sweeping conclusion of Weber's is frequently echoed
and elaborated in recent discussions without benefit of his vast
erudition or of contemporary empirical studies of the relation of
religious beliefs and practices to modernization. Indeed, this conclusion is frequently converted into modernizing policies and
value judgments that would have horrified Weber's scientific conscience. Yet, the most superficial observation of Asian religions
today indicates that they are far from being static, massive mono-
liths blocking the road to progress. Modern technology, at least, is
as quickly put into the service of religion as in any secular sphere:
neon lights shine in temples and shrines; the radio broadcasts
prayers and devotional songs; the motorbus, automobile, railroad,
and airplane take the pilgrim on his pilgrimage. And now a few
empirical studies are beginning to appear that show something of
the variety and complexity of the relations between the ethics and
theology of world religions on the one hand and political revolution, social reform, and economic enterprise on the other. (See
selected bibliography below.) These studies suggest, in fact, that
the relation of "ascetic Protestantism" to early industrial development, far from being a lonely exception, may turn out to be but
one of many cases of mutual interaction and adaptation between
religious and social change.

India offers a particularly rich field for the study of these in-
teractions and adaptations because of the strength, variety, and
long history of its religiosity and because of the intimate and free-
flowing connections between the popular religion of the masses
and the esoteric religion of the virtuosos. It is also an area where
social anthropologists, sociologists, and social and cultural historians have begun to identify the underlying processes involved in
the modernization of religious beliefs. Some of these processes are
described in the following panel discussion. The panelists are,
in addition to myself, Dr. Bernard Cohn, Associate Professor of

[1] Max Weber, *The Sociology of Religion* (Boston: Beacon Press, 1964),
p. 270. This is a translation of the original German work which was published in 1922.

History and Anthropology of the University of Chicago, and Dr. M. N. Srinivas, Head of the Department of Sociology at Delhi University, Fellow at the Center for Advanced Studies in the Behavioral Sciences, Stanford, California, for 1964–1965 and author of *Caste in Modern India.* The panel was recorded on the occasion of a conference on "Social Structure and Social Change in India," held at the University of Chicago's Center for Continuing Education, June 4–6, 1965. The Conference was cosponsored by the Wenner-Gren Foundation for Anthropological Research and the University's Committee on Southern Asian Studies.

PANEL DISCUSSION

SINGER: I am very happy that we were able to persuade Professor Srinivas to participate in this discussion of the modernization of religious beliefs in Asia. Dr. Srinivas, your contributions in this field have been especially influential, and I wonder whether you could say a little about the way in which you see this modernization occurring. I believe you have introduced the term "Sanskritization" for one of the important processes involved. Would you explain what you mean by that?

SRINIVAS: Sanskritization, as I see it, is a process by which the so-called low castes take over the beliefs, ritual, style of life, and certain other cultural items from those of the upper class, especially the Brahmans. And, as you are aware, this is a process that has occurred and is occurring all over India.

SINGER: What is the relation of this process to modernization?

SRINIVAS: Generally what happens is that when the desire to move up comes to a caste, especially a low caste, it initially takes the form of changing its rituals, style of life, and so forth in the manner of the upper castes, of local upper castes, and I think this is a prelude to westernization. It is interesting in this connection that the Brahman groups in some areas, especially in South India, are rapidly undergoing westernization. By westernization I understand that their beliefs regarding pollution and purity are becoming weaker. They are going into modern occupations such as law, government administration, and the academic professions, for example, and you also see certain important changes occurring in ritual. Would you like me to elaborate on this?

SINGER: Before you do, why don't we ask Dr. Cohn, who has also done research in villages in North India, to say whether he has found anything like the processes you are describing in these villages that he has studied?

COHN: Yes, I think Dr. Srinivas' remarks are certainly applicable to the area I did work in, eastern Uttar Pradesh. A few years ago, the village I studied had approximately two thousand people and two fairly large castes, one a dominant caste of Thakurs or landlords and a large untouchable caste of Chamars. The thing that struck me, particularly, on this point that Professor Srinivas is making is that you could very clearly see the formerly dominant landlords, Thakurs, partaking in the new urban industrial environment in the cities, moving in to become industrial workers and in a number of cases becoming clerks and teachers, taking on in their dress and manner, and certainly in their generalized religious outlook, what we would think of as a more westernized form of Hinduism. At the same time that this process was going on, the lower-caste Chamars were largely landless workers who, for generations, had been partially excluded from more regular forms of religious activity in the village (local Brahmans would not serve them). Their rituals formerly tended to be a very poor reflection of this upper-class landlords' rituals at times of marriage and birth. Through education, which they obtained in the local schools, and through a certain rise in their economic income, which had started during World War II and was continuing into the fifties, instead of turning to a westernized model of religious activity and general outlook, such as we could begin to see amongst the formerly dominant Thakurs, they were tending to become more Sanskritized, and certainly very much more like their former landlords. I think the point that Dr. Srinivas has made here is, of course, that we are not dealing with a dominant Brahman group, but with people who conceive of themselves as Rajputs or Kshatriyas, so that much of the outlook and values and religion that these lower-caste Chamars were taking up tended not to become a Brahmanization, but a Rajputization, but very much the same process that Dr. Srinivas has described.

SINGER: Thank you, Dr. Cohn. I think what he is saying is that in this village, while the upper castes are modernizing and westernizing their style of life and religious beliefs, simultaneously the lower castes are Sanskritizing and assuming more traditional forms of ritual and practice and belief.

SRINIVAS: That is a very interesting point, Dr. Singer. In fact, that is what I wanted to say, that Sanskritization and westernization are linked processes, and in the situation as it is in India today you cannot understand one without the other. As both of you are aware, Dr. Gould in a very interesting paper demonstrated that for the Brahman and other higher castes, Sanskritizing was an attempt to maintain the distance between them and the lower castes who are Sanskritizing; so the Brahmans are, in a sense, running away from the lower groups who are trying to catch up with them.

SINGER: Still another example of both of these processes occurring in a very large city—the city of Madras, where I have done some work myself recently—might be of interest here. In studying leading industrialists in Madras City, I was quite struck by the fact, for example, that there has been a decline of the fear of ritual pollution both in the office and in the factory. For example, in the factories different castes mix freely; at work they eat in the same cafeterias, they ride to work in the same buses, they go to trade-unions and political rallies freely with one another; and more striking than this, perhaps, is the fact that Brahmans and upper castes are actually going into fields of work that have been previously considered highly polluting; for example, the tanning of skins and hides.

COHN: Do these Brahmans actually tan the hides?

SINGER: One tannery I know has as its technical director a Brahman, and among the workers in the tannery are upper castes, clean castes, and some Brahmans. Now, let me not mislead you, because the situation in the factory is quite different from the situation in the home or social contacts, where the families of these industrial leaders and families of most other castes tend to keep up the traditional ritual observances and practices very much in terms of what Dr. Srinivas has called Sanskritization.

SRINIVAS: Dr. Singer, would you say, then, that these Indians whom you studied in Madras are culturally and socially amphibian?

SINGER: Perhaps "amphibian" is a good word for it. I like to think of it as a process of compartmentalization. Many of these leaders would say there is no conflict between their work in industry and their obligations as good Hindus because they are separate spheres. By this, I think they would mean not only that they were physically separate but that the spheres of office and the factory are separate domains where different standards of conduct and behavior and language apply. For example, they tend to wear Western dress, speak English, and follow European customs in the factory, and when they get home they change back to Indian dress, speak the local Indian language, and otherwise conduct themselves as good Hindus.

COHN: Dr. Singer, wouldn't you say this is fairly consistent with what we know of Indian society generally; that once life is built upon compartments, very often you have different roles that you play at the same time: you are a younger brother in one situation, you are a landlord in another situation, you have varying states of pollution; at one time you are polluted, another time you are unpolluted? So, this compartmentalization which you point to, is that different from real continuity in the society and culture of India?

SINGER: I think you are right. This is, perhaps, another or a new example of what happens in Indian society generally. There is this kind of compartmentalization; but I would like to point out, before we come back to the question of whether all this has happened before, that there are certain limitations to this compartmentalization—there are conflicts. You cannot work a full day in the office and at the same time be able to go to all the weddings and rituals and ceremonies that you went to before, so there is a conflict in time. There is also a limit, I think, to the extent to which any personality can divide itself up into all these different roles as father or industrialist or good Hindu, so there are "leakages" as a result of this conflict. I remember, for example, visiting one Brahman industrialist's home and noticing that there was a copy of the Bhagavad-Gita on his library shelves right next to an engineering manual; in his office, for example, I saw on his desk an image of Siva; and there are many other examples of such "leakages."

SRINIVAS: Would you say then, Dr. Singer, that on the one hand there is compartmentalization, and on the other there is the continuity that Dr. Cohn was trying to stress?

SINGER: I agree there is continuity, but it is not merely a kind of conservative persistence of tradition. It is an active, dynamic continuity that consists of people reacting to new conditions and trying to adapt to them. For example, most of these industrialists have tried to reinterpret such basic Hindu doctrines as the belief in rebirth, the belief in *dharma* or moral duty, the belief in personal fate or *karma,* in such a way that it applies to their industrial careers. To cite one or two examples, one of them said that when he is going to be reborn he would prefer to be an industrialist again, except that instead of taking a B.S. in geology he would prefer to have a B.A. in economics.

SRINIVAS: Wouldn't you say this process of reinterpretation of Hinduism has been going on ever since the beginning of the nineteenth century? As I see it, I notice two trends in the nineteenth-century Hinduism: On the one hand, there is increasing secularization, the thing you mentioned of contracting ritual, of leaving out some and emphasizing others, and what you have called "vicarious ritualization"—somebody else substituting for me in certain ritual activities; this is one aspect of it. On the other hand, there has been an attempt on the part of the Indian elite to acknowledge some institutions such as suttee and human sacrifice as evil and to put down these activities, and in doing this they have changed Hinduism in the process of reinterpreting it. Nationalism also came in handy in standing up to the Western colossus. Indians realized they should have their hands clean; that is to say, they should get rid of or reform institutions that the Westerners were condemning. What has happened today is that we have a purified and reinterpreted form of Hinduism, and this reinterpretation has not come to an end. It is going on.

SINGER: What you point out, Dr. Srinivas, is most interesting. I wonder if Dr. Cohn, who has been doing some historical studies himself, would like to comment on what you have just said.

COHN: I think Dr. Srinivas has pointed to a most important

cultural process that is going on. I would begin it at the nine-teenth century and would not end it in 1965. Again, going back to the village I worked in, which had been an area heavily proselyt-ized by the Arya Samaj in the early twentieth century, a reform movement such as Dr. Srinivas has described tried to go back to what the founder conceived of as the original Vedic Hinduism. This movement was most important in terms of setting standards for groups of both high and low caste who in various ways had drifted away from Hinduism and themselves had felt their reli-gion was becoming burdensome to them, so that they could not properly carry on with the older forms of religion in the changing environment that they felt in the early twentieth century.

It is striking again, I think, that those who became attached largely to these reform movements in the nineteenth-century Hin-duism can be subsumed under Srinivas' conceptualization of San-skritization or westernization because they were people, by and large, who were utterly mobile. I have just finished reading an in-teresting paper by Dr. Owen Lynch, of Columbia University, in which he describes the movement of a group of Chamar leather-workers in Agra City starting in the early twentieth century. They conceived of their movement first into the Arya Samaj as a means of becoming good Hindus. The interesting thing about this has been in recent years the rejection of the Samaj for two linked developments, the Neo-Buddhist movement on the part of the Chamars and their entry into politics. May I ask Dr. Srinivas a question on this point? The thing that strikes me particularly for some of these lower-caste groups who are now economically in a better position and certainly politically in a better position is this: is it not possible they may break out of the framework we have seen of Sanskritization as linked processes and move directly into a secular political world, in which they are going to fight for their rights, not in what we have believed to be the traditional cultural means, but with new political and economic means?

SINGER: Dr. Srinivas, would you wish to answer that?

SRINIVAS: I have a brief answer to that—necessarily dog-matic. I think Dr. Cohn would agree with me that this fight in secular economic realms, economic political realms, is already tak-ing place, and this will go on accentuating. Still, as far as the bulk of the original groups are concerned, I think they will also like to have their status validated in traditional caste terms.

In this connection, Owen Lynch mentioned the interesting process of "passing" occurring among groups not only in Agra, but as far south as Madura. All this is a fascinating universe, you see.

SINGER: If I may add a comment on this: of course, a secular alternative is available, and some of the lower castes and middle and upper castes are taking it; but it is also true that there are nonsecular alternatives that are non-Hindu. For example, Ambedkar's Buddhists are a case of many low castes opting for Buddhism. I believe there are other groups like the Moslems, the Indian Christians, the Sikhs, and others who are undergoing similar processes of modernization within the context of their specific cultural and religious traditions. Wouldn't you agree to that, Dr. Cohn?

COHN: Very much so. The thing that strikes me, Dr. Singer, is where we are left with a hundred years of European scholarship acting on Indian religion. Certainly if you look at the older works both of orientalists and some sociologists like Max Weber, there is the constant refrain that it is the cultural values and religion of India which are going to prevent any change. It is a static society and a static culture. Certainly the picture you draw of the industrialists and the processes that Professor Srinivas has mentioned indicate a highly flexible tradition in no way stopping a rapid development and change in the society.

SRINIVAS: Would you say that one of the things we are doing today is to shed the myths that had been acquired over the last fifty years about the characteristics of traditional Indian society and culture?

SINGER: Yes, I would agree there are many myths left to be shed, and what Dr. Cohn has suggested certainly should be emphasized again and again: that India and other Asian countries are very complex, changing societies; they have changed in the past and are still changing. Their basic religious and cultural ways are by no means static, and they are by no means incompatible with or obstacles to modernization. What we have been saying is that if you look at it closely, you will see that there are as many changes in ritual and beliefs as there are changes in industry and city life and in village life. These changes are not very different in principle and in form from changes that have been going on in a country like India for many hundreds, and possibly thousands, of years.

SRINIVAS: Yet I have a point here, Dr. Singer. Modernized and secularized India will not be America or Europe. It will still be India. What would you say to this?

SINGER: I would certainly agree with you. It is not going to be a carbon copy of America and Europe; and as America and Europe are different from each other, modernization in India will certainly have an Indian accent.

COHN: I certainly agree to that proposition. Dr. Srinivas, did you want to add anything by way of conclusion?

SRINIVAS: One thing I do want to emphasize here: it has struck me several times during the last eight months, while I have been working on the topic of social change in modern India, that educated Indians live with paradoxes. You remember that famous informant who told a British anthropologist, "When I put on my shirt and go to the factory I take off my caste. When I come home and take off my shirt I put on my caste." This dramatizes the paradoxes in which modern Indians live; secularization on one hand, Sanskritization on the other. A man who is studying for a Ph.D. in astronomy will still consult an astrologer if he wants to find a bride. I think that is a very interesting situation.

SINGER: I think most of us Westerners who visit India are very much struck by these paradoxes, and initially we think there must be very deep psychological conflict in the Indian soul, as some people say, underlying them. But I think further study has convinced me and many of my colleagues that there are indeed no very deep conflicts and that Indians are able to adapt to these paradoxes and go back and forth in these different contexts without schizophrenia.

COHN: I think I might argue that one of the underlying differences between Indian and American society is just in this point: that in the United States, in our society, there is a constant drive for role consistencies. A man's behavior should be consistent from one realm to another. In all my experience in India, I have felt the opposite. The Indians are much more tolerant of role conflict, and we perceive role conflict where they do not conceive any role conflict. There is not this kind of drive to make everyone in their lives one or to make everyone in the society one.

SRINIVAS: But, at the same time, Dr. Cohn, I feel—and perhaps I am completely wrong in this—Western sociologists and anthropologists who go to India assume that Western man is completely rational, whereas an Indian is a mixture of rationality and irrationality, and I would like to question this assumption. Is Western man so rational?

SINGER: Yes, I think we fall into the fallacy of comparing our own ideals with other people's realities, and we have to compare reality with reality and ideal with ideal.

Summarizing the discussion, I should like to suggest the following tentative conclusions on the relations of Hinduism to modernization.

1. Continuous exposure to European ideas and criticism from the sixteenth through the nineteenth centuries stimulated a number of reform movements within Hinduism, such as the Arya Samaj and the Ramakrishna missions.

2. Partly in reaction to these European influences and partly deriving from indigenous sources, particular individuals and groups increased their conformity to Hindu beliefs and ritual practices, that is, "Sanskritized" their style of life. In some cases, this Sanskritization was a prelude to westernization and modernization; in others, it followed upon entry into modern occupations and the acquisition of wealth, political power, and social status as an effort to close the gap between ritual and secular status.

3. European and modern models and influences have not been immediately fused with traditional models. They have rather been incorporated into Indian life and thought in separate spheres —for example, office and factory—where they have been permitted to develop as "foreign" innovations. Traditional Hinduism, on the other hand, has been maintained in the sphere of the home and social relations. This compartmentalization has minimized direct conflict between tradition and modernity.

4. The conflicts that have emerged from the coexistence of traditional and modern life styles tend to be resolved by abbreviating the time given to ritual observances, by delegating more of

the responsibility for ritual observances to those who have the time (for example, women and professional priests), and by reinterpreting traditional religious beliefs such as the doctrines of *karma, dharma, moksha,* and *ahimsa* to apply to the problems and conditions of modern life. Gandhi's use of these doctrines in the struggle for political independence, the abolition of untouchability, and the amelioration of poverty is a familiar recent example of this process of reinterpretation of Hindu beliefs. Less dramatic examples can be found among many Hindus engaged in modern occupations and professions.

5. The net result of these processes of reinterpretation, vicarious ritualization, Sanskritization, and compartmentalization is not yet a secularization of Hinduism, although the secular ideologies of socialism, communism, and rationalism are also found in India. The net result of these processes of interaction and adaptation is more accurately described as an ecumenical sort of Hinduism that is blurring sect and caste lines.

6. While these conclusions do not add up to a proof that Hinduism has caused modernization, they do reveal a capacity of Hinduism to adapt to changing conditions that casts serious doubt on the widespread belief that Hindu beliefs and practices are a major obstacle to modernization.

SELECTED BIBLIOGRAPHY

BELLAH, R. N. *Tokugawa Religion.* Glencoe, Ill.: The Free Press, 1957.
————. "Reflections on the Protestant Ethic Analogy in Asia," *The Journal of Social Issues,* 19 (1963).
————. *Religion and Progress in Modern Asia.* Glencoe, Ill.: The Free Press, 1965.
BINDER, L. *The Ideological Revolution in the Middle East.* New York: Wiley, 1964.
COHN, B. "The Changing Status of a Depressed Caste," in *Village India,* M. MARRIOTT, ed., Chicago: University of Chicago Press, 1955.
————. "Changing Tradition of a Low Caste," in M. SINGER, ed. *Traditional India.*
GEERTZ, C. *The Religion of Java.* Glencoe, Ill.: The Free Press, 1960.

GREEN, R. W., ed. *Protestantism and Capitalism: The Weber Thesis.* Boston: Heath, 1959.

GRUNEBAUM, G. VON. *Modern Islam.* Berkeley: University of California Press, 1962.

HARPER, E. B., ed. "Aspects of Religion in South Asia," *Journal of Asian Studies,* 23 (June 1964).

JANSEN, M. B., ed. *Changing Japanese Attitudes toward Modernization.* Princeton, N. J.: Princeton University Press, 1965.

SHILS, E. A. *The Intellectual between Tradition and Modernity: The Indian Situation.* The Hague: Mouton & Co., 1961.

SINGER, M. "Cultural Values in India's Economic Development," *The Annals* (1956).

————, ed. *Traditional India: Structure and Change.* Philadelphia: American Folklore Society, 1958, 1959.

————. "Weber on the Religion of India," *American Anthropologist,* 63 (1961).

————. "The Radha-Krishna Bhajans of Madras City," *History of Religion,* 2 (1963).

————. "The Social Organization of Indian Civilization," *Diogenes,* (1964).

————, ed. *Krishna: Myths, Rites and Attitudes.* Honolulu: East-West Center Press, 1966.

————. *et al.* "India's Cultural Values and Economic Development," *Economic Development & Cultural Change,* 7 (1958).

SMITH, D. E. *India as a Secular State.* Princeton, N. J.: Princeton University Press, 1963.

SPIRO, M. *Kibbutz: Venture in Utopia.* Cambridge: Harvard University Press, 1956.

SRINIVAS, M. N. *Religion and Society among the Coorgs of South India.* Oxford: Clarendon Press, 1952.

————. "A Note on Sanskritization and Westernization," *Far Eastern Quarterly,* 15 (1956).

————. *Caste in Modern India and Other Essays.* Bombay: Asia Publishing House, 1962.

————. *Social and Cultural Change in India.* Berkeley: University of California Press, 1966.

THRUPP, S. L., ed. *Millennial Dreams in Action.* The Hague: Mouton & Co., 1962.

WEBER, M. *The Sociology of Religion.* Boston: Beacon Press, 1964.

————. *The Religion of India, The Sociology of Hinduism and Buddhism.* Glencoe, Ill.: The Free Press, 1958.

WRIGHT, A., ed. *Confucianism and Chinese Civilization.* New York: Atheneum, 1964.

Chapter 5

The Modernization of Education

C. Arnold Anderson

Three slogans are now echoing around the world: independence, development, and modernization. These are today's cries of the leaders of new nations, the present-day versions of life, liberty, and the pursuit of happiness. Those of us whose nations came to birth under these latter aspirations recognize that the new aims are updated translations of our own ideals.

In some countries the leaders prefer to emphasize one of the goals, and most often that is independence. In other countries, development is put first, even if some independence is sacrificed. Usually leaders believe that independence, development, and modernization mean about the same thing. But we are supposed to be talking about modernization, even though that is an idea most difficult to define clearly. In some places, modernization means to the leaders admission to the United Nations, where their ideas are heard by the whole world, along with those of the most powerful nations. Elsewhere, modernization is thought of mainly in terms of airlines, steel mills, and a rising level of living. To still other leaders, enlightenment and science are the heart of modernization.

Machines are taken as the symbol of modernization by some men because they increase production; by others, because they symbolize science displacing superstition. But sometimes modernization means a strengthening of the old ways of life, as when literacy enables individuals to appreciate religious doctrines in their purer form, unmixed by superstition. Even if modernization is not a very clear idea, one theme runs through nearly every interpretation of it: modernization can be achieved only by improving and extending education. Why do the leaders of developing countries put so much emphasis on this point?

First, you must have education before you can obtain technological and economic progress. To boost food production, to operate factories, to apply science for improvement of life, or to trade in world markets, a country has to have a large group of well-trained people.

Second, to unify a collection of people and tribes into a nation, you also need education. Men cannot understand their fellow citizens and widen their loyalties beyond the village if they cannot communicate. They cannot identify with those who live in the next valley unless they or their neighbors have at least some notion of what it means to be a nation. They will have little influence on public affairs so long as they remain illiterate.

Third, a political state in the modern world can survive only if its officials can co-ordinate administration over large areas. The policies of the prime minister must extend beyond the range of his voice. It is interesting, indeed, that few nations today can imagine doing without something called prime minister or president; and this assumption is a commitment to a whole world of ideas and activities that can come into existence only through the work of literate public officials.

But it is not enough just to realize that education is needed. A people has to learn how to behave so that there can be an effective modern state and society. Peasants have to become more productive, enterprisers have to learn to become venturesome, officials have to learn how to carry on the public business promptly and in proper order. In all these situations, education is needed.

A careful look at education discloses that it has many functions. The results of education cannot be captured entirely by the economy or by government. Or, turning this the other way round, a society reaps many benefits that were not expected when it began to build up its school system. Several things happen to youngsters as they go through school.

Perhaps the most important thing is that children develop new conceptions of what kind of persons they are. They adopt new rules for their conduct and acquire loyalties to new ideas and new groups.

Schools also teach children various special skills—a craft, some science, how to run a household—but also some capabilities that can be interests for lifelong leisure: enjoyment of music, sports, or even the skills of controversy. Among the skills—but by no means the most important—schools help individuals to earn a living. And they prepare men to transform the occupational structure while they are working in it.

Education preserves intellectual systems: literature, art, law, science. And youth learn how to remold traditional intellectual systems into new forms with which to advance the material or nonmaterial aspects of modernization. At the same time, schools elaborate and reinforce the educational system itself.

In every society, including the most democratic ones, the schools help to single out those individuals who are to become part of the elite and instruct them in some of the special skills they will need to play their part as leaders. Education helps to select and train the culture bearers, the creative men, and the rulers.

Finally, since schools have important political purposes, we should point out that pupils are indoctrinated. Children learn to share the customs of their society and to accept certain political philosophies, and this is one of the chief means by which schools direct children's minds toward the future.

In all these directions, education contributes to the modernization of a society, but at the same time schools are also conservative agents. Whether on balance their effect is to strengthen old ways or to build new ones depends partly on whether education itself is being modernized, but it depends even more on what goes on outside the schools. When we trace the influences of education on the modernizing process, we have to remember that what is a very modern kind of education for one society may be exceedingly old-fashioned education in Old England or New England.

We should keep in mind, too, that education is not a magic medicine that can by itself transform a society. Social change is very complex, as can be seen by looking closely at some of the relationships between education and development.

It seems that today nearly everyone believes that national levels of education and of income are closely related. That faith is recorded in the documents of all the international agencies and in the scholarly magazines, and it is echoed in the popular press. In the long run, of course, no country can be prosperous unless it has a fairly large proportion of workers with something more than bare literacy. Countries cannot escape from poverty until their citizens become literate, learn to carry on complex technical and business operations, and can administer complicated organizations.

But before we conclude that a country should go all out for more education, we have to see just what those broad generalizations mean. It may help to keep some perspective on this problem if we recall that as late as 1890 less than 5 per cent of American youth finished secondary school. Yet by 1890 the United States was already one of the high-income countries, and it was certainly modernized; in fact, it was just about to launch the automotive revolution on the world. Or consider the Soviet Union, another country that has made great economic progress in recent decades. Yet in 1959, after a generation of industrialization, the average formal schooling of the working man in Russia was four years. Schooling, then, is necessary for development; but how much schooling? And will education bring development?

No country can move quickly from poverty to affluence or from backwardness to modernization. A nation climbs from one economic level to the next by small and halting steps. Long-run development is a series of short steps. In each short-run period, does education precede or follow rises in level of income? The answer seems to be that increases in income are followed by a rise in schooling. But each affects the other, for without improved training the rise in income would stop.

A country that has a little economic surplus above rock-bottom poverty can provide a little schooling. If put to good use—and that is a real *if*—that training can bring a small gain in productivity out of which to pay for more schooling, and so on. Depending on where we begin to look at the process of change, schooling can seem to be the cause or the result. But, of course, it is the step-by-step movement, as in walking, that brings the advance.

The first steps in educational improvement can be sterile. After all, the effects of schools depend on the motives for which people are willing to put their children in school and keep them there. The benefits depend also on how people use what they have learned. And so it is that the pay-off from education depends on all the supplementary influences and activities going on in the society around the school. This is true whether we measure the social value of schools by economic productivity, by how well the government is run, or by the wisdom of citizens when they vote. So, to be sure, the best-educated nations have the highest incomes; but this conclusion is so sweeping that it tells very little about what contribution education made to their modernization.

As we look backward one or two centuries in our own history, the typical individual did not have very much schooling, although the stock of educated men in England in 1750 or France in 1800 was larger than most people imagine. The countries that are starting today on the road of development probably need a relatively larger group of educated men than did England in 1750, for example, and for several reasons. The technology that is being borrowed today is more complex: radio instead of telegraph, plastics instead of paper. Today, also, it is important for every nation to have officials and technicians who can talk with the highly educated representatives of the developed nations.

Nonetheless, some of the developing countries set higher targets for education than they really require. They exaggerate the need for education and underestimate the importance of a stimulating social environment throughout the whole society. In some places, the faith that education is good in itself goes beyond reasonable bounds. And certainly the political pressures to open more and more schools is great.

Who would deny that education has worth-while results, whether it brings economic benefits or not? However, merely building up a stock of people with formal schooling is no guarantee of the hoped-for benefits. It takes generations to develop technical know-how, business experience, and productive habits of work. It is experience and effort that produce those qualities in a population; book learning is only a means to help acquire them.

We can say, then, that over much of the world we are witnessing a modernization *of* education that is not matched by an equal modernization *by* education. The "development gap" among the countries of the world that people speak about is not solely economic. There are other gaps: in the political maturity of citizens, in the skill of artisans, in business management, in administrative skill by tax officials. It will be easier to close the gap in schooling between countries than to level up the productive skills of ordinary peasants and workmen. All of this is another way of saying that school learning is only one part of the total education that is needed for modernization.

From a practical point of view, the problem may be clarified by posing three main questions: (1) How much education should a country have? (2) What kind of quality of education should its youth receive? (3) Who should receive that education if modernization is going to be pushed ahead?

How Much Education?

Since the long road from underdevelopment to modern ways of life must be traveled step by step, no matter how much help a country receives from the more advanced countries for its educational or other programs, in the long run it must pay most of its own way.

The resources that a poor country can spare for development are very limited. But, at the same time, the possible productive uses to which those resources could be assigned are many. Of course, the possibility of making wise investments is limited by the supply of people who know how to make productive use of such assets, whether in factories or in improving the educational system itself. No country can train a group of skilled men overnight. Education takes time, and the schools absorb a large share of the trained people to teach the new workers.

A country's shortage of skilled people can be relieved if it is willing to make use of well-trained foreigners during the decades in which its own citizens are being trained. But here we run into a clash between the desire for development and a country's determination to run its own affairs. Foreign teachers are often welcomed; but in most countries foreigners are not wanted in government or business, although they are also teachers of some of the rarest skills.

As a result, many countries set up crash programs to train people in the most-needed specialties; but crash programs are wasteful. If a country could bring itself to employ more trained foreigners, it could probably develop a more carefully planned education and training system. There would be more resources to put into other essential programs, such as roads or agricultural extension work. At the same time, there would be more money with which to employ foreign advisers to teach the refined skills of management and decision making that cannot be readily taught in schools. This leads us to a basic question: should we judge the modernization of an educational system in terms of its size and the number of graduates or in terms of how efficiently educational resources are used within the total program of modernization?

What, then, really are the educational needs of a country? The answer depends on what one expects education to accomplish. If youth are given a broad education, the supply of vocational skills will increase slowly. If, instead, an effort is made to turn out half-skilled men quickly, they will not be prepared to shift to new kinds of job. They will not know how to be citizens, and few will become public leaders.

The approach to education in terms of narrow training of specialized workers for an estimated need to fill a particular list of jobs is called man-power planning. Probably most of the predications of needed man power have been unreliable. Moreover, this approach is questionable because it does not prepare flexible workers. But the most important difficulty is that there is a danger of training more men than can be used, for it is much more difficult to find jobs for men than to teach them the skills. It is managers and employers, not workers, who are most lacking in developing countries. And then there is the related difficulty that some of the most important capacities are not taught in schools, but must be learned by experience on the job.

So the cautious answer is that a country needs a little more education than it has today. Five years from now, still a little more will be needed. Large forecasts look good on paper; but unless there is equal expansion in jobs, there will be much waste of resources by putting too much investment into training.

But, whatever the size of the educational system, there is also a problem of dividing it among the elementary, secondary, and university levels. One could find a strong argument for giving priority to any one of these. Unless the ordinary man is literate, for example, he will be cheated when he sells his crops, and he cannot read instructions for his job. As a consequence, many countries are now setting the goal of a universal six years of elementary education within a couple of decades.

On the other hand, there can be no government at all unless a country has many highly educated men to make policy, work in international agencies, conduct research, and run businesses. This way of looking at the problem would give higher education first claim on available resources.

But then we have to face the fact that a country needs about three to five middle-level technicians for every university graduate or senior manager. And the elite will be more capable if it is selected from a large pool of secondary-school graduates. In addition, most of the on-the-job training programs are intended for people with this middle level of schooling.

Among these three claims for educational priority, the case for university education is the weakest, provided a small number of really well-trained men and women are supplied. For example, at the time of the American Revolution, the United States had about one college man for every thousand of the population. Ghana (to take one example of a country with a comparatively large system of education) needs more than that, but does she need five times as many? In the same way, it can be suggested that a developing country does not need to put more than a small percentage of its youth through secondary school. Nobody can be given an exact numerical figure for the balance among these levels of school, but it is clear that most countries must resist the political pressures to overexpand the higher levels, unless one is so foolish as to say that a country needs as many educated people as it can produce.

However we define the need for educated people, we have to ask also how many a country can afford; and this brings in the idea of waste of resources. A basic test of how much education a country can afford is to ask what it would give up. For example, by expanding the upper schools rapidly, it would sacrifice potential primary-school teachers and reduce the supply of men to look after the upkeep of machines in its factories or to work at reforestation. The real cost of a program is what other possible projects would be given up to pay for the one chosen. By this test, a country can very easily slip into a policy of providing too much education. Also there are heavy costs and the possibility of much waste in having the wrong kind of education.

WHAT KIND OF EDUCATION?

In every country—not only in developing countries—there is a controversy between advocates of general education and those who emphasize technical training. The latter group deplore the bookishness of the usual kind of school. However, they forget that bookish schools have always been predominant in the United States. Those who favor general education at elementary and secondary levels point out that the schools in developing countries have all they can do to give children a basic education and get them ready to absorb vocational training.

After all, a country can accumulate a stock of skill in either of two ways. It can train a small number to a very high level of skill, matching the best-trained individuals in the advanced countries. On the other hand, it can train a larger number to an intermediate level of competence and only a few to the highest level. Many who have studied this question conclude that the second policy is the wiser one if the aim is to get the most development at the least cost and with the least damage to other kinds of development investments. In the field of health, for example, it has been recommended that a country provide many nurses, but only a few physicians to direct the program and train the nurses.

Another conclusion among some who have been thinking about the problems of vocational education is that whenever possible such instruction should be given to people who are already committed to jobs and at a point in time and place near where the skills will be put to use. That is, most vocational training should be given on the job. Thus, people are put to work and trained in the same broad program.

Often proposals are made to start people toward their jobs by giving them vocational training in primary school with lessons in gardening and manual training and then in secondary school moving on to such things as electronics. This is an unwise policy, for more reasons than can be mentioned here. For instance, long experience in many countries has shown that teaching agriculture in school makes children dislike farming; such skills should be taught to adults who are actual farmers and to older children who have chosen that calling. At the same time, it could be argued that agricultural extension work should receive major attention in nearly every country. Farm productivity will have to be raised, and this means that not all the training should be for industry. Another objection to giving vocational training in secondary schools is that it takes time away from science teaching, which is basic to all later technical education.

One clear conclusion from even this brief scanning of the situation is that an educational system should be flexible. One way to bring this about is to improve the quality of general education in order to turn out flexible graduates. At the same time, flexibility in training can be guaranteed by putting the training near the production operations whenever possible.

Very important is the question of the quality of education. Nearly all elementary schools in most of the world are of deplorable quality. Teachers are poorly trained; often they are little ahead of their pupils. Obviously foreign teachers cannot staff the primary schools, but must be used at higher levels, so the quality of primary schools can be raised only slowly.

At the upper levels, better quality can be obtained more easily. Here, foreign teachers can make a real contribution. And it will not be too difficult to produce comparatively well-trained local teachers fairly rapidly.

But quality refers to pupils as well as to teachers. This is one solid argument against too rapid expansion of postelementary schools, since a large proportion of those finishing elementary school will be barely literate. It does not follow, on the other hand, that good secondary or college students can be found only by using elaborate examinations. It is equally important to be generous in admitting students to secondary schools and colleges and then keep those who demonstrate the necessary ability.

What is really meant by quality in a pupil? What are the personal attributes found in men of initiative—men who will be productive workers on farms or in factories or as businessmen or officials? Over and above a solid schooling, such men need certain attitudes, certain traits of character, and a drive to make something of their lives. Schools do little to produce such qualities, which come also from family background, local traditions of enterprise, and the broad climate of public opinion. Schools are good tools for societies that know how to use them.

One more misconception should be laid to rest. The schools are often blamed for the fact that village youth drift off to the cities and try to become white-collar workers. But, after all, why should youngsters who have gone to school stay on the farms when their older kinfolk will not adopt better methods of farming? Why should people be satisfied with manual jobs if others pay more? Vocational aspirations are not produced by schools. They result from looking at the job market, from observing older people, and from ambition. If a country wants its youth to be farmers or extension workers or craftsmen, it will have to pay higher wages in those jobs. Few developing countries have yet learned this lesson.

Who Will Get the Schooling?

A poor country must try to get the maximum benefit from the comparatively small amount of investment it is able to put into education or any other development project. No one would define the benefits solely in economic terms, but economic goals must be high on the list if poverty is to be eliminated.

It is imperative to get the largest possible output from the schools in which the country invests its teachers and other resources. This will occur in only some parts of a developing country. Only in some districts are parents ready to put children in school and keep them there until they have learned something. Only some districts are willing to pay part of the costs of schools. Inevitably, then, some districts will have more schools, and their youth will receive more education than the children in less progressive districts.

But this means that not all the children in a developing country will have equal opportunities to attend primary schools. And of those who finish the elementary schools, children from homes and localities where education has become firmly established will show up better on examinations. Those children will make up a larger proportion of secondary and college enrollments. Hence an unequal distribution of opportunities; but so long as a country is poor, that inequality is unavoidable.

Even among the more fortunate children, there is a problem of how much freedom of choice in education and job selection a country should permit. Officials do have to decide how many places to provide in medical or engineering school, in liberal arts or agriculture. Inevitably some youths will not get their first choice. The problem for officials is in giving individuals as much choice as is consistent with procuring the needed supply of trained individuals. Of course it is not for some one official to develop the illusion that he really knows how many are needed.

Such are some of the relationships between education and different aspects of national development, some of the advantages and the shortcomings of various approaches to educational policy. There is a limit to what education can do for development unless it is strongly supported by other modernizing influences. Almost any kind of education would bring at least a few benefits to a modernizing country, but more definite and more comprehensive benefits are desirable and possible.

But, in the last analysis, education will upset traditional life at the same time it helps to lay the foundation for a new way of life. The more effective education is, the more sweeping will be the changes that result. Not all the effects will contribute directly to economic improvement, nor should they do so. Some of the effects will displease the political authorities. The best assurance for a stimulating and constructive educational system is to surround it with a society that has vigorous impulses toward change and initiative. Schools alone are weak instruments of modernization; but when well supported, they are powerful.

Chapter 6

Modernization
and Higher Education

Edward Shils

I

The success of the program of modernization of the new states is
to a large extent dependent on the performance of their university
systems. Like flags, anthems, armies, airlines, and atomic energy
commissions, universities are part of the paraphernalia of sovereignty. They are also emblems of modernity. But they are much
more than these. They are the institutional instruments for the
creation of modernity in polity, economy, society, and culture.
The large number of university graduates required for governmental administration and for economic planning and management, for numerous branches of technology, for statistical, medical, and agricultural services, and for geological and other natural
resource surveys renders it unlikely that the best universities in
the advanced countries could provide enough places for those
who seek higher education and whom their governments wish to
have trained at their expense. There are also strong economic reasons for providing university education at the undergraduate level
at home, because although initial costs are very high—probably
higher per student than they would be for training that same stu-

81

dent overseas—in a relatively short time the cost per student trained at home becomes more economical. There are, of course, very weighty political reasons to train students at home. The urge to be independent of the former colonial powers and the desire that a close contact be maintained between the prospective leaders of the country and the particularity of its situation necessitate the development of universities in the underdeveloped parts of the world. And, indeed, this is just what is happening. There are still a few underdeveloped countries in Black Africa which have more students pursuing their higher education abroad than they have at home, but this is only a temporary condition. Foreign study, particularly at the postgraduate level, is still necessary and will continue to be so; but the burden of preparing the educated elite of the future will fall increasingly and preponderantly on the universities of the underdeveloped countries.

The question is: Can they carry the burden?

II

Let us first consider their tasks a little more closely. The new states need, in the first instance, an effective machinery of government, and this means a competent higher civil service. They need trained scientists to conduct surveys of their mineral resources; they need technologists to invent ways of extracting and processing their mineral resources or to adapt imported techniques of extraction and processing. They need specialists in agriculture, trained in genetics, soil chemistry, plant diseases, veterinary medicine, agricultural economics, extension work, and so on. They need managers of industrial firms, chemists, and mechanical and electrical engineers; economists and accountants for their ministries of finance; economists for the drafting of economic plans and the evaluation of their implementation; demographers and statisticians for man-power surveys and numerous other activities. They need teachers for secondary schools; they need journalists, radio broadcasters and engineers; they need judges and lawyers, physicians and public health specialists, nutritionists and biochemists. They need university teachers, anthropologists, sociologists, historians, and linguists. Nearly all these occupations can be practiced adequately only on the basis of training at university level.

Even those occupations such as business management which, at earlier stages in the history of the advanced countries, were filled by persons without higher education, but are now coming to demand highly trained personnel, can no longer be staffed by men who have learned their craft exclusively by its practice. There is too great a gulf between the empiricism of the old-fashioned entrepreneur and the technology and organization of the modern industrial or commercial enterprise. What is more, the socialistic doctrinal affirmations of the leaders of political parties and of the governments obstruct the emergence of entrepreneurs in numbers large enough to satisfy the aspirations for economic expansion. Thus, even for business management, there must be a turning toward the universities.

Are the universities of the third world equal to the tasks that the program of modernization puts upon them? Can they produce graduates in sufficient numbers, of sufficiently high level, and of appropriate skills? Are they doing so at present?

Before attempting to answer these questions, it will be useful to say that it is not the modernization of the universities of the underdeveloped countries that is at issue. With the exception of the University of Al Azhar, the millennium-old university in Cairo, and a few old Latin American examples, like the University of Bogotá, the universities of the underdeveloped world are relatively young. Their problems are not primarily a matter of archaic courses of study.

Certain parts of the underdeveloped world do produce university graduates in large numbers. India, Indonesia, the Philippines, Pakistan, Egypt, and many of the Latin American countries do so. There are still quantitative shortages of university graduates in Indonesia, but at the present rate of production, this is only a temporary condition. The universities of the Black African countries and of Malaysia are still producing only a trickle of graduates. With respect to quality, it may be said that in general the universities or university systems which produce numerous graduates do not give them an education of a high standard, while those which produce only small numbers of graduates seem to adhere to a quite high standard of education.

This inverse correlation is not merely a result of the difficulty of educating large numbers. It is in part a result of the deliberate adherence to exigent standards of admission and examination in the African and Malaysian universities, as compared with the universities in the other parts of the underdeveloped world. The African and Malaysian universities and university colleges at Khartoum, Kampala, Nairobi, Leopoldville, Dakar, Freetown, Legon, Ibadan, Singapore, and Kuala Lumpur were founded by the then-ruling colonial powers not long before their departure. They were intended to have the same standard of intellectual proficiency, at least on the teaching side, as the universities of the metropolis. For a considerable period, many of them were linked by a "special relationship" to the metropolitan universities in order to assure their adherence to the standards observed in the metropolitan universities. (The University of Dakar is still a part of the French university system, being maintained financially by the French government and falling within the jurisdiction of the Ministry of National Education in Paris.) It is, indeed, their very insistence on high standards of qualification for admission that restricts the numbers of students being educated and graduated. The secondary-school systems of the Black African countries cannot produce enough students with qualifications that enable them to gain admission.

In the other countries where student numbers are large, qualifications for admission are not so exigent. The secondary-school systems of these countries, like those of Black Africa, are unable to train large numbers of their pupils at a high level, and this, coupled with a very liberal admissions policy, means that the student bodies of these countries are not prepared to pursue their studies at the same standards observed and required in the Black African universities.

For much of the underdeveloped world, therefore, the deficiencies are of quality, not quantity. There are enough or nearly enough persons who have the certification that enables them to fill the available posts; what is lacking is enough persons sufficiently well trained intellectually to enable them to do the jobs that have to be done. Of course, there are individual teachers and even whole departments—and in India, where the system of affiliated colleges prevails, whole colleges—giving a very good training, and there are often outstanding students who manage to get a good education despite their universities; but, on the whole, where university populations are large, the quality of graduates tends to be poor.

III

The universities and university systems with the largest numbers of students have grown very rapidly; the Indian university enrollment has increased from less than 150,000 in 1939 to 1,250,000 in 1964. These large and rapidly increasing numbers of students have required great numbers of teachers—and within a very short space of time. This brings us to one of the chief handicaps of the university systems of the underdeveloped world. There are simply not enough competent university teachers to fill most of the posts that have been created to meet the demands of mass university education. This shortage obtains also for the university systems of Black Africa, where student numbers are small. Even if expatriate university teachers from the metropolitan universities were available—and they are not, since the university systems of these countries are also expanding, and there is a great shortage of university teachers throughout the advanced countries such as the United States, France, Great Britain, and Germany—there is marked resistance to their employment. The idea of large-scale employment of expatriate university teachers does not even occur in India and Indonesia, or the Middle East or Latin America. It is only in Africa and Malaysia that expatriates make up a large proportion of the university teaching body—in senior posts, especially—and there, too, is found a growing dissatisfaction with the situation. The indigenous university teachers and many politicians are opposed to it, and this, in turn, makes such appointments less inviting to expatriate teachers who can find attractive posts in their own or other advanced countries.

It is in the underdeveloped countries with large student bodies that practically all university teaching is done by indigenous persons. Many of them are not very well qualified; but quite apart from that fact, the level of their performance is greatly pulled down by the large numbers they have to teach and the poor remuneration and working conditions provided for them. In Indonesia, very many of the teachers, in order to gain a livelihood, must teach in a number of universities simultaneously; or, alternatively, they must be employed in commercial or professional enterprises outside the university. In the Latin American universities, it is extremely common for university teaching to be no more than a part-time activity, employment in private business or professional practice providing most of the teacher's income and consuming most of his time. In India, most of the teachers in institutions of higher education teach many hours weekly for very small salaries, and many of them supplement their professional income by writing "notes" for students or by scrambling for examinerships. They have little time or motive for improving their knowledge and their manner of teaching.

All these factors—the poor training and hard living conditions of the teachers, confronting large numbers of students who themselves are ill prepared for university study—contribute to the low quality of education. Poorly stocked and crowded libraries, scantily equipped and crowded laboratories, crowded lecture rooms, insufficient space and time for personal meetings between teachers and individuals or small groups of students—all add to the handicaps of university teaching. Syllabuses and courses of study not brought up to date or carelessly planned are further aggravated by the delicate problem of the medium of instruction.

IV

In African and Malaysian universities, the medium of university instruction is English or French; in Africa, at least, thus far practically no one has challenged this arrangement. It has the great advantage of making available to the student not only up-to-date textbooks but the wide range of scholarly and scientific literature of the metropolitan language, which is indispensable for serious academic study on the undergraduate as well as the postgraduate level. It has the disadvantage that students often read slowly and with difficulty, and they follow with imperfect comprehension lectures delivered in a language that is not their mother tongue.

Yet, in Africa the present arrangement has gone unchallenged because there is no alternative. None of the African languages except Swahili is known by a large enough proportion of the population of any country to justify transferring to it without causing a violent reaction in all the sectors of the population that would be cut off by the choice of any one African language as the medium of higher education. And even if this obstacle did not exist, there is another that is likely to endure for a very long time; namely, that there is no scholarly or scientific literature, including textbooks, in any African language.

Throughout most of the rest of the world of the underdeveloped countries, the situation is quite different. There, instruction is carried on in the vernacular language, which means that the students are able to comprehend lectures but are then cut off from the main bodies of scientific and scholarly literature of the contemporary world and are condemned also to the use of textbooks written in the vernacular, which are largely inferior to those in the metropolitan languages. Their teachers, in addition to the reasons already cited, and because they do not have the time or linguistic facility, tend to confine their own studies to literature available in their own language. This does only a little harm in the study of indigenous languages and literatures, but in those fields where the major works of scholarship and science have been produced outside the particular country, the handicap to effective teaching is very substantial.

There are certain countries like India and Pakistan (and Ceylon, although the position is changing rapidly there because of the decision to go over to Singhalese as the medium of instruction at the University of Ceylon and the *pirivena* universities) where instruction is still conducted very largely in English. In these countries, the study of English is begun later in the preuniversity education than it used to be, and as a result the students and often younger teachers have a mastery of English that is inadequate for the effective teaching or learning of demanding subjects. The stu-

dents cannot readily follow the lectures, and the teachers' awareness of this often leads them to lecture in a manner that further
reduces the attractiveness of the subject taught. Where, on the
other hand, there has been a change-over to the mother tongue or
regional language as the medium of instruction, the teachers often
find it difficult to express themselves clearly in a language that is
undeveloped for scholarly or scientific uses; the students, for their
part, are confined to using textbooks of poor quality, and reading
supplementary to the textbooks is seldom done. It is true that they
are still expected to know and employ English and to have facility
in the use of books and articles in that language; but where the
change-over has occurred, English has usually been allowed to
deteriorate so that, in fact, they do not have easy enough command of it nor are they inclined or able to use it fruitfully.

Meanwhile, the pressure for a large-scale transfer to an indigenous language is gaining. The establishment since January 26,
1965, of Hindi as the official language of the government of India
(given the preponderance of government employment as the
chief occupational goal and opportunity for Indian university
graduates) will only add to the force of that pressure. With it,
facility in English is likely to decline further. It is most unlikely
that progress in the production of suitable textbooks, monographs,
and periodical literature and treatises in the various Indian languages will keep pace with the pressure for a change-over. All this
has the most serious implications for the future of higher education in India and for its capacity to provide persons of the level
and type of intellectual discipline required for the progress of the
country. This path has already been traversed in Burma; in Indonesia the process is now complete. The results are unfortunately
all too visible.

V

It is relevant at this point to refer to another factor affecting the
quality of the education received by college and university students in the underdeveloped countries. This is the state of student
morale. Although there are some striking exceptions, in the main

the university teachers in underdeveloped countries have not been able to inculcate in their students a love of learning or even an intense professional motivation. Much of the learning is rote learning of ill-understood matters. Few students seem to enjoy or love their studies. Most of them seem restless, discontented, and anxious. The restiveness of students in nearly all underdeveloped countries is legendary in its proportions. Strikes, processions, demonstrations, outbursts of violence, and denunciatory manifestoes are the order of the day throughout Latin America and much of the Middle East and south and southeast Asia. In many of these countries, the resentment of the students has a political focus; in others, such as India, it is aroused by all sorts of things having little to do with politics. It is easily understandable because the students are ill provided for as regards teachers who know and are interested in them, library and laboratory space, residential accommodations, messes, and amenities. Many of these countries also have traditions of vigorously active student participation in the independence movement during the period of foreign rule or hegemony. Yet, in Africa, too, where these traditions are much shallower because the anticolonial movements were of more recent origin and where, on the whole, the provision of facilities and amenities, especially in the English-speaking African countries, is far more ample (and, indeed, relatively luxurious), students tend to be hostile toward the existing government and even toward the governmental system. Although there is little to equal the magnitude of the student disorders in India, where particular universities are sometimes suspended for weeks and even months because the students' agitation prevents the conduct of academic life, many other universities of the third world approximate the Indian experience. In Latin America, for instance, the situation is quite similar. In Lagos, recently, the newly appointed Vice-Chancellor of the University of Nigeria was stabbed by students expressing their disapproval of his appointment. Similar instances could be cited without number. In a word, in addition to all the other impediments to a proper university education, the state of mind of the students is resistant to such education as is offered.

VI

No university system can be considered apart from the society in which it lives. Even in the advanced countries, the *de facto* autonomy of the universities and their long and rather well-established traditions of teaching and research do not eliminate the ties that bind them to their environing societies. The universities of the underdeveloped countries, which have not yet experienced the formation of strong traditions of teaching and research, are all the more susceptible to such demands and restraints.

None of the universities we are discussing has a substantial endowment. Apart from grants from foreign foundations, all are almost entirely dependent for their financial support on their governments (except for the University of Dakar, which is dependent on the French government). The governments are very conscious of their universities, which are considered relatively costly in relation to their tangible benefits, especially in countries where nearly everyone lives poorly. In Asia and Africa, the political elite also have high expectations of the universities. In Africa, the politicians are proud of their universities, which are showpieces and evidences of modernity. This is less true in the Middle East, in Latin America, and in much of south and southeast Asia, where politicians have had a longer experience of universities and have begun to act as if they have had their fill.

But, everywhere among the new states and in the older underdeveloped countries, whether the politicians like the universities or not, whether they are proud of them or not, whether they expect much or little from them, they are aware that the universities are critical of them. The universities are very frequently oppositional toward incumbent governments—not often revolutionary, but usually very critical, and sometimes bitterly so. Students, as already mentioned, are often up in arms against the politicians for one reason or another. The staff members are also down on politicians, whom they regard as having failed to deliver the goods they promised when they took over the rule of their countries on the occasion of independence, or whom they regard as hindrances to national modernization. Politicians are aware of this current of disapproval, and occasionally they indulge in reprisals which restrict the freedom of the universities. There have been drastic actions, such as that taken by General Ne Win when he destroyed the Rangoon University Student Union or when he closed the university; the various harassments inflicted by President Nkrumah and his radical supporters of the Socialist Youth Wing against the staff of the University of Ghana; the deportation action of the government of Sierra Leone against Mr. John Hatch of the University College of Sierra Leone; the savage attack of the Singapore Minister of Culture against Professor Dennis Enright; the action taken by the revolutionary government of Brazil against a considerable number of university teachers throughout the country; but fortunately such instances are relatively rare, all things considered.

Another source of tension between the academic and the political worlds arises from nationalistic sensitivity of the latter to the inherent cosmopolitanism of the intellectual community. Politicians in the new states are nationalists to a man; they could not have made a political career had they not been. Indeed, they would not even have entered on a political career. Being a nationalist invariably entails praise of the indigenous culture, which is a traditional culture. But, whatever else the universities may be teaching, it is not an indigenous traditional culture. They teach modern science and technology, modern economics and social science, and modern methods of studying traditional indigenous culture. When they teach about the sacred texts of their culture, they approach them in a way that differs radically from the traditional way. When they teach and study indigenous languages, they do so by modern methods. These new kinds of knowledge and technique are almost exclusively foreign creations, and in most instances they are drawn from the culture of the former ruling power. The universities of the new states are at present almost entirely dependent on imported culture for the substance of their teaching. They teach very little that has been generated or created in their own countries, and they also teach relatively little about their own country's history, society, and culture. This situation is not congenial to nationalist sentiments and often causes the universities to be accused by their radical critics of subservience to their former rulers.

The interest taken by politicians in the opportunities for patronage and for political support offered by university appointments is an occasionally distracting element which interferes with the proper conduct of academic work. The recent disturbance at the University of Lagos in connection with the appointment of a Yoruba to replace an Ibo as Vice-Chancellor, against the recommendation of the Senate of the University, is an instance of this practice. Intercommunal and intertribal animosities bedevil many of the universities, from Nigeria to Malaysia.

There are also difficulties which arise from the youth of the university institutions. Lay members of the governing bodies of universities have not yet learned to operate the university constitutions which they inherited or adopted from the metropolitan powers. They have not yet developed conventions which would facilitate a harmonious division of labor between themselves and the academic governing bodies. They have not yet accepted an arrangement whereby academic matters would be left in the hands of academics and nonacademic matters, such as the approval of the budget and plans for expansion, would be dependent on the assent of the lay council. As a result of this inexperience and an excessive literalness in the interpretation of the university constitutions, the lay councils have occasionally exceeded what should be their proper role in a well-run university.

Nonetheless, considering the hypersensitivity of the political elite, the alienation of many members of the university teaching staffs and student bodies from the regnant politicians, and the alien origin of the culture promulgated by the universities, it is still true that restrictions on academic freedom—that is, actions against members of universities for their views on political and cultural matters and interference with appointments for political and ideological reasons—have been relatively infrequent. As regards the substance of their culture, the universities of the underdeveloped countries are left fairly inviolate. (The universities suffer more from the pressure of public opinion, which demands not that they teach or believe particular things, but that they place no limits on the numbers of those admitted for study.)

On the whole, it may be concluded that the difficult position of the universities in much of the third world is not significantly attributable in any great measure to the positive misdeeds of the politicians. The deficiencies of these universities arise from having too many ill-qualified teachers teaching too many ill-prepared students. Insofar as they affect this situation, politicians do influence the quality of universities much more weightily, albeit indirectly, because of their unwillingness to take any measures that would restrict the numbers of students enrolled. Their reasons for this attitude are not unworthy. There are few boons that politicians of underdeveloped countries can give to their peoples, and university admission is one of these. Furthermore, any efforts by politicians to support restricted admission would be met with an outburst of wrath and a shift of loyalties to rival candidates.

The problem of numbers that so challenges the universities of the underdeveloped world outside Black Africa is not created by the politicians. It is a product of the desires of newly emancipated peoples, who believe that through education the lives of their offspring will be transfigured and improved. But it is this very desire that is making it hard for the universities to do what they could do for the enhancement of the life of their countries.

VII

It is often said that the concern for standards in some universities of the underdeveloped world is misplaced. The point is made that the underdeveloped countries need many competent but undistinguished persons who have mastered subjects of direct relevance to the needs of their countries. The universities are criticized for having an excessively stringent standard and for teaching the wrong kinds of skills. In reply, it might be well agreed that many of the underdeveloped countries have more graduates in law than they need for the legal profession, although some have far too few. But the critics imply that there should be many more technologists. Yet the fact remains that one of the features of the professional distribution in the underdeveloped countries is failure to employ technologists in technological capacities. Too many of them can-

not find technological employment and turn instead to administration, so that their presumably urgently needed skills are left
unused.

The argument that the underdeveloped countries need an infrastructure of technicians is valid. To provide this class of skilled
persons requires diversification in the courses of study in the
higher educational systems, and especially in the secondary
schools. But it certainly does not constitute a valid argument that
standards at the universities should be relaxed, that less intellectual exertion should be demanded of students, and that less
knowledge of relevant kinds should be expected to be produced in
their examinations. The underdeveloped countries suffer from
slackness in performance; and if a small minority of their young
people are not educated to overcome this slackness, the sloth and
disorganization that injure these countries at present will continue, and modernization will be hindered.

VIII

But universities are not mere producers of trained persons. They
are not expected to confine themselves to the transmission of
knowledge already established and confirmed. They are expected,
if they are to qualify as modern universities, to create new and
important knowledge through the use of up-to-date research techniques.

It is most necessary that the universities of the third world
become research centers; otherwise, they will not produce the research workers required to perform the tasks that are integral to
modernization. The development of new strains of plants and ani-
mals, the prospecting for minerals, the inventory of economically
relevant flora and fauna, the adaptation of foreign technology and
medical knowledge to local conditions, the development of economic methods for utilizing local resources—all these research
tasks are of pressing practical importance.

There are also the tasks of interpretation based on research
by current methods on the traditional indigenous culture, of writing enlightened, modern history that does justice to the internal

dynamics of the country's developments, instead of presenting it simply as the scene of the expansion of Western powers. These are essential for the proper establishment of a national culture, which is in turn an essential part of the complex of modernity. But it is not only for the sake of knowledge that research must be carried on in the universities of the underdeveloped countries. Without such research the universities will not gain self-respect and self-confidence and attract to their teaching staffs outstandingly talented and well-trained young men and women. Unless some of the best members of the younger generation join the university as teachers, and unless they are enabled to develop their best potentialities, the universities will not be respected. They will arouse no enthusiasm for learning in their students, and they will not be able to meet their obligations to their countries.

To attract and retain these creative young scientists and scholars, they must, in the present climate of intellectual life, be provided with the time, facilities, and resources to do research. If these are withheld, the universities will become dead institutions, and the best of the oncoming academic generation, particularly those who have had the costly advantages of further study in foreign universities and laboratories, will look abroad for the opportunities they are denied at home. India, which is rare among the new states in having already a considerable number of highly qualified scientists, is already experiencing a "brain drain"; many of its very able young scientists prefer to work in America or western Europe because of the superior opportunities there. Pakistan, too, is having this experience. Latin America is in the same position; and so are some of the other countries of the third world, as their best-endowed young men are trained as scientists in metropolitan universities.

But are the universities of which we speak in a position to do the research which their own situation and their countries' needs require? They are not. Even India, which has the largest scientific system of any of the underdeveloped countries, is far from being able to do so. It is still excessively dependent on foreign scientific and technological knowledge. Moreover, it has made the mistake of concentrating far too much of its scientific research in research institutes from which the universities are, in the main, cut off.

Indian universities do not offer favorable conditions for research, in equipment, in time, or in atmosphere, although there are outstanding individuals in a variety of fields of science and scholarship. The amount of scientific research done in the universities of the other underdeveloped countries is, broadly speaking, meager in quantity and slight in quality.

They have neither established a scientific community nor formed a scientific tradition of their own. A scientific tradition can be formed only around a center of creativity; it needs a creative intellectual personality to form a nucleus of protégés, some of whom will become creative in their own turn. This demands stability and, above all, some density of intellectual settlement. The more creative individuals are far too widely scattered within each field in India; in a continent as sparsely settled scientifically as Africa, or in areas like the Middle East or southeast Asia, the dispersion of individuals into isolation is even greater. The circles of interaction are too small within any particular field of specialized research. Stimulation tends to come predominantly from the overseas metropolitan centers, and the maintenance of close and continuous ties is more costly than the underdeveloped countries can afford. Yet, these handicaps must be overcome; otherwise scientific research will not develop in these countries, the universities will not grow into genuine modern universities, and the process of modernization will turn into stagnation.

IX

If we grant that the role of the universities of the underdeveloped countries is vital to their development, and if the universities are not at present doing what is necessary in the way of teaching and research, how can the situation be bettered? Can the universities raise themselves by their own bootstraps? I think that the prospect is not hopeless.

For one thing, in most of the underdeveloped countries, there are young men (and perhaps women) of outstanding talent, and there are even some with distinguished accomplishments to their credit. They are often rendered academically ineffective by being diverted into government administration, in which they play a useful role, or else they remain in academic life and become demoralized by their isolation from stimulating colleagues and by the frustration of university bureaucracy and intrigue as well as by the burdensome struggle for a livelihood. In countries where there are numerous universities, one remedy could be found in "concentration" of the actually and potentially creative workers in certain fields into one institution. The tasks of teaching could be made more attractive by differentiation of admissions policies, so that the institutions with the most outstanding staffs would also receive a disproportionate share of the livelier and more promising students. Such a policy would not affect the principle of maximum access to higher education to which countries like India, Indonesia, and others are committed. Yet this policy would enable at least one first-class university to develop in the country—a university that could serve as a model and a spur to the others and in the course of time supply the personnel they all need.

Furthermore, the universities of the advanced countries have a major part to play by seconding some of their best young men for periods of several years and by offering the services of some of their retired members who still have many years of valuable service to offer. Co-operative research projects, in which members of universities in the advanced and underdeveloped countries unite, offer additional possibilities for fixing the teachers and research workers of the underdeveloped countries firmly into the international intellectual community.

The main objective is to fortify the intellectual will of the university teachers of the underdeveloped countries. This fortification of will is not, however, just a matter of institutional rearrangement and the exercise of solicitude and responsibility by the universities of the advanced countries. It also calls for strength of character on the part of the university staff members of the underdeveloped countries. They must strengthen their resolve to avoid the temptations of indolence and of political and academic intrigue. If they can do this, then, despite large numbers, difficult working conditions, and political distractions, the future is not without promise.

Chapter 7

Communications
and Development

Ithiel de Sola Pool

Developing nations need many things all at once. They need to improve agriculture and also to build industry. They need to invest in public health and also in education. They need transportation, and they also need new media of communication. When scarce resources cannot meet all the needs at once, the difficult problem is to choose. As an aid to selecting wisely, let us evaluate the importance of one of these many competing needs; namely, the means of communication. How much and in what ways can investment in communication contribute to the process of development?

When new roads, newspapers, radio, television, movies, or books come into a society, powerful effects can usually be observed over time. Changes follow in the way people think and in the things they value. There have been a number of studies of what happens in a village when a road comes in to link it with the outside world. Among these are the work of Daniel Lerner in Turkey,[1] Y. V. L. Rao in India,[2] Oscar Lewis in Mexico.[3] Life changes. People begin to travel to work in nearby towns or to market. They see new things; they buy new things. Officials and enterpreneurs come into the village more often; a doctor may come where previously he refused. Newspapers can be delivered. The young consider new alternatives in life that may shock the old. Manufactured products are brought in and put up for sale, displacing village crafts. Politicians come around seeking votes. Soon a bus line will be formed; the drivers and bus owners may become a new part of the elite. Nothing could be more revolutionary than a road.

Telephones, radios, television, movies, also come into traditional villages and produce similar changes in the way of life. While they do not physically bring in people, they bring in words that carry advice on agricultural practices or public health. The media show what opportunities exist for using new commodities such as electricity, refrigeration, or automotive transportation. They undermine traditional values, introducing new kinds of music, new kinds of drama, new political beliefs. They may also be used in the classroom; radio and television teaching can put the resources of a large community in the hands of a village teacher.

These observations from experience and common sense are further supported by a growing series of studies that correlate modernization with access to the media of communication. All over the world, it has been found that those individuals and villages that have access to the printed page or radio have more modern attitudes, are more progressive, and move into modern roles faster than those who do not. For literacy, this is almost so obvious as to be banal. An illiterate in a white-collar or professional job with wide knowledge of the world is almost inconceivable. For radio, it is less obvious, but the results are very striking. Much of what comes over the air may be entertainment or music;

[1] Daniel Lerner, *The Passing of Traditional Society* (Glencoe, Ill.: The Free Press, 1958).

[2] Wilbur Schramm, *Mass Media and National Development* (Stanford: Stanford University Press, 1964), pp. 48 ff.

[3] Oscar Lewis, *Life in a Mexican Village: Tepoztlan Restudied* (Urbana, Ill.: University of Illinois Press, 1951).

the person who hears it may be illiterate; but still we find that where radio goes, there modernizing attitudes come in. Correlation studies show few variables as predictive of modernization as the measures of mass media exposure.[4]

If it were all that simple, we might recommend as a formula for development that a nation invest large sums in diffusing radio and other mass media; but it is not that simple. Many developing nations do not really push communications development. In the first place, as already noted, the process of development requires many things at once. The effects of investment in communication may depend on how it is integrated with investment in transportation and also with political organization, as we shall see a little later. In the second place, communication investments have different effects on various aspects of the process of development. Modern communications may be important to unify a country, but have less significance for exploitation of natural resources. The importance of new mass media depends on what one wants to do. In the third place, communication investments are not all of one piece. Putting in a road facilitates personal contact; installing telephones permits the conduct of business; putting in radios may entertain and educate; teaching literacy in school may have profound effects, but only as new generations grow and assume leadership. One must be precise as to what kind of communication investment one has in mind. In the fourth place, policy decisions must be made about various other aspects of a communication system. How far shall it be free, and how far dominated by the state; how does one train the skilled personnel needed to run a modern communication system; does one use it for mass propaganda or for sophisticated discussions among the intelligentsia?

Modern means of communication seldom replace the previously existing means. Television has not eliminated radio; radio has not destroyed the printed book; the invention of print has not stopped us from writing letters by pen and ink; and teaching people to be literate does not make them any less inclined to converse. Each new mode of communication is superimposed upon the old. It may take over certain functions, but other functions are retained by the former mode.

[4] Cf. Schramm, *op. cit.*, p. 47.

Thus, in the communication systems of the most highly developed societies, there is a complex interaction between the modern mass media system and the traditional network of personal word-of-mouth communication. A modern society is not an anomic depersonalized mass society free from primary groups. It is an elaborate system of families, clubs, ethnic groups, classes, political organizations, and friendship groupings.

The dissemination of any new idea or practice in such a society depends not only on the publicity it is given in the mass media but also on conversation and discussion about it among people, face to face.[5] The mass media provide people with basic information; but before people will act on such new information, they need to be encouraged by persons in their immediate environment whom they know and respect. Farmers may learn about a new agricultural practice from hearing a broadcast. They are likely to adopt it only when they see a neighbor getting a better yield by using the practice.

Much recent social science research has been devoted to the relationship between the mass media and word-of-mouth communication. We know that the mass media alone can have a profound effect on what people pay attention to, the information they have, their tastes, and their images of the world. We know that, on the other hand, the mass media by themselves are less effective in changing their attitudes or leading to action.

The situation with regard to attitudes is complex. On many matters, people have rather weak and ill-defined attitudes. Mass media messages may, indeed, shake these, but usually in a transitory way. For example, experiments have been carried out telling students about minor political leaders of remote foreign countries through the mass media. Having no special reason to doubt the message and having no concrete views on the matter, persons in these experiments conclude that the man is good if the media have told him he is good, or bad if the media have told him he is bad. That, however, is a casual attitude of no particular significance and likely to be soon forgotten. But even such casual information, if repeated again and again for a long period of time, may

[5] Everett Rogers, *Diffusion of Innovation* (Glencoe, Ill.: The Free Press, 1963).

create an attitude set, particularly if the information thus conveyed is never contradicted. For example, millions of people have a favorable attitude toward the Riviera as a pleasant, sunny place. Most of them have never been there, have no knowledge at first hand, and do not care very much; but this represents a noncontroversial consensus, and frequent hearing has built an attitude that sticks.

More significant is what happens to attitudes that are highly meaningful to people, that impinge on important aspects of their lives, and that are controversial. Such attitudes are seldom changed by the mass media alone. The media may din propaganda into people incessantly, but if their friends and relatives preach different values, the mass media are not likely to win. The persistence of belief in God in countries where atheist propaganda has gone on for decades is an example in point.

In securing action, the mass media are even less effective in the absence of personal reinforcement. Advertising may lead a shopper buying soap to pick up one brand rather than another, but this is an action that has no particular significance to him. However, to get people to act in ways that conform to new values almost always requires that mass communications be reinforced by personal influence. An example was provided by J. C. Mathur and Paul Neurath in an experiment on securing adoption by Indian peasants of new agricultural practices.[6] The All-India Radio broadcast agricultural advice programs. In one set of villages, listening groups were assembled to discuss the suggestions following the broadcast. Sometimes the suggestions were rejected, but at other times they were approved. When they were approved, action often followed. In another set of villages without group listening, though radios were tuned in, no action resulted. It took a combination of information through the mass media and reinforcement by personal discussions to get the peasants to act. The same thing is found in all spheres of life. Advertising alone will not sell a novel product; it requires other forms of promotion—for example, by salesmen—to build upon the ads. In politics, broadcasts and editorials do not lead people to act unless a party organ-

[6] *An Indian Experiment in Farm Radio Forum* (Paris: UNESCO, 1959).

ization with local political workers reinforces the broad propaganda. In community development, the mass media help the local action agents by providing a background of knowledge, attention, and predisposition. Mass media development, then, can be an important part of any program of development; but, depending on the objectives to be served, it must be linked with organization.

Given a proper mix of communication, transportation, and organization, there are many functions that a modern system of communications can perform: (1) Modern media provide accurate and permanent records. Newspapers, films, books, magazines, and magnetic tapes are available for reference and verification years later. (2) The modern media are extraordinarily rapid. Events are reported all over the world within minutes after their occurrence. (3) The modern media extend the scope of a man's empathic comprehension of ways of life that he has not experienced at first hand. Newspapers and radio enable people to conceive what it is like to be a ruler, or a foreigner, or a millionaire, or a movie star. (4) The modern media co-ordinate the interpersonal groups that constitute the network of face-to-face contacts in a society. The leaders of these various groups are provided by the media with similar clues as to what is going on, similar images, and a similar sense of what is important. The media establish this common file of mutually understandable information simultaneously over large areas. A mass media system welds the segments of the personal contact network into a single national whole capable of integrated action.

For example, mass media help make possible national political parties. These must somehow find platforms, slogans, and policies that will win them votes all over the country. A local village or town leader can maintain his leadership by serving local needs without reference to ideology. He may win support by providing a better water supply. But unless this action can be generalized into an example of a broad policy, it has no meaning to anyone elsewhere. A well in one town, a favor to an influential man in another, adherence to the dominant religious sect in the third— these alone do not constitute a national platform about which the mass media can talk. The mass media need formulas, slogans, and policies that will be meaningful everywhere. A well in one town, a road in another, a clinic in a third, can be generalized under the ideology of modernization. Then the mass media and the political parties can treat them as matters of national politics. An alliance among local leaders then becomes possible in each of their own communities. It is no coincidence that everywhere in the world the growth of political parties and the growth of the press have historically gone hand in hand.

In other fields, too, modern communication systems make possible the co-ordination of life over wide geographic units. The city-state was the natural political unit for ancient Greece because, as Aristotle and Plato pointed out, it was the unit within which citizens could communicate with each other. Modern communications make the natural units larger. Quick, up-to-the-minute price quotations make possible wide markets. Radio, telephones, and roads enable police to maintain legal order over areas that would in the past have been the domain of local bands or barons. Radio communication is essential to an air transport system. Between 15 and 25 per cent of the capital cost of air transport facilities is for communication. A modern communication system is essential for the conduct of international trade. Not only do developing countries need feeder roads and communications into villages; they also need access to the world-wide system of communications. Importers and exporters, salesmen and buyers, need hotels and air lines, international telephones and wireless.

More subtle than all these obvious uses of modern communications for defense and security, for politics and trade, are the effects of a modern communication system on the ways in which people think. Such effects, while hard to trace, are no less profound. Consider, for example, the impact of having a press on the development of an intelligentsia. If there are newspapers and magazines, motion picture companies and radio, there are jobs for a certain number of modern young men as writers, editors, and producers. It is from this class of the literate intelligentsia that has come much of the political leadership for nationalist movements. At the time of colonial rule, there were few openings for bright, modernized young men that did not require them to compromise themselves in the service of their rulers. Those who became civil servants or acquired positions in industry were not free to be the leaders of a new ferment of national consciousness. Only autonomous professions, such as sometimes the law, but even more often journalism and mass communication, provided a channel for expression of early nationalist development.

So here is an indirect but important way in which the growth of modern communication has changed the thinking of people in developing countries. But the most obvious and direct means has been through the exposure of the audience to new and unfamiliar ways of life described in the media. It is in reading, movies, and radio that people in villages and impoverished cities everywhere have discovered a land of their heart's desire and have come to know that there is a different way of life from their inherited rut.

In modern countries, saturated as they are with the mass media, what Marx called rural idiocy has disappeared. In the United States today, there is no difference between knowledge of the world in the city and in the country. There are as many television sets as there are families; more radio sets than there are people; more than one-and-a-half times as many telephones as there are families; and an average of 1.4 newspapers are read per day by each adult in the population, thereby using more than sixty pounds of newsprint per capita in the course of a year. In addition, the typical adult spends almost three hours per day watching television. That is an extreme case of a society saturated with mass media. Although some individuals are more participant than others, still no sector of such a society, rural or urban, rich or poor, agricultural or industrial, fails to be exposed to modern life and the facts of the world.

In a developing economy, there are segments of the society just as fully exposed to the modern mass media as is generally the case in the United States, Japan, or western Europe. Educated middle-class people living in cities read newspapers every day, have radios with short-wave reception, go to a choice of movies at will, subscribe to magazines, and read books. Given differences in ideology, tradition, and culture, still the image of modern life available to them is essentially the same as that which comes through the mass media to all the citizens of media-saturated countries.

But developing economies are dual societies. In them, the city dweller and the villager are not alike in knowledge or in basic images of life. As one moves from the port town or capital to the squatter settlements on their outskirts, filled with men just out of the village, and then on into the village itself, one finds knowledge of the modern world disappearing. Many surveys have found remote villages where the majority of the people could not name the president of their own country, not to mention naming the leading cities of the world or the names of other leading statesmen.[7] The mass media change this situation. They disseminate awareness of aspects of life that are not part of the personal experience of the reader or listener or viewer himself. Those who fear this phenomenon call it a demonstration effect or revolution of rising expectations. The media create knowledge of desirable things faster than these things themselves can be produced. It is easier to bring in movies, newspapers, and even radio than it is to bring in housing, automobiles, bicycles, and medical facilities. The effects of the mass media are therefore legitimately feared. Like all revolutionary forces, they prepare men's minds for new desires more rapidly than those new desires can be satisfied. So media development cannot stand alone. If the media are to do more than to add to frustration, they must be part of a program of sustained development.

Media development can be many different things. Providing television in schoolrooms will produce one set of effects; building a plant for newsprint will produce others; putting telephones into villages will produce a third. Space does not permit us to consider more than a few of the many possibilities.

Let us look at one of the simplest systems designed to reach into villages otherwise completely beyond the domain of the modern communications. For such isolated villages, off the road, there are severe limitations for even battery-transistorized radio sets that are relatively cheap (perhaps ten dollars) and portable. To keep live batteries in such sets costs perhaps twenty to forty cents a month. In contrast, in South Korea, entrepreneurs have found that they can set up wired loud-speaker systems in villages, charging only fifteen cents per month to each householder who

[7] Cf. Schramm, *op. cit.*, pp. 70 ff.

chooses to rent one.[8] The loud-speakers cost about a dollar, and the entrepreneur connects them with a single, central, battery-operated tuner-amplifier and perhaps tape-recorder unit that he owns, using army wire that costs only about thirty cents per hundred feet. The village is thus provided with music most of the day and with whatever other agricultural and educational programs the national broadcasting system puts on. In addition, the loud-speaker system permits announcements of local interest and the playing by record or tape of selections the villagers particularly like to hear.

An alternative exists if a telephone line links the village to the outside world. A loud-speaker system for broadcasts can come into the village on the phone line, although at a substantial deterioration of broadcast quality. A phone in a village, even if used only a few times a day, can give the government rapid communication, provide reporting of market information, and handle emergency medical and similar calls. The rest of the time the line can carry broadcasting.

Thus, at the most elementary level, a development plan might call for every village to have at least one telephone and a system of loud-speakers connected either to it or to a radio tuner. All this can be done at a cost that almost any village can bear over time.

A higher level of development is identified by UNESCO as a minimal goal: namely, that every country should seek to have at least ten daily newspapers, five radio receivers, two cinema seats, and two television receivers per hundred inhabitants. Two-thirds of the population of the world are in countries that fall below these goals. Except for radio, which is spreading rapidly, the prospects of reaching these ideals are remote. Yet UNESCO has estimated that they could be achieved by spending $3.4 billion over the next twenty years.

A quite different type of investment in modern communication is found in American Samoa, where resources are going primarily into education. At a cost of many millions of dollars, television has been installed in all schools. Television teaching by a few

8 William L. Eilers, *Rural Radio in the Developing Countries* (unpublished manuscript).

expert teachers reaches daily into all the villages. The initial out-
lay is high; but by comparison with what would have been spent
to train enough teachers to an adequate standard for all those
schools, the cost is low, and to wait for teacher training would
have meant a delay of at least a decade. Now, for the first time,
there is the prospect of universal literacy among Samoan children.

In countries at the next level of economic development, television may play a tremendously significant role not only in schools
but also in homes. In many countries of the world, there are
shanty towns and slums capped by forests of television aerials.
Television is expensive. The sets are expensive; production is expensive; transmission is expensive. It requires a great deal of electricity and employs vast amounts of talent in writing, in acting, in
repair and maintenance. Wherever the government has kept television noncommercial, financing has been difficult, for the cost of
keeping an adequate supply of interesting material in production
to fill the air waves for many hours a day is horrendous.

Radio is a much cheaper medium. Furthermore, where governments have barred commercial operation and have attempted
to broadcast only what they felt the audience should hear, the
listeners have been able to frustrate this restriction by virtue of
the extremely long-range reception capability of short-wave radio.
Foreign broadcasts are available if the domestic broadcasts wax
too dull or pedantic. With television, however, that is not the case,
for the signals are only locally receivable. The development of
communication satellites may ultimately make it possible to receive television programs internationally, but that is a prospect for
the future.

The argument for commercial sponsorship is not just that the
advertiser provides some of the resources necessary for expensive
production. Advertising itself may also be a powerful instrument
of development. It is a way of facilitating the distribution of commodities, broadening the market, and making people aware of
possibilities with which they would not otherwise be familiar.

On the other hand, there is the eternal problem of maintaining quality in the mass media. Not enough talent exists to keep all
the outpouring of print, radio, and television at a high level of

culture and art. Mass media are bound to show some effects of mass production to be a mixture of both good and bad.

There has been disagreement among the experts on the significance of this fact for development.[9] Some argue that what goes to the masses in new knowledge stimulates development, even if it comes in comic books and film songs whose standing as art is questionable. Others hold that what developing countries need most is a leadership provided with knowledge and understanding of the very highest quality. They insist that not comic books and film songs will modernize a country, but rather literary and sophisticated dailies and magazines, helping to create a new leadership.

The truth is, once more, that development requires many things all at once. Metropolitan dailies aspiring to the excellence of the New York *Times*, weeklies aspiring to the standards of the *Economist*, journalists of the highest education and the highest character, are needed for a nation's progress; but so is a mass press, often in another vernacular and addressed to the level of the new literates, and so are popular radio and movies.

[9] Cf. papers by Edward Shils and Ithiel de Sola Pool in Lucien Pye, *Communications and Political Development* (Princeton, N. J.: Princeton University Press, 1963).

Chapter **8**

The Modernization
of Social Relations

Neil J. Smelser

The subject of economic development is very much in the minds of political leaders in the new nations; it also preoccupies the policy makers of advanced Western countries; and it is a subject of keen interest to social scientists who are attempting to fathom the panoply of social changes that are revolutionizing the contemporary world.

Because this idea of economic development has become such an everyday concept in our mid-twentieth-century outlook, we are likely to be tempted to think of it as a simple, unitary type of process. But economic development is neither simple nor unitary. When we employ the term, we usually have at least four distinct but interrelated processes implicitly in mind: (1) In the realm of technology, a developing society is changing *from* simple and traditionalized techniques *toward* the application of scientific knowledge. (2) In agriculture, the developing society evolves *from* subsistence farming *toward* the commercial production of agricultural goods. This means specialization in cash crops, purchase of nonagricultural products in the market, and often agricultural wage labor. (3) In industry, the developing society undergoes a transition *from* the use of human and animal power *toward* industrialization proper, or men working for wages at power-driven machines, which produce commodities marketed outside the community of production. (4) In ecological arrangements, the developing society moves *from* the farm and village *toward* urban concentrations. Furthermore, while these four processes often occur simultaneously during development, this is not always so. Agriculture may become commercialized without any appreciable changes in the industrial sector, as was the case in the colonial countries in which the dominant powers strove to increase production of primary products. Industrialization may occur in villages, as it did in early British industrialization and in some Asian societies. And cities may proliferate even where there is no significant industrialization, as has happened in some parts of Asia and Africa. The lesson forced upon us by these observations is that the causes, courses, and consequences of economic development must be expected to vary widely from nation to nation.

Economic development, moreover, is only one aspect of the complex of social change experienced by the emerging nations. The term "modernization"—a conceptual cousin of the term "economic development," but more comprehensive in scope—refers to the fact that technical, economic, and ecological changes ramify through the whole social and cultural fabric. In an emerging nation, we may expect profound changes (1) in the *political* sphere, as simple tribal or village authority systems give way to systems of suffrage, political parties, representation, and civil service bureaucracies; (2) in the *educational* sphere, as the society strives to reduce illiteracy and increase economically productive skills; (3) in the religious sphere, as secularized belief systems begin to replace traditionalistic religions; (4) in the *familial* sphere, as extended kinship units lose their pervasiveness; (5) in the stratificational sphere, as geographical and social mobility tend to loosen fixed, ascriptive hierarchical systems. Furthermore, these various changes begin at different times and proceed at different rates in a developing nation. A modernizing country, then, displays a multiplicity of institutional changes; and no matter how carefully social change is planned, some institutional changes will always lead the way, and others will always lag behind. Thus a developing nation, if it could be depicted graphically, would resemble a large, awkward animal lumbering forward by moving each of its parts, sometimes in partial co-ordination and sometimes in opposition to one another.

Some of the typical institutional changes and discontinuities that are part of the modernizing process includes changing work relations, changing family relations, and changing community relations. It is impractical here to elaborate widely, and dealing only in generalities may do some injustice to the complexity of the developmental process. But within these limitations, we may point up the relations among the various institutional changes and discontinuities and suggest some of the reasons why we should expect a high potential for social and political unrest in the developing nations.

CHANGING WORK RELATIONS

In preindustrial societies, production is typically located in kinship units. Subsistence farming predominates; other industry, such as domestic manufacture, is supplementary to farming, but still attached to kin and village. In some societies, occupational position is determined by an extended group such as the caste. Exchange relations are also outlined by traditional kinship and community obligations. In short, economic activities are relatively undifferentiated from the traditional family-community setting.

Economic development means, above all, the segregation of economic activities from this traditional setting. In agriculture, the introduction of money crops means that, as a basic change from subsistence farming, the goods are consumed in households different from those in which they are produced. Agricultural wage labor, in which individuals rather than families are likely to be hired, often undermines the family production unit. In industry, handicraft production and cottage industry, like commercial farming, mean that individual families do not produce for themselves, but for other, unknown families somewhere in the market. And when manufacturing and factory systems arise, the worker is segregated not only from the control of his capital but also from other members of his family, since he is placed side by side with individual workers recruited in the labor market. In these ways, modernization separates economic activities from those of family and community.

As a result of these changes, the worker's relations to economic life are greatly altered. He now receives cash for services performed and spends it for goods and services in the market. More and more of his income and welfare come to depend on the pay envelope and less and less on the traditional rights and obligations expected from and owed to kinspeople and neighbors. This means that the worker in a modernizing market faces a number of problems of adjustment.

First, he finds that a new basis of calculation is foisted upon him. From the standpoint of allocating his productive time, he may no longer work at his own pace; he must adjust to the notion of a workday and a work week, and, on the job, he must conform to the rhythm of the machine rather than the rhythm of his own mind and body. From the standpoint of allocating his wealth, he must think in terms of budgeting a weekly bundle of cash; on the face of it, this would not appear to be much of an adjustment; but when we contrast the requisite level of calculation required with the day-by-day flow of economic activities in the traditional setting, in which cash payments scarcely figure, it is possible to appreciate the significant changes in outlook required of the new urban-industrial worker.

Second, he finds the definition of his economic security greatly altered. In a traditional system of agriculture or domestic manufacture, a worker is likely to be underemployed rather than unemployed as a result of market fluctuations. In this case, he works somewhat less and turns to kinsmen, tribesmen, and neighbors for help. In the urban-industrial setting, however, the worker is likely to be laid off and totally unemployed when economic activity is slack. In the new setting, then, he is subject to sharper, more severe fluctuations in welfare and security, even though his average income may be higher than it was in the traditional setting.

Third, with respect to consumption, the worker in the modernizing market is faced with continuously changing standards.

The urban market provides a veritable flood of new items: sweets, beer, gadgets, bicycles, transistor radios, and the like. As the worker is simultaneously drifting away from traditional expenditures—such as the dowry—and being exposed to new forms of gratification, he is likely to experience confusions and disorientations. It goes without saying that opportunities abound for merchants to market shabby products and to swindle inexperienced consumers.

A fourth need for adjustment is imposed on the traditional sector. Many urban-industrial workers visit or migrate back to the countryside. While in the urban-industrial setting, they are probably ambivalent about its demands and opportunities; but surely they often paint a beautiful picture of city life to their kinsmen and former neighbors who have remained in the countryside. Insofar as this occurs, it is likely to prove unsettling to the traditional way of life, especially if conditions are not good in the countryside, and to augment social conflicts between urban and rural sectors as well as between younger migrating generations and their elders who remain in the country.

I do not mean to exaggerate the differences and discontinuities between the traditional and modern sectors. Many halfway arrangements between the two hypothetical extremes are worked out in the modernizing process. Migratory labor, for instance, is a kind of compromise between full membership in a wage-labor force and attachment to an old community life. Cottage industry introduces extended markets, but retains the family-production fusion. The employment of families in factories, which is a more frequent phenomenon than is commonly appreciated, maintains a version of family production. The expenditure of wages on traditional items, like dowries, also manifests the half-entry into the full urban-industrial structure. The social and psychological reasons for these halfway houses are many; but, whatever the reasons, we may expect that in the compromise arrangements, the adjustments and discontinuities just discussed are lessened accordingly.

CHANGING FAMILY RELATIONS

One consequence of the removal of economic activities from the family-community setting is that the family itself loses some of its previous functions and becomes a more specialized agency. As the family ceases to be an economic unit of production, one or more members leave the household to seek employment in the labor market. The family's activities become more concentrated on emotional gratification and socialization.

The social implications of these simply described structural changes in the family are enormous. The most fundamental of these implications—imposed mainly by the demands for mobility of the family—is the individuation and isolation of the nuclear family. If the family has to move about through the labor market, it cannot afford to carry all its relatives with it or even to maintain close, diffuse ties with extended kin. Thus, connections with collateral kinsmen begin to erode; few generations live in the same household; newly married couples set up homes of their own and leave the elders behind. One of the social problems that arise as a consequence of these kinship changes concerns the place of the aged. No longer cushioned by a protective kinship unit, the older folk are thrown onto the community or the state as "charges" in greater numbers than before. Because of the social isolation of the aged, new institutional arrangements, such as pensions and social security programs, become imperative.

I do not want to oversimplify the process of decline of the extended kinship unit. In many cases—Japan would be a good example—it survives intact for quite a long period of industrialization; in other cases, some features of extended kinship (for example, reciprocal working) erode, but other features (such as mutual visiting) survive. Even the most advanced industrial societies still show some viable extended kinship structures. Despite these qualifications, however, it must be remembered that advanced urban-industrial market conditions and full-scale extended kinship systems are inimical to each other in many respects.

Simultaneously, the relations between parents and children undergo a transformation. The father, who now has to leave the household for employment in a separate establishment, necessarily loses many of the economic training functions he previously enjoyed over his children. Correspondingly, apprenticeship systems which require the continuous presence of father and son decline as specialized factory production arises. Often, it is claimed, this decline in economic authority spreads to a decline in *general* paternal authority, though these claims have proved difficult to substantiate empirically. The mother, often being the only adult in the presence of young children during large parts of the day, develops a more intensive emotional relationship with them. Her role in socialization thus becomes more crucial, for she has almost sole responsibility for forging the early emotional life of the children.

However concentrated the relations between mother and children in the early years, this period is short-lived. An advancing urban-industrial society demands more complex technical skills than the family is able to provide. Hence, the family tends to surrender many of its training functions to formal educational systems. The nuclear family very early loses control of its children to primary school (or even nursery school); by adolescence, the child has outside contacts not only with education but also with some parts of the labor market. Furthermore, children may have married by their late teens or early twenties, set up a new household of their own, and become even more independent of their parents.

One ramification of these changing relations between parents and children is the "gap of adolescence," when the youth has been freed from the intensive parental ties of his early years, but has not yet become fully engaged in adult occupational, marital, and civic roles. He thereby experiences a few years of loose role involvements. Psychologically, this means a period of uncertainty for the young person; and this uncertainty typically produces a number of symptoms of disturbance, such as random protest, compulsive search for love and security, faddism and experimentation, lethargy and apathy, and so on. Many commentators have pointed to the historical fact that urban-industrial societies invariably witness a growth of adolescent protest and delinquency. The explanation for this historical fact cannot be appreciated, however, until we grasp the simultaneous and interrelated changes that occur among the economic, educational, and familial structures in a modernizing society.

A further ramification of the revolution in kinship relations in the urban-industrial setting concerns the formation of new families. In many traditional settings, marriage is closely regulated by elders; the tastes and sentiments of the couple to be married are relatively unimportant. The basis for marriage, then, lies not in love, but rather in more practical arrangements, such as the availability of a substantial dowry or the promise of marrying into a choice parcel of land. With the decay of extended kinship ties and the redefinition of parental authority, youth becomes emancipated with respect to choosing a spouse. This emancipation, however, simultaneously produces a "vacuum"; if some variety of arranged marriage is not available as an institutional mechanism for forming new families, what criteria are available? Having posed the question in this way, we may better appreciate the social importance of "romantic love" as the dominant basis for marriage in urban-industrial societies. The feeling of being in love provides an alternative criterion for choice in an uncertain situation in which other institutional arrangements are lacking.

In sum, modernization tends to encourage the development of a family unit that is formed on emotional attraction and built on a limited sexual-emotional basis. The family has been removed from other major social spheres except for the segmental, external ties of individual family members. The family, being thus isolated and specialized, impinges less on these other social spheres; nepotism as a basis for recruitment into other social roles tends to become at most corrupt and at least suspect, whereas in traditional society it was the legitimate basis for recruitment into roles. Finally, within the family, the complex and multifunctional relations of family members to one another tend to be pared down to more exclusively emotional ties.

CHANGES IN COMMUNITY AND ASSOCIATIONAL LIFE

In the simplified model of traditional society that we have been using for analytic purposes, community and associational life is closely knit with the ascribed bases of social existence: kinship and clanship, and tribal and caste affiliations. Formal organizations such as trade-unions, social clubs, voluntary associations, and special interest groups seldom develop. Most of social life and its problems are worked through in the multifunctional ascribed groupings themselves.

These traditional bases for community and associational life retain much vitality, even as the urban and industrial complex begins to emerge. When industrialization occurs in villages, for example, or when villages are built around paternalistic industrial enterprises, many ties of community and kinship can be maintained under industrial conditions. Furthermore, some evidence shows that migrants to cities display what might be called the "brother-in-law" syndrome; they seek out relatives or tribesmen, reside with them while seeking employment and sometimes after finding it, and limit their social life primarily to them. The invariable development of racial, tribal, and ethnic "ghettos" in the growing cities of the world, it seems to me, reveals both outright residential discrimination and a search for community in cities.

The persistence of exclusively traditional ties in the urban-industrial setting, however, appears not to be a sufficient basis for community and associational life. After a time, these traditional ties come to be supplemented by the formation of more specialized organizations, such as clubs, unions, mutual savings associations, football clubs, chapel or church societies, and so on. The names of these groups, which would suggest special purposes for each, should not obscure the fact, however, that, especially in the early days of their formation, they are frequently multifunctional organizations. The friendly societies of eighteenth-century England, for example, were simultaneously trade-unions, insurance societies, and drinking clubs. Many of the loose formal organizations among African urban migrants are simultaneously tribal associations, trade-unions, football clubs, and social centers. Furthermore, these organizations tend to be quite unstable in their early days. They may begin as a tribal association, turn next into a savings association, and then take an interest in nationalism. As time passes, however, the fluidity of these organizations diminishes, and more "functional" groupings, based on economic or political interest, begin to replace them.

DISCONTINUITIES IN MODERNIZATION AND THE GENESIS OF SOCIAL UNREST

The various economic and social changes so far described are disruptive to the social order for several reasons.

First, structural change is, above all, uneven during periods of modernization, as we noted at the outset. In colonial societies, for instance, the European powers frequently revolutionized the economic and political framework by exploiting economic resources and establishing colonial administrations, but at the same time encouraged or imposed a conservatism in traditional religious, class, and family systems. In a society undergoing postcolonial modernization, similar discontinuities appear. Within the economy itself, rapid industrialization bites unevenly into established social and economic structures. Social institutions also display a pattern of growth that produces leads, lags, and bottlenecks. For example, most of the colonial nations, upon attaining independence, more or less immediately established some form of universal suffrage, thus entering instantaneously into the modern era. This action immediately created a crisis in education, since a mass electorate rests on the assumption of a literate electorate with a sense of citizenship and an ability to participate in the policy.

The establishment of a mass education system, however, itself demands a developing economy, both to supply educational facilities and to absorb trained individuals into occupational roles commensurate with their training. Social change thus moves ahead by a complicated leapfrog process, creating recurrent crises of adjustment. The first paradox of development, then, is that a developing society must change in all ways at once, but cannot conceivably plan such a regular, co-ordinated pattern of growth. A certain amount of social unrest is inevitably created.

Second, the development of new kinds of social and economic activities creates conflicts with traditional ways of life. For example, when factories begin to mass-produce items that compete with the same items produced domestically, the market is flooded with cheap goods, depriving the domestic workers of their means of livelihood. In theory, this should drive domestic workers into more remunerative lines of wage labor. In practice, however, the process of converting domestic labor into wage labor is a very slow and painful one, sometimes taking several generations to complete. To take another example, the growth of a class of highly trained doctors poses a threat to traditional medicine men and magicians as well as many revered domestic cures. The second paradox of modernization, then, is that when economic and social advances take place, many people in the society turn out to be at least ambivalent and possibly openly hostile toward these advances. This continuing conflict between modern and traditional ways is a further source of social unrest.

Third, attempts on the part of governments of the new nations to contain and handle social unrest often create the conditions for even further unrest. Most of the effective efforts to integrate and develop societies come from the centralized governments. It seems to me that, given the severe and pervasive problems of integration faced by these nations, it could scarcely be otherwise. But, insofar as central authorities establish themselves as viable governments, they simultaneously become threats to local, caste, regional, and other traditional types of authority. These threats underlie the apparent tendencies to Balkanization in some of the developing countries. The third paradox of development, then, is that even the effective exercise of authority creates unrest and conflict with competing authority systems.

The moral that might be drawn from these paradoxes is that developing nations face a danger if they conceive—as they are likely to do—economic development simply in terms of developing as fast as possible. To focus unduly on this criterion is likely to create social costs—expressed in terms of unmanageable levels of social unrest and political instability—that may in the end defeat the very effort to develop. If speed is the only criterion, the developing nation may destroy too rapidly various traditional forms of integration and unleash explosive levels of unrest. Furthermore, if too much speed is fostered in any one institutional sphere—for example, the economic—the society is likely to create an unbalanced pattern of growth, which is also a source of social unrest. It seems to me that the key problem in successful development is not to focus on a single criterion of growth, but rather to balance and measure development according to several different economic and social criteria.

Chapter 9

The City
and Modernization

Norton Ginsburg

All definitions of "modernization" refer in some measure not only to change, but, more important, to conceptions of efficiency, increased human and spatial interaction, and extraordinary complexities of social relationships, broadly interpreted. Invariably, these ideas also have come to be associated with the city and the process by which cities grow and societies become increasingly urbanized. This is as it should be, since cities, as we know them, are associated with the more efficient production and provision of a heterogeneity of goods and services and with a multiplicity of contacts among peoples and places. Cities mean large numbers of people concentrated in relatively small areas and therefore many more potential contacts among urbanites than are possible where populations are thinly distributed.

For example, if one assumes a population density of 50 per square mile (the average for the world in 1960), the number of people inhabiting a circular area ten miles in radius would be 15,700. On the other hand, if one assumes a population of 8,000 per square mile (the average of the central cities in the metropolitan areas of the United States), then the population of that same area would be over 2,500,000; and if one assumes a density of a Manhattan Island, then the total population in the area soars to close to 24,000,000.[1] The complexity of an urban entity with such population densities is immense, and the problems attendant upon organizing its population so that they can survive and prosper staggers the imagination. Population densities of this order in many large urban agglomerations are not uncommon in many parts of the world, chiefly the more highly developed countries, and they may be regarded as the principal hallmark of the modern society.

Yet, cities have existed on the face of the earth from the earliest historical times. The city is at once both very old and very new, both evolutionary and revolutionary. The cities that came into being in the Fertile Crescent of Southwest Asia over five thousand years ago were associated with the modernization of that period, just as the cities of medieval Europe were associated with modernization then, and the cities of the contemporary world, with modernization today. Modernization is a phenomenon found in every era; so is the growth of cities. One can reasonably propose that every major change in history (as opposed to prehistory) leading to the more rational use of resources, to increased efficiencies in production of goods and services, and to increased spatial interaction has been associated with urbanization, that is, with the growth of cities and the roles that cities have played in given societies.

The last few decades have witnessed a more rapid pace of both modernization and urbanization than had ever been experienced before. If the proportion of persons living in cities—that is, the rate of urbanization—is regarded as an index to modernization, then the decades between 1900 and 1960 may be regarded as the most rapidly modernizing of all history. Whereas in 1800 it is estimated that only about 3 per cent of the world's population lived in urban places of 5,000 or more and in 1850, 6.4 per cent, by 1900 this percentage had increased to 13.6 per cent, by 1950 to a phenomenal 30 per cent, and by 1960 to an estimated 32 per cent,

[1] Philip M. Hauser, "Urbanization: An Overview," in Philip M. Hauser and L. Schnore, eds., *The Study of Urbanization* (New York: Wiley, 1965), p. 11.

nearly one-third of all the people on the globe.[2] Clearly, some parts of the world are more highly urbanized than others. With some exceptions, these regions are associated with the industrialized, higher-income countries of the Western world, a large proportion of whose populations live in cities, and increasingly in cities of large size. In the United States, for example, which in 1790 had only 5 per cent of its relatively small population living in urban places of 2,500 or more, 70 per cent of the entire population in 1960 lived in such places. Moreover, during the first sixty years of the present century, when the population of the United States increased from 75,000,000 to 180,000,000, the increase in urban population, as Philip Hauser points out, "absorbed 92 per cent of the total increase in the nation," and the increase in metropolitan population, that is, in the larger cities, accounted for about 85 per cent of the total population growth.[3] The intensity of concentration in metropolitan areas reached a maximum between 1950 and 1960, when the twenty-four metropolitan areas in which lived over a third of the nation's population alone accounted for 60 per cent of the total national population growth. In short, in the United States, more people are living in large metropolitan agglomerations than ever before, and it is likely that during the next few decades the metropolitanization of this country's population will continue.

The United States represents an extreme case in many ways, and its relative youth and wealth among the nations of the world have an important bearing on the rates at which its urban population has grown; but, in principle, similar developments have been taking place in most of the countries of western Europe, in Australia, in Canada, and in Japan. Since all these countries have been experiencing rapid industrialization and have both created and utilized modern technologies to the full, there appears to be some strong relationship between modernization, urbanization, and industrialization. This proposition appears to be borne out by the strong inverse relationship between economic underdevelopment or poverty, however measured, and urbanization. Few of the poorer countries of the world have high proportions of their

[2] E. Lampard, "Historical Aspects of Urbanization," in *ibid.*, p. 524.
[3] Hauser, *loc. cit.*

populations living in cities, although many of them display so rapid a growth of large cities that they are sometimes said to suffer from what some authors have called "overurbanization." If this observation seems paradoxical, it may be so because a distinction must be made between urbanization and urbanism, in the first instance, and between the growth of individual cities and urbanization, in the second. To cast some light on these semantic issues, let us examine some of the reasons for the existence of cities and the functions they have performed at different times and in different places.

All cities are called into being to perform certain functions that cannot be carried out by other types of settlement units. From the dawn of history, cities have performed two primary or basic functions. The first of these is the administrative function; the second, the commercial. Both are associated with the concentration of certain kinds of activities in nodes or central places. All cities of the ancient world may be assumed to have exerted administrative authority over a tributary or subservient area. In the case of the larger cities, this hinterland might have encompassed a far-flung empire; in the case of the smaller towns, it might have been a province, county, or other minor civil division of a larger polity.

Cities with predominantly administrative functions were also centers of exchange, but the goods that flowed into them from rural areas were, more than not, in the form of tribute, not true trade goods. These goods often took the form of taxes in kind, such as grain and other agricultural produce, which were necessary to keep the residents of the cities alive and presumably at higher levels of living than those held by the rural populace in the tributary area; but the principle holds that the city dominated its rural hinterland politically, and by coercion or appeal to religious authority it forced the flow of presumably surplus goods from farm and village to town. The origin of this surplus (and, indeed, the question whether or not it even existed) is far from clear. Some authorities maintain that the cities could not have come into being until a surplus existed. Others argue that forced levies of grain resulted in famine in rural areas. Still others claim that the city encouraged the creation of a surplus in one or both of two ways: either by forcing the farmer or herdsman to cultivate larger areas or go farther afield to graze his flocks (in short, to work harder and longer); or by providing technological means for increasing productivity—for example, by constructing large-scale irrigation, flood control, or water conservancy works that diminished the hazards and variabilities in agricultural production. If we accept the third view for the moment, it appears that, at minimum, the predominantly administrative center paid for the imports from its hinterland with administrative services, albeit often unwelcome and tyrannical, some of which, as in the case of large-scale public works, made greater production possible. These public works were paid for, of course, by the goods that came from the rural areas. In short, the cities were a device for accumulating and organizing capital for productive uses.

The accumulation of capital in the form of grain and other types of storage was one of the major functions of most early cities. It was Lewis Mumford who suggested that the history of civilization could be written in terms of the kinds of containers that given cultures created for themselves—containers for the storage of grain, water, or wine; for the channeling of irrigation water or the control of floods; for the cartage and movement of goods and people; for the containment and shelter of kings and prelates, soldiers and servants, tradesmen and artisans. Almost from the first, the city was a central place for the storage of wealth. Consequently, it was also a central place for the distribution of that wealth and in this capacity assumed the commercial function of distributing goods drawn from certain parts of its hinterland to other parts of the hinterland that did not produce them. It also exchanged some of its wealth with other cities, which had different kinds of wealth, and in the process its people became familiar with the products and ways of life of other places. Not inevitably, but usually, the city thus became a center in which new ideas circulated and where change therefore became possible, or at least more so than in rural areas. Thus, almost from the beginning, the earliest cities were centers of modernization, in the sense that modernization means in part change leading to new permutations, combinations, and innovations in economic and related activity.

Such cities as these also provided substantial markets for goods that were not imported directly from the countryside, but had to be produced—manufactured, in the literal sense of the term—within the city itself. The market consisted chiefly of the holders of power, the elite groups, royal or priestly, and their retainers residing either within the cities or in urban outposts elsewhere in the hinterland. The concentration of artisans in these cities led to some economies of scale, but for the most part the market was too small for these to become significant except in certain trades, such as the weaving of fine cloths, the manufacture of arms, and the construction trades. In short, although cities of this type were manufactural, they were for the most part *not* industrial, in that production was for a market of limited size, technological innovations were slow to develop, units of production were minute, specialization of manufactural occupation was more by craft than by tool or process, and animate energy underlay almost all production.

In this situation, an urban-rural dichotomy was much less clearly defined than one might have supposed. On the contrary, a state of ecological symbiosis existed between city and countryside, the latter supplying food and other agricultural products, the former supplying services—some of them productive, some onerous, but all helping to bind the two together. In fact, except for perhaps the very largest of the cities of the early world, such as Rome and Ch'ang-an, one of the hallmarks of the type of city here described was the strength of its bonds with its tributary area, which was almost always contiguous with it.

Nevertheless, all such cities were not necessarily as highly autonomous ecological entities as this description might suggest. In large countries where there were long-term political stability, peace, and effective government, numerous cities appeared, each linked with the others by means of transportation networks based on rather primitive technologies, to be sure, but effective, nonetheless. Such was the case of the Roman Empire. Such also was the situation in China during the Han and later dynasties, when a national transportation network, based in part on the extensive system of inland waterways designed initially to move tax grain from producing areas to the national capital region, helped in the establishment of what might properly be termed a system of cities grouped by size, administrative functions, and commercial importance into an urban hierarchy. Most of the cities in this hierarchy were multifunctional—administrative, commercial, manufactural—despite some specialization in areas possessing special resource endowments. In most respects, the larger cities were like the smaller ones, only more so; or, to put it another way, the smaller cities were lesser copies of the larger, both in form and function.

Although the type of city just described presumably characterized most cities in the ancient world, it also represents a model of most cities everywhere until the eighteenth century. Indeed, as recently as the turn of *this* century, many cities in the non-Western world resembled the model to a high degree, and even at present some cities, in Asian countries in particular, continue to carry certain of the characteristics of the model, especially in their morphology.

Some scholars call this ideal-typical model the "preindustrial city" and associate with it not only the characteristics just noted but also a marked bias toward traditionalism rather than change.[4] But this appellation, though useful and suggestive, obscures what may be most important in this discussion: the role of the city throughout history as a central place, a nodal point, in which spatial interaction, one measure of modernization, was maximized and through which the world view of all affected by it was enlarged. What is perhaps most significant in this context is the fact that even when cities of this kind flourished, they were themselves so few and the numbers of people living in them and/or directly affected by them were so small that the import of their modernizing influences directly affected only a small proportion of the world's population, which continued to be engaged in agricultural activities, cut off from the wonders and stimulation of the metropolis by poor accessibility and illiteracy.

The modern Western city closely resembles in many ways the type called preindustrial, and to a considerable degree it continues to fulfill many of the same functions. It also serves a usually

[4] Gideon Sjoberg, *The Preindustrial City: Past and Present* (Glencoe, Ill.: The Free Press, 1960).

contiguous hinterland, often maintains administrative offices, carries on what have come to be called "central-place" or commercial and service functions, and possesses densities of population that are not very unlike those of the earlier models.

Its spatial structure, however, is in most cases markedly different, especially if it is a relatively new city, founded and developed primarily after the beginning of the nineteenth century. For one thing, commercial activities tend to dominate the central portion of the city—and the larger it is, the more so—instead of governmental buildings and religious edifices, although these two can still be found there. In other words, there is a Central Business District, instead of a market or series of markets in outlying locations. On the peripheries of the city are usually found a spate of predominantly residential suburbs, tied economically with the central city, but often politically independent of it. Moreover, these suburbs are inhabited largely by persons in middle- or often upper-income groups, instead of the lowest-income groups found on the outskirts of the more traditional cities. The modern city is much larger than its predecessor, and there are many more of them in any one country than ever before, so that as a type it tends to directly affect many more people proportionally. Some of these cities specialize in certain kinds of activity, much more so than had been true in the case of the earlier towns, and almost all of them carry on manufacturing to a degree not known in the past. In fact, manufacturing, in addition to administrative and commercial and service functions, is of basic significance among the various roles that the city plays in modern societies.

The development of the modern city is associated, then, with industrialization, with the development of manufactural processes based, not on the artisan's shop, which most often was his home as well, but on the factory, in which productive processes are concentrated to the exclusion of other functions. Most modern cities, therefore, have substantial portions of their territories devoted to industrial land uses, and an important sector of their populations is employed in secondary or industrial activities. They are also much more efficient producers of manufactures than the earlier cities, which depended, not on the factory, but on skilled artisans.

The factory and the modern city, alike, are associated with

the application of sources of inanimate energy to both manufacturing and the movement of goods and people. Prior to the invention of the steam engine, water power and, to some extent, wind were the prime sources of inanimate energy. Since hydraulic energy was not directly transportable for any distance, such activities as relied on it were bound to sites at which water power was available. The steam engine, utilizing wood and particularly fossil fuels that could be brought to it, introduced a flexibility into the spatial arrangement of manufacturing activities and at the same time greatly increased the capacities of men to produce. The steam boiler was a container, different from those referred to previously, in that it was a generator of energy, and not merely a storage device. When applied to transportation, the steam engine, and later the electric motor and the internal combustion engine, provided a means of moving goods and people rapidly and relatively cheaply from place to place. This meant not only that raw materials could be marshaled at central locations at minimal costs; it meant also that labor was no longer tied to its places of residence, but could live in one location and work in another. Labor also became associated with *means* of production, that is, types of tools and machines, rather than types of goods produced. Thus, labor not only accumulated in increasingly large pools as cities grew, which meant economies for those industries dependent on it; it also came to possess considerable mobility, and this condition in turn permitted the location or relocation of manufactural activities at new points of optimal value. Another hallmark of the modern city, therefore, is the separation of place of work from place of residence.

Historically, these developments in western Europe, at least, had their roots in a period when Europe was expanding over the face of the globe and by conquest or persuasion came to control many of the surpluses in other parts of the world, which previously had been restricted to individual countries and cities within them. The resulting accumulation of capital made it possible for Britain and the other metropolitan powers to invest in the necessary overheads and external economies that are essential for factory-based manufacturing. The city became less dependent than ever before on its immediate hinterlands for raw materials, and improvements in transportation technology, even preceding the railroad and the steamship, brought areas thousands of miles away into the respective spheres of the larger cities. At the same time, the accumulated wealth helped create, in turn, more substantial domestic markets for manufactures, raised levels of living in the Western countries, and permitted entrepreneurs to invest in ways that previously had been impossible. Moreover, the beginnings of modern science and rapid improvements in technology brought additional resources into play, most of them in or emanating from the cities, which continued to be central places for learning and knowledge as well as for other types of productive services.

Of course, this description is not intended to be a complete explanation. It simply notes some of the factors that were brought into play at a particular time in human history. Just why these events took place probably never will be known completely; but it is clear that there was a noteworthy period of what has been called "technological convergence" during the nineteenth century, and in the present century the rate at which technological knowledge has grown continues to increase at exponential rates. Moreover, the nineteenth century, as well as the nearly two centuries immediately preceding it, represented a period of intense competition among the countries of Europe, and this struggle for power meant, *inter alia,* a struggle both for access to extranational resources *and* for increasing efficiencies in the production of goods, whether used for facilitating over-all economic development or as material for war.

The modern city lies within a network of world-wide interconnections, within which different cities tend to play rather specialized roles. No doubt, there would be even greater specialization if national boundaries did not exist, since the division of the world into independent states encourages the duplication of functions beyond that made necessary by distance and transport costs. Within countries, the modern city tends to be part of a remarkable hierarchy of cities of varying sizes, each offering complexes of services and performing types of functions that differ with their size as well as their location. A great metropolis like New York is the headquarters of most of the larger corporative business enterprises in the United States, and the economy of the country is controlled from it to a large extent. This would be even more the case if New York, like London or Paris, were the national capital, since the influence of the place would be greatly increased if it were the center for governmental as well as commercial decision making. To a considerable degree, New York is also the nation's wholesaler, specialized retailer, and cultural center. It is a great industrial center, as well, and it is a vast market for its own products, although its industrial role is distinctly subordinate to these other "central-place" functions, since its location is somewhat marginal to the national market taken as a whole. Not only is the hinterland of New York the entire United States, but since its sea and air connections give it convenient access to most of the rest of the world as well, one can argue that, to some degree, its hinterland includes every part of the world that is free to trade. The same can be said of London, Paris, or Stockholm, for example, or even of many other cities that are not dominant within their countries. The hinterland of Chicago, the nation's second city, as seen, for example, in the origins and destinations of goods that pass through the port of Chicago, also may be described in terms of a world-wide network of production, transportation, and consumption.

In other words, the modern city is no longer dependent on its immediate hinterland for foodstuffs, raw materials, or markets. In turn, what had been or might have been urban hinterlands, in the traditional sense of the term, can now play more specialized economic roles. They can become increasingly urbanized and suburbanized, as is happening along the eastern seaboard of the United States (which one geographer has called "Megalopolis"), or they can engage more readily in specialized agricultural production; for example, for national or international markets. Within such agricultural areas, however, as in the grain-growing Great Plains of North America, cities, though sometimes large, tend to play the role of regional service and processing center, in close symbiotic relationship with the immediate hinterland and performing a middleman function between that hinterland and the rest of the country and the world.

The Industrial Revolution, as it unfolded in the eighteenth

and nineteenth centuries, first in western Europe and then in the United States, resulted in the concentration of industrial production in one of two types of locations: either (1) in established cities where wealth and markets were already concentrated or (2) in newly established or expanded urbanized areas such as the British Midland or the Ruhr, where raw materials, particularly bulky fossil fuels, were naturally located. Of the two developments, the second was certainly the more conspicuous, and many of the cities that developed during this period were predominantly industrial in function. However, technological changes since the turn of the century, with regard to both transportation and the generation and transmission of energy, have greatly broadened the range of locational choices available to plant managers, who are no longer as rigorously bound to sites where given natural resources are available. Increasingly, location near the market has become more important than location near raw materials. Thus, proportionally, more and greater varieties of industries with close linkages to each other are finding their most economic locations within the metropolitan areas that contain higher proportions of a country's population.

At the same time, the range of locational choices within or near the metropolitan areas has been greatly enlarged by improved transportation technology, and space-demanding industries are tending to locate in less densely occupied areas along the margins of the great cities or even at some distance from them. Closely linked industries need not be contiguous as before, and trends are toward a more diffuse pattern of industrial localization than was ever thought possible. This, in turn, has resulted in a more rapid suburbanization of rural areas near the great cities, based less on commuting of workers to and from the central cities and more on employment in the peripheral areas themselves.

As a result, the point has been reached where the notion of the "dispersed metropolis," composed of a number of specialized nodal centers connected by an efficient transportation network composed of highly automated railways and limited access to highways, can be seriously considered for planned metropolitan development. In fact, this writer has had occasion to recommend the development of such a dispersed metropolis to the Governor of Okayama Prefecture in Japan, where a new multicentered metropolitan area, including much agricultural and other open land, has already come into administrative being.[5]

Despite these developments, two-thirds of the world's population continues to live in rural areas, especially in those regions described variously as the "non-Western" or "underdeveloped" areas. In Asia, only about 13 per cent of the people reside in cities; in Africa, only about 10 per cent; and in Latin America, 25 per cent, a figure that may reflect the partial "Europeanization" of that geographic realm but is still low as compared with North America and Europe. This is not to say that there are not very large cities in these regions or that large numbers of people are not urban. On the contrary, it is estimated that about 35 per cent of all the people living in cities of 100,000 or more are Asians alone, and that percentage may well rise to nearly 50 per cent by 1975. What does this mean?

It means, first, that the populations in certain Asian countries —China, India, Japan, Pakistan, Indonesia—are very large and that even low rates of urbanization mean large numbers of urbanites. Second, it suggests that large cities may have long been a part of the cultural historical fabric of certain Asian countries. This is true notably of China, Japan, and India; it is less true of other Asian countries.

At the same time, one is confronted with the seeming paradox that there are many large cities in certain countries that have not had a long tradition of urban life—countries that are most certainly neither industrialized nor modernized and are not highly urbanized in general, in that the vast majority of their people do not live in cities at all. In fact, the coast of southern and even eastern Asia, other than Japan, is dotted with numerous large cities, most of them ports, in which the largest proportions of their urban populations are in fact concentrated: Karachi, Bombay, Colombo, Madras, Calcutta, Rangoon, Bangkok, Singapore, Djakarta, Surabaya, Manila, Hong Kong and a number of coastal Chinese cities of which Shanghai, Ch'ing-tao, and Tientsin are perhaps the most noteworthy. All these cities, with one exception, are

[5] Norton Ginsburg, "The Dispersed Metropolis: The Case of Okayama," *Toshi Mondai* (*Municipal Problems*), (June 1961), 67–76.

relatively modern, in that their periods of most rapid growth and development took place within the last century or so. Furthermore, all were products of the expansion of Europe into Asia, in the form of either direct conquest or indirect political and/or commercial control. To a considerable degree, then, these very large cities developed, not to serve immediately contiguous hinterlands, but in order to act as linkage points between the European imperialist powers, on the one hand, and the territories they controlled, on the other. To this extent, despite the fact that the overwhelming majority of their populations are Asian, they represent or represented what might be regarded as alien enclaves, and not indigenous urbanism.

As the formerly dependent territories in southern Asia won independence, chiefly after World War II, many of these cities became national capitals and Primate Cities—that is, cities overwhelmingly larger than the next-largest cities and in which most national urban functions were concentrated. This proposition must be modified, of course, in discussing China, which has possessed large cities and a stunted urban hierarchy for millenniums, and India, for which the same statement holds to some extent and where the British had established an interior capital at the old Mogul capital city of Delhi.

Despite their development due to foreign initiative and their commercial linkage roles, morphologically and organizationally, these cities, even today, more nearly resemble the hypothetical "preindustrial" city model than the modern city. Their spatial distribution of population by socioeconomic classes is less clear than that by ethnic, caste, or occupational characteristics. Suburbanization is relatively slight, and Central Business Districts are underdeveloped. Industry either partakes of many of the qualities of the artisan type of manufacturing or is located in larger modern plants almost entirely on the outskirts of the urbanized areas. In some cases, as in Indonesia, one may speak of the "ruralization" of the city, in that, except for somewhat greater densities, large portions of the urbanized areas resemble the rural villages from which many of the residents have come within the past few decades.

Almost all Asian cities, like those in Africa, too, and many in

Latin America, have been inundated with migrants driven from their homes in the first instance by rural unrest and insecurity and more recently by the higher levels of living that characterize the towns and the seemingly greater opportunities for employment. Yet, industrial employment in almost all cases is at best at low levels, as might be expected in countries where industrialization, as known in the West, has just begun. In instances where it is now under way, as in Malaya, industrial employment is higher, of course. But, for the most part, immigrants to the cities find their chief sources of livelihood in service occupations. It is generally agreed that most of them are underemployed, if not unemployed, that they are not in a position to take advantage of the benefits of urban living, and that the degree of interaction to which they are subject is much lower than in the cities of the West. The cities are even more overburdened with in-migrants than are the cities of the northeastern United States and far less capable of assimilating them or bringing them into productive roles within the national economy. Urbanization is taking place, in that cities are growing, especially the largest ones; but *urbanism* as a way of life is another matter.

For all these reasons, the cities of much of Asia and of the other poorer countries in the world tend to be much less effective modernizing media (although they are, of course, to some degree) than are cities in the Western world. Without the relatively rapid economic development of their countries themselves and the industrialization that presumably will accompany it, these cities, sometimes called "colonial cities" and identified as a separate type of urban phenomenon, cannot play the same modernizing role that has characterized the cities of the West.[6]

On the other hand, these cities are experiencing their rapid growth under technological circumstances different from those of, say, the nineteenth century. Public health measures, transportation technology, and administrative rationalization can all be applied, theoretically, in ways not possible a century ago. Even so, these require investment in overheads in their own right, and

[6] T. G. McGee, "The Rural–Urban Continuum Debate: The Pre-Industrial City and Rural–Urban Migration," *Pacific Viewpoint* (September 1964), pp. 59–82.

many of the countries concerned cannot afford these measures given the present state of their economies.

It remains to point out, however, that at least one Asian country—Japan—has not only industrialized and to a considerable extent modernized its society but also shifted from being a predominantly agrarian to a predominantly urban country. In 1960, nearly two-thirds of Japan's population lived in officially designated cities, and about 44 per cent lived in so-called Densely Inhabited Districts, roughly the equivalent of the Standard Metropolitan Statistical Area in the United States, but including many smaller places. In fact, about 25 per cent lived in the four largest such districts.

One cannot say that the modernization of Japan, albeit having taken place in distinctively Japanese ways, was the *result* of urbanization, even though the two went hand in hand. More likely the reverse was true; that is, modernization, along with industrialization, was a major cause of urbanization. At the same time, Japan had the advantage of beginning its modernizing period free from even indirect foreign domination. It also possessed several large cities and a considerable number of smaller ones, and "urbanism as a way of life" was far more deeply imbedded in Japanese society a hundred years ago than is the case in Southeast Asia today, for example. Furthermore, as the cities grew, they created opportunities for increasing the efficiencies of industrial production, processing, and marketing and provided Japanese entrepreneurs with ever greater opportunities to exploit growing labor pools, tap publicly provided overheads, and maximize the linkage effects in industrial location.

That Japan has been able to accomplish ends of this sort does not mean that other countries can do the same or do it in the same ways. After all, it is almost a hundred years since Japan embarked on its mission of becoming a modern nation in Asia, and the entire world setting has changed since that time. Yet, the Japanese case suggests that cities, by providing an environment with high interaction potentials and large aggregations of people in small areas, may well be the necessary, if not sufficient, condition for economic progress in the developing world.

Chapter 10

The Modernization of Man

Alex Inkeles

The main purpose of economic development is to permit the achievement of a decent level of living for all the people. But almost no one will argue that the progress of a nation and a people should be measured solely by reference to gross national product and per capita income. Development encompasses the idea of political maturation as well, as expressed in stable and orderly processes of government resting on the expressed will of the people. And it also includes the attainment of popular education, the burgeoning of the arts, the efflorescence of architecture, the growth of the means of communication, and the enrichment of leisure. Indeed, in the end, the idea of development requires the very transformation of the nature of man—a transformation that is both a *means* to the end of yet greater growth and at the same time one of the great *ends* itself of the development process.

But what is the modern man, and what makes him what he is? The answer to this question is inevitably controversial, and almost no one enters on a discussion of it without arousing a good deal of emotion. The reasons are not hard to find. In the first place, the change from more traditional to more modern qualities in man often means someone must give up ways of thinking and feeling that go back decades, sometimes centuries; and to abandon these ways often seems to be abandoning principle itself. For another thing, the qualities that make a man modern often do not appear to be neutral characteristics that any man might have, but instead represent the distinctive traits of the European, the American, or the Westerner that he is bent on imposing on other people so as to make them over in his own image. In the third place, many of the characteristics that are described as modern, and therefore automatically desirable, in fact are not very useful or suitable to the life and conditions of those on whom they are urged or even imposed. These are most serious issues, and we shall return to them briefly after sketching some details of what we mean by modern man.

The characteristic mark of the modern man has two parts: one internal, the other external; one dealing with his environment, the other with his attitudes, values, and feelings.

The change in the external condition of modern man is well known and widely documented, and it need not detain us long. It may be summarized by reference to a series of key terms: urbanization, education, mass communication, industrialization, politicization. These terms signify that in contrast to his forebears living in the traditional order of his society, the modern man is less likely to work the land as a farmer and is more likely to be employed in a large and complex productive enterprise based on the intensive use of power and advanced technologies. The various economies yielded by the concentration of industry in certain sites and the further demands of those industrial concentrations make it likely that the contemporary man will live in a city or some other form of urban conglomeration. Here, he will experience not only crowding but access to all manner of resource and stimulation characteristic of urban life. Inevitably, one of these stimuli will be the media of mass communication: newspapers, radio, movies, and perhaps even television. His experience of new places and ideas will be augmented by the impact of schooling, if not directly for him, then for his children, who may carry the influence of the school into the home. He is much more likely to have some connection with politics, especially on the national scale, as he is more exposed to mass communication, more mobilized in the surge of urban life, more courted by the competing political movements that seek his support as he may enlist their aid to replace that of the chief, the patron, or the family head whose assistance he would ordinarily have sought in his native village. Indeed, another mark of the contemporary man is that he will no longer live enmeshed in a network of primary kin ties, perhaps supplemented by ties to a small number of fellow villagers, but rather will be drawn into a much more impersonal and bureaucratic milieu in which he is dependent for services and aid in times of distress on persons and agencies with which he has a much more formal and perhaps tenuous relationship.

These are all attributes of his life space that may impinge on the modern man, but in themselves they do not constitute modernity. The densest urban centers may still shelter the most traditional network of human relations; the media of mass communication may mainly disseminate folk ideas and traditional wisdom, factories may run on principles not far different from those of the estate or the hacienda, and politics may be conducted like an extension of the village council. Although his exposure to the modern setting may certainly contribute to the transformation of traditional man, and although that setting may in turn require new ways of him, it is only when man has undergone a change in spirit —has acquired certain new ways of thinking, feeling, and acting —that we come to consider him truly modern.

Although there is no single standard definition of the modern man that all accept and use, there is quite good agreement among students of the modernization process as to the characteristics that distinguish the more modern man from the more traditional. To convey my impression of his traits, I have chosen to describe him in terms of a series of attitudes and values that we are testing in a study of the modernization process among workers and peasants in six developing countries. This permits me not only to present the characteristic profile we define as modern but also to indicate some of the questions we are using to study its manifestation in concrete cases. The order in which these characteristics are presented here is not meant to suggest that this is the actual sequence in the process of individual modernization. So far, we are not aware that there is a clear-cut sequence, but rather have the impression that the process develops on a broad front with many changes occurring at once. Neither does the order in which the characteristics are given suggest the relative weight or importance of each characteristic in the total syndrome. Here, again, we have yet, through our scientific work, to assess the relative contribution of each characteristic to the larger complex of attitudes, values, and ways of acting that we consider modern. We do, however, assume that this complex of attitudes and values holds together: that in the statistical sense it constitutes a factor, and a relatively coherent factor. In time, our scientific evidence will show whether or not this is a reasonable assumption.

The first element in our definition of the modern man is his readiness for new experience and his openness to innovation and change. We consider the traditional man to be less disposed to accept new ideas, new ways of feeling and acting. We are speaking, therefore, of something that is itself a state of mind, a psychological disposition, an inner readiness, rather than of the specific techniques or skills a man or a group may possess because of the level of technology they have attained. Thus, in our sense, a man may be more modern in spirit, even though he works with a wooden plow, than someone in another part of the world who already drives a tractor. The readiness for new experience and ways of doing things, furthermore, may express itself in a variety of forms and contexts: in the willingness to adopt a new drug or sanitation method, to accept a new seed or try a different fertilizer, to ride on a new means of transportation or turn to a new source of news, to approve a new form of wedding or new type of schooling for young people. Individuals and groups may, of course, show more readiness for the new in one area of life than another, but we can also conceive of the readiness to accept innovation as a more pervasive, general characteristic that makes itself felt across a wide variety of human situations. And we consider those who have this readiness to be more modern.

The second in our complex of themes takes us into the realm of opinion. We define a man as more modern if he has a disposition to form or hold opinions over a large number of the problems and issues that arise not only in his immediate environment but also outside of it. Some pioneering work on this dimension has been done by Daniel Lerner,[1] of the Massachusetts Institute of Technology, who found that the individuals within any country, and the populations of different countries, in the Middle East varied greatly in their ability or readiness to imagine themselves in the position of prime minister or comparable government leader and thus to offer advice as to what should be done to resolve the problems facing the country. The more educated the individual and the more advanced the country, the greater was the readiness to offer opinions in response to this challenge. The more traditional man, we believe, takes an interest in fewer things, mainly those that touch him immediately and intimately; and even when he holds opinions on more distant matters, he is more circumspect in expressing them.

We also consider a man to be more modern if his orientation to the opinion realm is more democratic. We mean by this that he shows more awareness of the diversity of attitude and opinion around him, rather than closing himself off in the belief that everyone thinks alike and, indeed, just like him. The modern man is able to acknowledge differences of opinion without needing rigidly to deny differences out of fear that these will upset his own view of the world. He is also less likely to approach opinion in a strictly autocratic or hierarchical way. He does not automatically accept the ideas of those above him in the power hierarchy and reject the opinions of those whose status is markedly lower than his. We test these values by asking people whether it is proper to think differently from the village headman or other traditional leader and, at the other end, by inquiring as to whether the opinions of a man's wife or young son merit serious consideration when important public issues are being discussed. These questions prove to be a sensitive indicator in helping us to distinguish one man from another and, we believe, will be an important element in the final syndrome of modernity we shall delineate.

A third theme we deal with at some length is that of time. We view a man as more modern if he is oriented to the present or the future, rather than to the past. We consider him as more modern

[1] Daniel Lerner, *The Passing of Traditional Society* (Glencoe, Ill.: The Free Press, 1958).

if he accepts fixed hours, that is to say, schedules of time, as something sensible and appropriate, or possibly even desirable, as against the man who thinks these fixed rules are something either bad or perhaps a necessity, but unfortunately also a pity. We also define a man as more modern if he is punctual, regular, and orderly in organizing his affairs. These things can be very complicated, and this is a good opportunity to point out that it is a mistake to assume that our measures of modernity differentiate between traditional and nontraditional people as they would ordinarily be defined. For example, the Maya Indians had a better sense of time than their Spanish conquerors, and they preserve it to this day. The qualities we define as modern can, in fact, be manifested in a people who seem to be relatively unmodern when you consider the level of technology or the amount of power they have. We are talking about properties of the person, which in turn may be a reflection of the properties of a culture that could emerge in any time or place. Indeed, when I described this list to a friend of mine who is doing an extensive study of Greece, he said, "My goodness, you are talking about the ancient Greeks!" He said there were only two respects in which the Greeks did not fit our model of the modern man. And, of course, the Elizabethan Englishman would also fit the model. So, this concept is not limited to our time. "Modern" does not mean merely contemporary in our approach.

A fourth theme that we include in the definition is planning. The more modern man is oriented toward and involved in planning and organizing and believes in it as a way of handling life.

A fifth, and important, theme we call efficacy. The modern man is the one who believes that man can learn, in substantial degree, to dominate his environment in order to advance his own purposes and goals, rather than being dominated entirely by that environment. For example, a man who believes in efficacy is more likely to respond positively to the question, "Do you believe that some day men may be able to develop ways of controlling floods or preventing destructive storms?" The more efficacious man, even though in fact he has never seen a dam, would say, "Yes, I think that some day man could do that."

Sixth, an element we consider part of the modern complex

and include in our set of themes is calculability. By our definition, the modern man is one who has more confidence that his world is calculable, that other people and institutions around him can be relied on to fulfill or meet their obligations and responsibilities. He does not agree that everything is determined either by fate or by the whims of particular qualities and characters of men. In other words, he believes in a reasonably lawful world under human control.

The seventh theme that we stress is dignity. The more modern man, we feel, is one who has more awareness of the dignity of others and more disposition to show respect for them. We feel this comes through very clearly in attitudes toward women and children.

The modern man has more faith in science and technology, even if in a fairly primitive way. This provides our eighth theme.

Ninth, we hold that modern man is a great believer in what we call, for this purpose, distributive justice. That is to say, he believes that rewards should be according to contribution, and not according to either whim or special properties of the person not related to his contribution.

You could easily extend this list; you could also divide some of these items into still others; but I think this will serve to give an idea of the complex of attitudes and values that we consider important in defining the modern man. We have chosen to emphasize these themes because we see them as intimately related to the individual's successful adjustment as a citizen of a modern industrial nation. They are qualities that we feel will contribute to making a man a more productive worker in his factory, a more effective citizen in his community, a more satisfied and satisfying husband and father in his home.

We must, of course, acknowledge that the nine themes just described are not the only way to approach the definition of modernity. Although we have stressed certain themes that cut across numerous concrete realms of behavior, some students of the problem prefer to emphasize attitudes and behavior relating mainly to certain important institutional realms, such as birth control or religion. Their position is certainly reasonable, and in the research we are conducting at the Harvard Center for International Affairs, we have therefore included questions on such themes as restrictions on family size; treatment of older people and obligations to one's parents and relatives; the importance of social change; the role of women, especially the rights of women; how to bring up a child; attitudes toward religion; attitudes toward the consumption of material and physical goods; social and political problems of the community, the nation, and the international realm; educational and social aspirations, including aspirations for social mobility; and contact with media of mass communication. For each of these realms, one can define a position that can be considered more modern and an attitude one can define as more traditional, although at times the process of definition becomes very complex.

There is, for example, a very widespread notion that people lose their religion merely because they leave the countryside and go to the city. As a matter of fact, exactly the contrary is very often the case. There are two forces that bring this about. In the first place, really to practice your religion well, you must be a reasonably well-composed, well-contained individual. The person who is emotionally disturbed neglects his social obligations and involvements. Despite the idyllic image that many people have of the countryside, the great majority of the world's peasants are in a state of culture shock produced not by modernity but by the hard conditions of rural life. When a man goes to the city, and especially if he secures a job in industry, he comes to have much more respect and become much more self-controlled. This makes it more feasible for him to practice his religion. He turns to things that he previously neglected in his effort just to hold himself together. He reintegrates himself, if you like, with the formal things around him, one of which is his religion.

The second factor that may contribute to facilitate religious practice in the city is economic. To practice your religion generally costs something. For example, you may have to buy candles. If there is a religious ceremony, usually the religious specialist who performs the ceremony must be given some kind of payment. Something is required of you. If you are living a sufficiently marginal existence as a peasant, this may be one of the costs you forego. When you get to the city and earn a more stable and steady income, you may be more willing to underwrite these costs.

So, on this issue we are actually taking a rather unorthodox position and predicting that our city workers are going to be more rather than less religious, if not in spirit at least in terms of performing their formal religious obligations.

So much for our conception of the qualities that make a man modern. What can we say about the forces that produce such a man, that most rapidly and effectively inculcate in a population those attitudes, values, needs, and ways of acting that better fit him for life in a modern society? Just as modernity seems to be defined not by any one characteristic, but by a complex of traits, so we find that no one social force, but rather a whole complex of influences, contributes to the transformation from traditional to modern man.

Within this complex of forces, however, one certainly assumes pre-eminence: namely, education. Almost all serious scientific investigations of the question have shown the individual's degree of modernity to rise with increases in the amount of education he has received. Some reservations must be introduced, of course, to qualify this statement. In many countries, the weakness of the nation's resources permits schooling to be only of very poor quality, and the pressures on the poorer people force the children to be quite irregular in their attendance. In a number of countries, it has been observed that if children can obtain only two or three years of schooling, and especially if they do so under conditions where their environment does not particularly reinforce or support the school, there the effects of education on modernization will be very modest indeed. Similarly, the degree of traditionalism of the school itself plays some role. Little or no change toward modernity is evident in the more traditional schools that devote themselves mainly to passing on religious practices or to inculcating and preserving traditional lore and skills. This is a characteristic of schools not only at the primary level; it may apply to those offering nominally advanced education. The "finishing" schools for young ladies from polite society in the United States may be taken as an example. Allowing for reservations of this sort, we may still say that education, especially in schools emphasizing the more modern type of curriculum, seems to be the most powerful factor in developing a population more modern in its attitudes and values. This effect depends in part on the direct instruction provided, but we assume as well that the school as a social organization serves as a model of rationality, of the importance of technical competence, of the rule of objective standards of performance, and of the principle of distributive justice reflected in the grading system. All these models can contribute to shaping young people in the image of the modern man as we have described him.

There is little agreement as to the rank order of influences other than education that we see affecting the degree of modernization of individuals. Many analysts of the problem propose the urban environment as the next most important input. The city is itself a powerful new experience. It encourages, and indeed to some degree obliges, the individual to adopt many new ways of life. By exposing men to a variety of ways of living, a wide range of opinions and ideas, increased mobility, more complex resources of all kinds, it accelerates the process of change. At the same time, in the city the prospect is greater that the individual will be relatively free from the obligations and constraints placed on him in the village by his extended kinship ties, the village elders, and the tight community of his neighbors. These structural differences free the individual to change; but, of course, they do not in themselves guarantee that he will change in ways that make him more modern. In many cities, there are powerful examples of rationality, of the use of technology to master the physical demands of life, of rewards adjusted to technical skill and competence, of the value of education, and of the guarantee of human dignity under law. But many great cities also provide powerful lessons that run counter to these modernizing influences on every score. If they breed a new type of man, they hardly make him in the image we have called modern. In addition, under conditions of very rapid growth, the city is often unable to absorb and integrate all the in-migrants, so that on the outer edges or in the older districts of the city, huge slum communities may develop in which people are in the city but not of it, cut off from many of its benefits and from the modernizing influence of urban life.

One source of modernization which generally accompanies urbanization but is also an independent influence is mass commu-

nication. Almost all studies of the growth of individual modernization show that those who are more exposed to the media of
mass communication have more modern attitudes. Since such exposure, especially in the case of the newspaper, depends on literacy and education, it is important to stress that the modernization
effects of the mass media can be shown to exert their influence
within groups at almost any educational level. Of course, there
remains the possibility that it is the man with modern attitudes
who seeks out the mass media, rather than that the media make
the man modern, but there seems little reason to doubt that the
influence is at least mutual. These media greatly enlarge the range
of human experience with which the individual can have contact,
even if only vicarious. They constantly present and illustrate new
tools, items of consumption, means of transportation, and a myriad of new ways of doing things. They show examples of efficacious behavior of the most powerful kind in the building of dams,
the taming of floods, the irrigation of deserts, and even the conquest of space. They also provide models of new values and
standards of behavior, some of which are far beyond the reach of
most men, but many of which can be copied and do influence
behavior directly. As in the case of urban influences, we must acknowledge that the media of communication can and often do
carry messages that mainly reaffirm traditional values, beliefs, and
ways of acting or disseminate a concept of the new that is nevertheless not congruent with the model of the modern man here
described.

Another source of modernizing influence is the development
of the national state and its associated apparatus of government
bureaucracy, political parties and campaigns, military and para-
military units, and the like. The more mobilized the society, the
more dedicated the government to economic development and
spreading the ideology of progress, the more rapidly and widely
may we expect the attitudes and values of modernity to expand.
Some of the agencies of the state—in particular, the army—may
play an especially important role in introducing men to the modern world, both in the direct instruction they offer and indirectly
in the model of routine, scheduling, technical skill, and efficacy
that inheres in many of their operations. Here again, however, we

must acknowledge that the power of the state may also be used to reinforce more traditional values: politics may be conducted in a way that hardly sets an example of modern behavior, and armies may be run so as scarcely to induce a man to exert himself, to practice initiative, or to respect the dignity of others.

One last source of modernizing influence that we may cite— one that holds a central place in the research we have been conducting at Harvard—is the factory or other modern productive and administrative enterprise. Certain features of the modern factory are relatively invariant, and they communicate the same message, no matter what the cultural setting in which they may be installed. In them there is always an intense concentration of physical and mechanical power brought to bear on the transformation of raw materials; orderly and routine procedures to govern the flow of work are essential; time is a powerful influence in guiding the work process; power and authority generally rest on technical competence; and, as a rule, rewards are in rough proportion to performance. In addition, a factory guided by modern management and personnel policies will set its workers an example of rational behavior, emotional balance, open communication, and respect for the opinions, the feelings, and the dignity of the worker which can be a powerful example of the principles and practice of modern living.

In modern times we are experiencing a process of change affecting everything, yet controlled by no one. It is, in a sense, strictly spontaneous; yet it is in some ways the most strictly determined process history has yet known. Since no one can escape it, no one may be unconcerned with it. Man himself is being transformed. Many evils are being erased, but no end of new forms of corruption and wickedness may be loosed in the world. Some people in backward countries are ready to believe that any change is for the good. Others feel that much they now have is superior to what is being offered, and they are deeply convinced that many of the changes the contemporary world is introducing into their lives are no improvement, while others are positively disastrous. I have pointed to a set of qualities of mind that I call modern, which I believe have much to recommend them. They are not compatible in all respects with qualities that are widespread in traditional cultures, but I believe they are qualities men can adopt without coming into conflict, in most cases, with what is best in their cultural tradition and spiritual heritage. I believe they represent some of the best things in the modernization process. But whether we view them as positive or negative, we must recognize these as qualities that are fostered by modern institutions, qualities that in many ways are required of the citizens of modern societies. We must, therefore, come to recognize them, to understand them, and to evaluate them as important issues in contemporary life.

III

THE
MODERNIZATION
OF POLITICS
AND
GOVERNMENT

Chapter 11

The Modernization
of Law

Marc Galanter

In the past two centuries, the whole legal landscape of the world has altered dramatically. Throughout the world, there has been a proliferation of governmental responsibility and a growth of new areas of law; social life is regulated increasingly through law, rather than through market pressure, custom and informal controls, fiat, or force. During this period, the industrial-izing nations of the West have developed and consolidated unified national legal systems of a kind not known before. And in the poorer parts of the earth, the nineteenth and early twentieth cen-turies have seen an influx of foreign law unprecedented in scope (even by the acceptance of Roman law in medieval Europe). The incorporation of large blocs of civil and common law in the nine-teenth century has been followed, since World War II and the end of Western dominance, by the reception of new constitutional models and by a postindependence wave of reform and rationali-zation.

In both older and newer nations, the development, expan-sion, and consolidation of these national legal systems seem to involve certain common directions of change. Laws are applied

over wider spatial, ethnic, and class areas; personal law is replaced by territorial law, special law by general law, customary
law by statute law. Corporate rights and responsibilities are replaced by individual ones. Religious sanctions and inspiration are
replaced by secular motives and techniques; moral intuition is replaced by technical expertise. Law making and law applying
move from authorities with local accountability and diffuse responsibility to specialized professionals representing central national power.

In speaking of modern law, one may mean many things. The
term "modern" is used here to refer to a cluster of features that
characterize, to a greater or lesser extent, the legal systems of the
industrial societies of the last century. Many of these features are
to be found elsewhere; some of them are absent to some degree in
one or another advanced industrial society. However, I am putting forth, not a description, but a model. Modern legal systems
differ in many important respects. This model attempts to isolate
their common salient features.

Let us begin by considering the kinds of legal rules.

First, modern law consists of rules that are uniform and unvarying in their application. The incidence of these rules is territorial rather than "personal"; that is, the same rules are applicable to
members of all religions, tribes, classes, castes, and localities and
to both sexes. The differences among persons that are recognized
by the law are not differences in intrinsic kind or quality, such as
differences between nobles and serfs or between Brahmans and
lower castes, but differences in function, condition, and achievement in mundane pursuits.

Second, modern law is transactional. Rights and obligations
are apportioned as they result from transactions (contractual, tor-
tious, criminal, and so on) between parties rather than aggre-
gated in unchanging clusters that attach to persons because of
determinants outside the particular transactions. That is, legal
rights and duties are not determined by factors such as age,
class, religion, sex, which are unrelated to the particular transac-
tion or encounter. Such status clusters of rights and obligations as
do exist are based on mundane function or condition (for exam-

ple, employer, a business enterprise, wife) rather than on differences in inherent worth or sacramental honor.

Third, modern legal norms are universalistic. Particular instances of regulating are devised to exemplify a valid standard of general applicability, rather than to express that which is unique and intuited. Thus the application of law is reproducible and predictable. Cadi justice is replaced by Kant's Categorical Imperative.

Now let us consider the kind of institutional arrangements and techniques for administering these rules.

Fourth, the system is hierarchical. There is a regular network of courts of first instance to apply this law and a regular structure of layers of appeal and review to ensure that local action conforms to national standards. This enables the system to be uniform and predictable. This kind of hierarchy, with active supervision of subordinates, is to be distinguished from hierarchic systems in which there is a delegation of functions to subordinates who enjoy complete discretion within their jurisdictions. Independent legal fiefdoms are transformed into provinces.

Fifth, the system is organized bureaucratically. In order to achieve uniformity, the system must operate impersonally, following prescribed procedures in each case and deciding each case in accordance with written rules. In order to permit review, written records in prescribed form must be kept in each case.

Sixth, the system is rational. Its procedures are ascertainable from written sources by techniques that can be learned and transmitted without special nonrational gifts. Rules are valued for their instrumental utility in producing consciously chosen ends, rather than for their formal qualities. Theological and formalistic techniques, for example, in the field of evidence are replaced by functional ones.

Seventh, the system is run by professionals. It is staffed by persons chosen in accordance with testable mundane qualifications for this work. They are full-time professionals, not persons who engage in it sporadically or avocationally. Their qualifications come from mastery of the techniques of the legal system itself, not from possession of special gifts or talents or from eminence in some other area of life. The lord of the manor and religious dignitaries are replaced by trained professional jurists, by police, examiners, and other enforcement specialists.

Eighth, as the system becomes more technical and complex, there appear specialized professional intermediaries between the courts and the persons who must deal with them. Lawyers replace mere general agents.

Ninth, the system is amendable. There is no sacred fixity to the system. It contains regular and avowed methods for explicitly revising rules and procedures to meet changing needs or to express changing preferences. Thus it is possible to have deliberate and measured innovation for the achievement of specific objectives. Legislation replaces the slow reworking of customary law.

Finally, let us consider the relation of law to political authority.

Tenth, the system is political. Law is so connected to the state that the state enjoys a monopoly over disputes within its cognizance. Other tribunals for settling disputes, such as ecclesiastical courts and trade associations, operate only by the state's sufferance or in its interstices and are liable to supervision by it.

Eleventh, the task of finding law and applying it to concrete cases is differentiated in personnel and technique from other governmental functions. Legislative, judicial, and executive are separate and distinct.

By modernization I mean the development of the features mentioned above or sustained movement toward these features. Such a movement may be discerned in Europe as far back as the reception of Roman law, beginning in the eleventh century. But the development of national legal systems of this kind gathered momentum in Europe at the very end of the eighteenth century and spread over most of Europe in the early part of the nineteenth century. The foundations of such systems were laid in many other parts of the world in the nineteenth century. Thus, the "modern" legal experience in most of the world began only a short time after the European. Although in many non-European nations modernization has been intimately connected with the importation of European law, developments in Europe and elsewhere should be seen as phases in a world-wide transformation to legal systems of this "modern" type. This sort of modernization continues today in both new and old states.

It must be emphasized that this process of modernization is still going on in the West. There is no shortage of examples in the contemporary United States: the abolition of racial classifications in the law, the persistent trend to bring state law into line with federal standards in racial matters and in criminal procedure; the movement to make state laws in commercial fields uniform; the movements toward professional judges at the lower levels of the legal system. In the newer nations, the process goes on even more rapidly, more visibly, and often more painfully. But the point is that all legal systems are comprised of these "modern" features in uneven mixtures with traditional ones, just as modern and traditional features are interwoven throughout almost every society.

Our model of modern law emphasizes its unity, uniformity, and universality. Our model pictures a machinery for the relentless imposition of prevailing central rules and procedures over all that is local and parochial and deviant. But no actual legal system is really so unified, regular, and universalistic. Let us look, then, at the sources of diversity, variety, irregularity, and particularism in legal systems.

Every legal system that embraces a diverse population faces the problem of accommodating local norms and giving expression to local concerns while securing uniformity. Again, any legal system that extends over a wide area must be multilevel. It must have at centers of political power some superior agencies that are acknowledged to be authoritative and are engaged in formulating and elaborating important social norms. But it must also have a multitude of lesser and local agencies to apply this law to everyday occurrences in many places. Finally, any legal system must take account of the fact that at any given time there is inevitably a discrepancy between the highest normative standards that are embodied in the law and the going usages of officials, lay people, and legal professionals themselves.

Thus we come to the basic sources of diversity and discrepancy between the law in books and the law in action—the multiplicity of legal agencies themselves, the necessity of accommodating local interests and concerns, the necessity of accommodating values and interests that are not explicitly acknowledged by the legal system. These basic sources of diversity and deviance may be handled very differently by different legal systems. What we have characterized here as modern law can be thought of as one fairly distinct style of balancing unity and diversity, the center and the periphery, the legitimate and the disapproved.

So far, we have talked lawyers' law—the law on the books. But we know that there is no exact correspondence between the law on the books and the law in action. To understand how this modern system works and how it is really different from earlier legal systems, we must ask what happens when we put it in context—where this official lawyers' law is juxtaposed with local legal tradition, deviant practices, and divergent popular attitudes.

The lawyers' law is not the whole of the law. By lawyers' law I refer to those elements of the legal system that are national, formal, impersonal, written, refined, and elaborate, articulated and applied by specialists arranged in a hierarchic network of communications and involving reference to universal norms and independently verifiable facts. On the other hand, the going practice of any legal agency or locality involves local standards and understandings, informal relations, and personal judgments. There are some legal systems that are so simple that no such lawyers' law is differentiated as a distinct and recognizable entity from going practice; for example, the self-contained traditional communities studied by students of primitive law. On the other hand, there are legal systems in which this official lawyers' law has in the main absorbed and effaced the local law traditions. In both of these situations, "official" law is well integrated with popular attitudes about legality; lawyers' law is indistinguishable from local law. Most theories of law, strangely to me, are based on the assumption of a high degree of unity of this kind. Law is said to be the command of the sovereign or the expression of the jural postulates of the society.

But these highly unified legal situations are extreme or ideal types. Plainly there is an intermediate type in which there is an unresolved tension between the national and local, the formal and the informal, the official and the popular. The clearest instance of this is when a colonizing power superimposes uniform law over a territory formerly governed by a diversity of legal traditions. But it is important to recognize that this kind of legal colonization may come from within as well as from without, as it did in Japan in the nineteenth century and Turkey in the twentieth century and as it proceeds today in the reforms instituted in many new nations or in the United States. We may call this intermediate type the dualistic legal situation.

In a relatively homogeneous society, one may visualize law as the expression of shared social norms. But in a heterogeneous society (differentiated horizontally by culture or region or vertically by caste or class), the law expresses primarily the aspirations, not of "the society," but of the groups and strata that promulgate, formulate, and apply the law. The official law embodies norms and procedures that are congenial to the governing classes and may be more or less remote from the attitudes and concerns of many of the people ruled by it. As an astute Nigerian lawyer recently observed, "The law and the constitution of a people are an expression of the social consciousness of their leaders." [1]

A gap between official law, on the one hand, and popular or local law on the other, is not a rare phenomenon. It is probably typical of most large political entities or those with intensive social differentiation. This dualistic legal situation is present with special intensity in the newer states, but it obtains in most modern societies to a greater or lesser degree.

This multilayered legal situation is not new; it long antedates modern systems of law. What is distinctive is how modern law deals with this situation and the processes of change that it sets in motion. There is a striking contrast between modern and premodern law in the way in which the higher and most authoritative elements in the legal system address themselves to the local and discordant elements.

Take the example of India, where there has been and continues to be legal pluralism on the most massive scale. In the Hindu law system, before the coming of the British, law was for the most part a local matter. Besides the courts of kings, there were innu-

[1] H. O. Davies, "The Legal and Constitutional Problems of Independence," in Peter Judd, ed., *African Independence* New York: Dell, 1962, p. 328.

merable tribunals, formal and informal, applying myriad bodies of customary law to their respective castes, localities, and guilds. There was classical Hindu law or *dharmaśāstra*, a widespread and prestigious system of law. But in spite of the plenary power of the kings' courts, official or higher law did not operate to override and displace local law. *Dharmaśāstra* itself incorporated the widest tolerance for local law. The king was instructed to recognize the binding authority of these lesser bodies of law. The fact that *dharmaśāstra* was the only body of law that was written, studied, and systematically cultivated combined with the prestige of its Brahman expositors, the patronage of royal authority, and the striving of many groups for social advancement to spread this "higher" law to more groups on more topics of law. But this was by absorption and acceptance, not by imposition. At the same time that custom was gradually aligned in some respects with śāstric standards, the textual law itself was continuously reinterpreted to accommodate a variety of going usages.

Thus, in the Hindu system, the existence of royal courts and a refined and respected system of written law did not serve to unify the system in the way that national law did in the West. In Europe and America, local law was absorbed into and gradually displaced by law promulgated by state authorities. But Hindu law did not visualize the respective authoritativeness of its governmental, śāstric, and local components in a way that supplied either the techniques or the ideology for the ruthless suppression of local law. The relation of the highest and most authoritative parts of the legal system to the lower end of the system was not that of superior to subordinate in a bureaucratic hierarchy. It was perhaps closer to the relations that obtain between Paris designers and American department-store fashions, or between prestigious universities and smaller colleges, than to anything in modern legal experience. Instead of systematic imposition, there is a general diffusion by example and persuasion, by the filtering down (and up) of ideas and techniques, by some conscious imitation and imitation of imitations.

Hindu law, then, is the prime example of the ancient maxim that "special law prevails over general law." Let us take another premodern example: that of Muslim law. Here, too, we find a body of authoritative and universal legal norms worked out in an elaborate and refined legal literature. But here, too, we find that the local, the particular, the deviant, the customary, are accommodated, not, as in the Hindu system, by simply absorbing them and conferring legitimacy on them, but rather by an elaborate series of technical devices to make the law comport with going practice and by a delimitation of spheres by which troublesome matters were left to custom or to royal prerogative.

In modern law, the relatively stable and slowly changing balance between higher and local components in a legal system is shattered beyond repair. In earlier systems, there was a mutual influence and interchange between higher general law and special local law. The higher law might deflect the local and might be deflected by it. They might coexist without much friction. Now, as we shall see, there is an end to the possibility of coexistence and there is an acceleration of the rate of influence in one direction and an inhibition of influence in the other.

In a modern system, there is a strong and persistent tendency toward the replacement of local and popular law by official lawyers' law. The most powerful agency of dissemination is a hierarchical system of courts. The nationwide rules and standards propounded at the upper reaches of the hierarchy are applied by local courts. The decrees of these courts can be enforced by compulsory process, independently of local opinion. Even where official courts attempt to apply indigenous law, the latter is transformed in the process. Hindu or Moslem law, applied in courts with different rules of procedure and by judges with different training, preconceptions, and traditions, takes on a new character. And this even more so with unwritten customary law. From an orally transmitted body of precepts and precedents, subject to variable interpretation and quasi-legislative innovation at the discretion of village notables, it becomes a body of fixed written laws to be applied by a professional court. Variable sanctions imposed with an eye to the total situation of the parties are replaced by the compulsory and drastic execution of the decree of the official court.

This process of modernization is accompanied by characteristic discomforts. In nineteenth- and twentieth-century India, we hear complaints that are strikingly reminiscent of those in medieval Germany at the time of the reception of Roman law, applied by professional judges—judges unfamiliar with local customs, delay, expense, unnecessarily complicated procedure.

In this process, the official law does not remain static. If official law is borrowed, it is refined more or less to distill out some of the localisms of its original historic embodiment, as the common law, in being transplanted to India, was stripped of technicalities and historical anomalies and rendered symmetrical and orderly. Again, the lawyers' law must be elaborated to assimilate new kinds of persons and transactions, as the English law of crimes had to deal with new kinds of offenses and new kinds of property in India and Africa. The dissemination of lawyers' law is not wholly a one-way process. But official law is limited and contained by the very conditions of its success. The law on the books does not represent the attitudes and concerns of the local people. The demise of traditional law does not automatically bring the demise of traditional society. People learn to manipulate it for their purposes, to make it express their concerns and serve their ambitions. They devise new patterns of avoidance and evasion of the rules promulgated at the upper reaches of the system. The law in operation is always a compromise between lawyers' law and parochial notions of legality.

Every legal system purports to cover everything under the mantle of elevated general standards. But it always has pockets in which to accommodate local and parochial interests and attitudes. In premodern systems, the smaller groups enjoyed autonomy in their own law work, and the government tended to absorb and apply local standards. Under a modern system, these methods are no longer available.

A modern system breaks the tie of law with local and group opinion; this can be liberating for the dissenter and the deviant. The individual is freed from the prescriptive usage of the local group; the group itself must now be responsive to norms of a much wider collectivity. Local attitudes and concerns can no longer find direct embodiment in law. They become law only when mediated through ideas of remote lawmakers and the techniques of professional judges. The legal world is transformed from congeries of more or less independent chapels into a few hierarchic churches.

In this new dispensation, parochial interests and concerns find expression in new ways. Federalism, limitations on government, rules of contract, and voluntary association all provide enclaves; influence through representation at the law-making centers makes official law responsive. Devices like juries, and locally elected judges and prosecutors, permit differences under the veneer of uniformity. Selective nonenforcement, planned inefficiency, *sub rosa* compromise, tolerated evasion, and, finally, corruption—all these permit the local, the particularistic, the deviant, to assert themselves while maintaining the fiction that the law is uniform and unvarying.

In spite of its discomforts, there seems to be a certain irreversibility in this process of forming a modern legal system. Schemes to revive the "simplicity" of local customary law by reconstituting village courts cannot put together the broken vessel of traditional law. Legal revivalist movements such as those in Ireland, Pakistan, and Israel, whatever their limited success in changing substantive norms, seem similarly doomed to have little effect on the basic character of the legal system.

It is instructive to compare the fate of colonial law with that of colonial languages. While the languages of the colonizing powers sometimes recede from their former pre-eminence as a medium of public business and public life, the tide of modern law that colonization brought in its train continues to advance. For modern law includes techniques for eroding away and suppressing local law by official law; it accomplishes its own imposition, even inadvertently. And this imposition seems to be enduring in a way that language is not. An official language does not become a household language; each generation must undergo anew the process of estrangement. But the official language does not necessarily gain at the expense of household languages. On the contrary, we find in India, for example, an enrichment and development of indigenous languages during British rule. However, official law of the modern type does not promote the enrichment and development of indigenous legal systems. It tolerates no rivals; it dissolves away that which cannot be transformed into modern law and absorbs the remainder.

But it should be emphasized that the process of modernization does not continue relentlessly until it produces a legal system that corresponds to our model in every detail—that is, completely unified, uniform, hierarchic, and so on. As society becomes modernized in all spheres, new kinds of diversity and complexity are generated. Intense concentrations of population, mobility, occupational specialization, mass media of communication—all create counter pressures that demand differentiation, responsiveness, and flexibility in the law. So the very factors that encourage modernization of law and are encouraged by it finally impede and undermine it.

Modern societies develop new devices to blunt and deflect the drive toward modernization of law—new techniques of local autonomy through federalism, voluntary associations, and contractual undertakings; new methods of making law flexible and responsive, such as we find in juvenile courts, administrative agencies, and arbitration. Modern law as we have depicted it in our model is not a destination, but rather a focus or vector toward which societies move. But the very forces that support this movement and are released by it deflect it from its apparent destination.

This should warn us that our model does not represent a goal to be pursued for its own sake: these features of a modern legal system are not necessarily a good thing per se.

Law is in its nature a halfway thing—part principle and part power—and the problem is to get an acceptable combination: that is, to get a principle that is acceptable to the people concerned and to the wider collectivity and is supported by the power of that collectivity. The classic problem of traditional law was that where matters were decided locally, there might be either no power to secure enforcement or no principle, but only force. Where decided by a remote political authority, there was sufficient power, but it might be unconnected to any principle that commended itself to those concerned. The modern legal system attempts to combine power and principle in a new way: by making the local decision maker responsive to the wider society, rather than to local power. This gives modern law an unprecedented but not unlimited power to shape opinion and deflect practice. But this can be successful only when that law is responsive to the concerns and interests of the diverse groups that make up a modern society. This has tended to be a difficult problem because of the close association in modern law of the moral authority of the law with its universality and uniformity.

But, as we have seen, no legal system can be entirely uniform and unvarying in operation. Each society must find for itself an appropriate balance between unity and diversity. In part, this is a problem of ensuring feedback through responsive representative institutions so that the law does not move too far ahead or lag too far behind opinion. Beyond this, it requires realistic assessment of human diversity and imagination in fashioning the law so that the inevitable disuniformities of the legal system correspond to those desirable disuniformities of human behavior.

Chapter 12

Administrative Modernization

Ralph Braibanti

Administrative and Political Modernization

Administrative modernization is closely related to the larger activity of political modernization. The nature of that relationship—that is, whether administration can or should be modernized without inducing change in the total political process—depends on what is meant by political modernization. Judging from characteristics of successful political systems that have existed for several generations or even centuries (mostly in the Western world), we can say that political modernity embraces the following qualities: (1) the existence of a legal structure that has the potential (though it may not have the present capability) for transforming valid expressions of popular will into actions fairly predictable and consistent with the system's basic polity; (2) the broadening of popular participation in the political process and the enrichment of the quality of such participation in terms of understanding, responsibility, and orderly pursuit of change; (3) the capability of maintaining national integration through orderly accommodation of cultural, religious, and similar divisive forces; (4) the capacity to blend administrative expertness, responsibility, and rationality with the popular will into an effective amalgam and to carry out that amalgam in a regularized manner subject ultimately, though not immediately, to neutrally imposed canons of equity and justice.

The intellectual dilemma facing administrative modernization in new states is that of the unequal pace of these four attributes of modernization. Some scholars assume that the rapid expansion of popular participation is the most important of these four elements and that foreign assistance programs should deliberately and actively create and support so-called "popular governments," that is, those alleged to have a maximum of popular participation. On the other hand, it may be that the emphasis given to this aspect of "popularity" neglects such factors as the nature of the relationship between the masses and political movements, the quality of responsibility, knowledge—in short, the low state of civic culture that prevails in most new states. It is my assumption that administrative modernization, while it depends ultimately on the larger process of politicization, cannot wait for the maturation of that process, but must proceed irrespective of it.

This is precisely what is happening in many new states. Even without deliberately inducing change in all four sectors, interpenetration occurs. It is commonly overlooked that the modernization of administration usually sets in motion powerful forces that activate modernizing irritants in the political realm as well. Moreover, the rapid modernization of administration increases the capability of balancing the newly awakened public will with a higher quality of rationality. It is true that it may actually temper, perhaps even delay, other aspects of political modernization. Some would view such a possibility with alarm. But, since it is manifestly impossible to achieve symmetrical development of all four aspects, it seems to me to be the greater evil to develop "popular government" at the expense of a viable administration capable of carrying out an amalgam of the mass and elite wills.

In sum, political modernization embraces administrative modernization. But, while efficient administration may actually depress some aspects of politicization, such sedation may be beneficial in the long run. Further, while it may quiet some sectors of politicization, it may also accelerate other sectors. Such sedation and acceleration occur in different proportions in various settings. It is as much an oversimplification, however, to assume that rapid administrative progress necessarily impedes politicization as it is to assert that it necessarily enhances it.

CHARACTERISTICS OF COLONIAL ADMINISTRATIVE SYSTEMS

However controversial this relationship between political and administrative development may be, it is quite clear that, except for India, most new states have inherited asymmetrical political systems in which administration was paramount. The strength of administrative apparatus left by French and British imperial rule, particularly, has been an advantage in orderly demission of power. But its very strength also constituted something of an impediment to attitudinal change. Its ideological roots are a distinguished blend of Confucian concepts of rule by superior virtue, the institution of guardians espoused by Plato, and the notion of gentlemanly power wielded by a small elite group steeped in a tradition of equity, regularity, and respect for precedent in the conduct of government business. In most of the new states, the administrative system was more highly developed than the legislative process or the activities of political parties and often commanded greater prestige than even the judiciary. Certainly, the civil servant had higher status in society than members of the professions and those engaged in business. In India, Pakistan, Ceylon, and Burma, for example, an ambitious mother's aspiration for her son was not that he enter politics, law, medicine, or teaching, but rather that he enter the higher civil service. In some countries, the elitist quality of the service conjoined with ancient notions of caste, and higher civil servants, like indigenous castes, were referred to as "heaven-born" or "twice-born."

A significant characteristic of preindependence administrative systems was the all-encompassing power the bureaucracies possessed. In this respect, many ex-colonial countries can be said to have been administrative states. Government did virtually everything that needed to be done. It was the only significant employer. It ran universities, hospitals, and transportation and employed physicians and professors. Virtually the only persons outside the ambit of direct employment by government were lawyers, landlords, and businessmen. A pluralistic society as known in some Western countries, in which various activities and institutions exist independent of government, in competition with each other and with government, was virtually unknown in the new states before independence. This monopoly of activity by government produced a corresponding attitude of abject reliance on the bureaucracy for the generation of activity. This reliance was encouraged further by the elitist, exclusivist attitude of administrators who, resenting the rise of an assertive political process, felt that only they could understand government and the needs of the state. Thus, there was virtually no interplay of forces between the public and administrators.

A closely related characterisitc was the exaggerated elitist quality of the higher bureaucracies, or, as they are more commonly called, the elite cadres. In the five Asian states formerly under British rule—India, Pakistan, Ceylon, Malaya, and Burma —officers of the elite cadres numbered about two thousand of the nearly nine million persons employed in government service. While the total public service was somewhat insulated from the society it governed, the degree of insulation diminished as the hierarchy of rank descended. At village levels, for example, government officials were hardly distinguishable in dress, language, and way of life from the villagers themselves. The total public service drew its inspiration, its values, its very breath of life, from the upper reaches—the elite cadres. The fact that these upper reaches were oriented toward Western culture, functioned entirely in English or French, and reflected values of administration neither understood nor shared by the rest of society tended further to draw administrative officials away from their own society, although, as we have noted, the pull was weak at the lower levels. The highest officials, who really made policy, were not only insulated from the public but separated from the rest of the public service by several circumstances. In the first place, they belonged for the most part to a different race; they had superior language skill in the language of government; they had superior managerial

technology, higher salaries, and more generous related perqui-
sites. Most importantly, they were not a part of the familial, clan,
or tribal organization of the society they governed and hence
could detach themselves more easily from the web of entangled
personal relations.

A third characteristic was the condition of security of office
that these administrative systems had. For the most part, civil
servants at all levels were admitted to government service by
competitive examination rather fairly administered by independent public service commissions. Once admitted, however, promotion to superior positions outside clearly defined caste groups was
out of the question. It was, therefore, impossible to work one's
way up the ladder from clerk to executive. A clerk would retire as
a clerk, and an executive would have commenced his career as a
junior executive. Thus we find in these colonial systems a mixture
of what modern literature of sociology calls achievement and
ascriptive criteria. A civil servant was admitted to service by
achievement, more or less objectively determined. But, once in
the service, his status was determined by ascription, that is, by the
group to which he belonged. It is not widely enough appreciated, by Americans especially, that the mere fact of ascriptive
status of government employees contributed immensely to the
power, prestige, and stability of the administrative system. This
was especially true for the elite cadres, whose important policy
decisions naturally were subject to strong outside political pressures. Certainty of status within the system enabled executives to
resist mounting pressures of politicians who became more important as independence approached. Another advantage of ascriptive criteria was the reduction of rivalries within the system.
These bureaucratic values of security and absence of competition
fitted in with cultural values which, largely because of economic
circumstances eliciting specific validating religious doctrines, appeared to deplore open competition in any sphere and to emphasize harmony and consensus. While the qualities of insulation and
detachment had distinct advantages, there was also the serious
disadvantage of engendering attitudes of haughtiness and even
arrogance which the public, especially after independence, re-
sented. In most of the ex-colonial states, these attitudes have been

eroded by the impact of politicization. Yet, in Pakistan, the problem remains an important one, and as recently as 1962 in the National Assembly, one legislator said of Pakistan's elite cadre that it possessed powers not even enjoyed by the President and that "all the hatred in the hearts of the people against any Government is due mainly to the self-conceited and haughty behaviour of these functionaries."

Still another quality of the colonial bureaucracies was the belief that good administration was an art, rather than a science. Pope's couplet "For forms of government let fools contest. Whate'er is best administer'd is best" would not have been out of place as the dominant motif of administration. The classical-literary tradition of the omnicompetent, itinerant generalist was the tradition held dear. Administrative training was virtually non-existent; technical specialists were subordinated to gentleman generalists to an exaggerated degree. Above all, rigorous empirical methods, such as organizational and procedural analysis and use of statistical data, were not highly regarded.

To some extent, this was the consequence less of ideological inclination than of the insulation of the colonial areas from the dynamic changes occurring in "scientific administration" in the West, particularly in the United States in the period starting in the nineteen-thirties. Moreover, this period of dynamic change in administration elsewhere occurred just at a time when the colonial powers were preoccupied with staving off independence movements; there was no time for concern for change in administrative technology. It is also commonly said of the colonial administrative systems that they were oriented entirely to the maintenance of law and order and the collection of revenue, hence did little or nothing in the way of economic development. To some extent this is true, though a causal relationship between the relative absence of vigorous economic development measures and the disposition of the bureaucracies certainly has not been clearly established. In fact, some economic planning did take place. Again, aggressive state planning did not emerge in Western countries until the nineteen-thirties, when the colonial powers were concerned with holding a disintegrating empire together and, in the next decade, with war. Nevertheless, whether the reasons were those of deliberate colonial policy or those of having been cut off from the dynamics of change in administration and planning in the West, the attitudinal inclination of the colonial administrators was toward maintaining law and order. Above all, they were ill prepared in mindset to meet the disarray, competition, and challenge to omniscience that an activated political process, based on sovereignty of the people, brought into play.

POSTINDEPENDENCE PROBLEMS

The most urgent problem faced by the administrative systems following independence was replacing foreign officers—whom we shall call expatriates—in top-level policy-making positions they had occupied. Indigenization in administration had occurred at a somewhat slower pace than in the judiciary, education, commerce, medicine, or the practice of law. Immediately before independence, 53 per cent of the officers in the higher civil service of India (including what was later to be Pakistan) were British. In Malaya, the percentage was 66 per cent; in Burma, 56 per cent; and in Ceylon, 56 per cent. The average for all five countries was 52 per cent. After independence, there was a rapid departure of expatriates. During the first few months after independence, participation by expatriates shrank to 22 per cent, most of whom were in Pakistan, where the staffing problem was the most acute. By 1952, fewer than twenty expatriates remained in the service of these five states. The problems presented by this rather dramatic fading of the British presence was aggravated by the simultaneous expansion of government activity resulting from sovereignty and concern for economic development.

To cope with this, the new states had to replace about three-quarters of their old expatriate officers with their own nationals and had to add to the total size of the bureaucracy as well. From 1947 to 1964, India's elite cadre alone expanded by nearly 350 per cent, Pakistan's by nearly 200 per cent. Burma doubled the size of its higher bureaucracy, and Ceylon and Malaya increased their higher ranks by 48 per cent and 14 per cent, respectively. For these five states, there was an average increase in elite cadre strength of nearly 200 per cent. The consequent strains on the administrative system were severe. The discipline and power of the British were no longer factors conducive to order. New entrants had received poor training in universities that had been disrupted by independence movements. Inexperienced officers were catapulted into positions of responsibility not normally assigned for ten or twenty years. Above all, the buffer of colonial rule was gone; native officers now directly bore the brunt of the people's expectation that sovereignty would solve problems of economic distress as well as other difficulties. Finally, the competition for power between the new nationalist leaders, who were typically politicians or lawyers, and career administrators, who appeared to remain neutral during independence movements, was a problem. But this problem resolved itself, sometimes by domination of one elite, sometimes by absorption of parts of one elite into the power structure of the other. The whole administrative apparatus creaked under the strain, which was worsened in Pakistan, Burma, and Ceylon by unstable political conditions. In most new states, the administrative machinery barely functioned, holding the state together in precarious unity. Given the circumstances in most new states, and viewed in retrospect, it is a tribute to both the legacy of colonial—especially British—power and the capacities of the states themselves that the administrative systems did not break down completely. Such were the features and conditions in administration when foreign—particularly American—aid programs began to gather momentum in the late nineteen-fifties.

AMERICAN HELP IN ADMINISTRATIVE MODERNIZATION

As economic planning and related substantive aid activities expanded, it became evident that modernization of the administrative apparatus was essential. Without such modernization, aid could not be effectively used. Yet, it was not easy to convince the new states that such modernization was essential. They had been conditioned to view administration as a gentlemanly art, and they felt unfamiliar with and even disdainful of American education and administrative practices. Moreover, administration was not merely the "cutting edge" of government; it was the very heart of government, closely bound up with social classes, education, familial ties, and political issues. The complexity of this enmeshment in the web of society was not generally understood by most Americans, who tended to regard administrative modernization as simple acceptance of certain well-tried practices in the United States. The need for administrative reform was recognized not only by the United States in its various foreign aid programs but also by the United Nations Technical Assistance Programme, by the Ford Foundation, and by other countries giving bilateral aid under the Colombo Plan or other arrangements. The magnitude of effort in such transnational inducement of administrative modernization is certainly worth noting.

In this respect, the activities of the United States Agency for International Development (USAID) dwarf those of other agencies. In terms of money spent, the USAID public administration program is roughly fifteen times that of the United Nations and fourteen times that of the Ford Foundation. The United Nations program has operated in over eighty states; in 1962, the USAID program in public administration operated in some sixty countries, but concentrated nearly one-third of its expenditure in four: Liberia, Peru, Pakistan, and Ecuador. The Ford Foundation has operated similar programs in fewer than twenty states and has concentrated more than half of its public administration commitments in three areas: India, West Africa, and Pakistan. These three agencies together during the decade of 1951–1962 spent throughout the world nearly a quarter of a billion dollars in administrative modernization, supported some seventy-five training institutions, and trained at least seven thousand persons in public administration. These figures are minimal, and if local currency expenditures and related activities such as community development, welfare, agricultural, and educational administration were included, the figures might be a third higher. However we compute the magnitude of the operation, it is a major part of foreign aid operations, and it reflects the great reliance placed on administrative modernization as a means of achieving a better life in the new states.

Efforts of the USAID to assist in modernizing administrative systems in developing states reveal a pattern of principles and action, or format, which I shall now try to describe.

Administrative reform effort of the last decade owes much of its inspiration to what we can loosely define as codified doctrine. This has been formulated into prescriptions in two United Nations handbooks and a manual of the USAID. The mere fact that enough universal agreement has been achieved to allow such convenient codification is important, for a packaged doctrine of inter-related elements usually facilitates propagation and acceptance. Other factors bear on the manner in which reform ideas are propagated. The medium of transmission is quite different now from what it was before independence in the nineteen-forties. Under colonial rule, ideas were diffused largely through a highly personalized and intimate relationship embodied in teaching or in apprenticeship. Whatever adaptation between the new idea and the cultural milieu occurred was usually the result of an intimate intellectual process in a single human mind. But the transmission of administrative techniques in modern times is marked, first of all, by a much greater speed of diffusion. This may result in greater difficulty in integrating the new with the old. It is one thing to have sent a Nehru for seven or eight years of secondary and university education and another to send a person to London or New York for a three months' training course.

On the other hand, this problem may not be so severe as suggested here, for there has emerged the concept of "institution building" as a matrix in which new and old ideas jostle together and are adjusted. Thus, institutes of administration, administrative staff colleges, university departments of public administration, and professional societies have been established in virtually every country in which the United States has helped administrative reform. The pedagogical techniques of research papers, seminars, syndicates, and workshops have created a highly dynamic setting in which acculturation of new ideas presumably takes place. For example, at the National Institute of Administration in Vietnam, a seminar on case studies drawn from Vietnamese experience was a significant educational experience that resulted in

compilation in 1959 of a bilingual casebook on Vietnamese administration. Very little is known about the results of this process. For
this reason, we look with great interest on a research program in
institution building being conducted by four American universities supported by both the Ford Foundation and the USAID.

Secondly, it is quite clear that in this aspect of help, as in all
foreign aid, technical and financial assistance is given only upon
request by the host government and in accordance with a plan or
design worked out by both governments. It is equally clear that
American efforts scrupulously avoid dealing with ideological
forces, involving political theory, that undergird the administrative systems of the West. For example, while we appear to have
favored certain governments because of their alleged "popular
base," we have, in fact, operated in a variety of contexts of such
diverse degrees of politicization as Pakistan, Indonesia, India,
Thailand, and Nigeria. This neglect of the ideological factor may
be a serious deficiency in the whole program of administration
modernization because it is doubtful if mere technical efficiency
can long be sustained in isolation from its ideological roots.

Probably, in the long run, there must be deep belief that
good administration is a means of securing justice in the whole
social order. This is the logical outcome of belief in human dignity. Be that as it may, we have made no efforts to manipulate or
mold ideology. That is too delicate and hazardous an operation
and is too closely connected to internal political issues and to historical and social forces better understood by the emerging state
than by an outside power. Our expectation is that a superstructure
of procedure and technique of sound administration will be encouraged and that eventually this technique will find support in a
compatible ideological underpinning which will emerge from the
new countries' own constitutional system and from its own systems of belief.

Another characteristic of American help in administrative reform is that very little effort has been directed at short-range reform. On the contrary, most of the activity has focused on long-
range consequences usually measurable in terms of attitudinal
change, rather than in terms of finite output criteria. As a conse-

quence, there has been some impatience both in the governments of the new states and in the USAID with such programs which appear to yield no observable increase in efficiency. But if anything has been learned from technical assistance experience, it is that there must be reluctance to judge results too soon. A base of iceberglike dimensions must be constructed first before the peaks in terms of measurable efficiency are even observable. For example, in Pakistan, it took several years to get accurate statistical reporting recognized as a need, to get statistical units built into the governmental structures, to get statisticians trained, and to compile statistical data. Finally, in 1964, after nearly a decade, the first scientific census of government employment in West Pakistan was completed. For the first time, the number of employees classified by rank and position was known to within 5 per cent of accuracy. This observable peak would not have been possible without ten years of hard work which officials often wanted to curtail because it seemed to be leading nowhere. This generation of statistical activity, combined with advisory services given by the Ford Foundation to the Planning Commission since 1951, made it possible for the Foundation to say in its 1965 report on its work with the Commission that "the documentary basis of Pakistan's development plans is now considerably above that of most emerging countries."

Another discernible feature of the American program is that technical personnel are in most cases advisory. They do not hold positions of responsibility in the host government. This is quite different from the United Nations OPEX program, which recruits officials who actually hold down operating jobs within the administrative system of the host government. The American advisory role has been criticized by many as a slow, ineffectual technique, and many advisers have privately wished they were operating a specific program, rather than advising the responsible official. But an advisory relationship is really the only respectable relationship between two sovereign nations, however frustrating it may seem in the short run. Two types of advisers are used. First are regular United States government employees assigned to various USAID missions whose offices are usually in the USAID headquarters but who may also serve as advisers to certain offices in the host government. The second type of adviser is one employed for a short term (up to two years), drawn from an American university or management consulting firm, to work more closely with the host government on a specific project. This second type of adviser is, by the very nature of his work, much more immersed in the affairs of the host government and much less oriented toward the USAID mission than is the permanent USAID official. It is precisely because he is able to achieve this somewhat less bureaucratic relationship that so much reliance is placed on this second type of adviser. Such advisers are employed through contracts between the USAID and universities. In 1960, for example, there were 105 such contracts in force with fifty-eight American colleges and universities. Of these, 13 contracts were in the field of public administration. This does not include other contracts with such organizations as management or research organizations or individual consultants.

Principal reliance for inducing administrative reform has been on training officials at all levels, both in newly established institutions in the host country and in the United States. The assumption is that such training will be reflected in corporate institutional change in attitude, structure, and process. One of the problems has been to develop the respectability of training as a continuous process. This has been very successful in Pakistan, which now has a clearly defined training policy, tied in with promotion patterns for all levels of officers and three different types of institutions. Most of the country's programs have also emphasized the performance budget, organization and methods analysis, supervisory methods, filing and record keeping, auditing and the use of statistics. In a few instances, large-scale plans for total administrative reform were prepared under USAID auspices, but more typically this was done by Ford Foundation projects while the USAID concentrated on training of personnel.

Perhaps one of the most important contributions has been in fostering the concept of public administration as a field of study and as a profession, with learned journals and with research that has operational utility. This has broken the monopoly that a few people in government claimed to have on administrative knowledge and skill. As the science of administration is further diffused in universities among persons who are not themselves government servants, this may help in establishing a better climate of bureaucratic responsibility to the public.

The last decade of rather vigorous activity in modernizing the administrative systems of developing nations has revealed some hard truths. In the first place, it is evident that administration cannot be plucked out from the tissue of culture in which it is embedded. The total social order is implicated in government administration. There must be a settled constitutional system with settled allocation of powers, so that administration can function within the context and the boundaries of such allocation. There must be relative stability and order in society, especially freedom from war and revolution, which tend to cancel modernization efforts. Above all, the other institutions of the social order must be functioning effectively. Universities must turn out students who have attended classes and who have submitted to personal and intellectual discipline. Unless there is an output of such students, new recruits into the service will transfer the irresponsibility of their training to the bureaucracy. There must be open and responsible channels of communication, especially a vigorous press, for this is a means of keeping bureaucratic power in check. There must be some means by which the citizen can seek and get redress for bureaucratic grievances through the judiciary: an institution like the Danish *ombudsman* or the French *Conseil d'État*. A further requirement is the development of the economy to such an extent that government employment no longer serves a social welfare function. There must be competition for good talent in occupations other than government service. It is obvious that few of these optimum conditions are found in any single developing state. Their absence places an unnatural strain on the administrative system, which must discipline and rectify itself with little responsible help from other sectors of society.

It is now also clear that there are some clichés of administrative "misbehavior" which, although they excite much attention, cannot be helped much or at all by mere administrative reform.

Some of these clichés, such as corruption, overstaffing, overcentralization, and democratic or egalitarian behavior, are deeply rooted in economic circumstances or in social structure.

For these reasons, the emphasis on training personnel and building institutions that can generate and continue to support the results of training seems to be the most promising means for achieving systems capable of functioning efficiently. Even so, the results cannot be measured, perhaps, for some time to come.

Chapter 13

National Integration

Howard Wriggins

The focus of this discussion will be one aspect of modernization: that concerned with national integration. What do we mean
when we speak of national integration? The dictionary says that
to integrate is to make whole or to complete by bringing together
the parts. National integration, then, suggests the bringing together of the disparate parts of a society into a more integrated
whole, or to make out of many small societies a closer approxima-
tion of one nation.

There are many ways in which emerging states will experience national integration if they are to succeed as nation-states.
For example, most emerging countries reveal marked social diversity. Men and women find their real loyalty and sense of oneness,
not within the nation as a whole, but within their special small
regional, ethnic, language, or religious group. National integration
will lead to a drawing together of these diverse elements into
something more cohesive, with the parts linked more closely together. The trend to be foreseen is what one might call "from
many small societies to one large society."

In most emerging countries, the rulers are at a substantial

distance from the people in their way of life, their education and training, and their awareness of their populace as individual human beings. Over the long-run future, however, one can foresee that the leaders will draw closer to the people.

National integration has another meaning. In many new states, the executive government is barely able to assert its authority throughout the country. There are often areas of dissidence beyond the reach of government. Sometimes they are isolated, mountainous areas into which the government's servants and national economic life, education, and social ways hardly penetrate. Over time, there is likely to be an increase in the government's ability to have its way, even in the farther, frontier areas. National integration, then, may mean a growing ability of the government to exert its authority throughout the realm.

There are other possible ways of looking on the problem of national integration. But, for our purposes, I should like to concentrate on the first type of national integration; that is, the transition from many small societies into one large society.

A walk down the main street of the capital of any developing nation will dramatize how diverse is the society. The men from the country wear clothes quite different from those of the city. It is often possible to tell whence a man comes, what religion he follows, and his line of work by his clothes or by the way he walks or even by his facial features.

But these visual contrasts are unimportant by comparison with deeper, more subjective differences. These are often called mosaic societies, made up of countless pieces, each neatly defined and separated from all the others. In many countries, indeed, men are set apart from each other by more than what binds them together.

Everyone is familiar with the facts of language differences. India has over two hundred languages. Even Nepal, with only ten million people, has some six substantial language groups. In Ghana, with only 7.5 million people, there are over five major languages spoken. Fellow feeling is difficult to develop when language differences isolate one from another.

Regional loyalties and differences, too, remain strong, and status groups are marked off from one another. Men feel themselves to be part of their region, tribe, or caste before they sense loyalty to the wider nation. One's region is one's place of origin, and in that place one's family finds its home. One's self develops its peculiarity and esteem from relations with others in the village. Or one's family or clan may be part of a status group including relatives in many villages but set off from others by traditional distinctions that tell who is above one and who below.

Differences between the city and the country are also marked. These are differences of locality, of where one lives, of the social group one works with and lives within. Also represented are differences of value and perspective that are hard to bridge. The leaders in the city often look overseas for models of how life should develop and be managed. In the countryside, one looks to tradition and the ways of elders. In the city, men and women increasingly deal with one another according to their skills and the utility each has for every other. In the countryside, men still deal with one another with a deep and intuitive knowledge of each man's family, the network of relatives that binds him to others and determines his status, and his inherited position, rather than by what he can accomplish. The man of the city often considers the man from the country backward, superstitious, and primitive. The countryman looks on the city as materialistic, lacking in proper respect toward elders, harboring an immorality devoid of the restraints and disciplines that give to life in the countryside its links to traditional religious beliefs.

It is easy to exaggerate these differences. Most city men do retain some links to their villages of origin. Family status still largely affects social relations in the cities. But there are, nevertheless, very substantial differences, and only as national integration progresses will they diminish.

Thus, cleavages are marked, and they often reinforce each other. In modern societies, men associate with one another in many different circles. They belong to one group for religious worship, to another for earning a living, and in all probability to still another for living; to a fourth for educating their children and yet another for recreation. One's life is lived with individuals from many groups, and one's participation in any one involves but one part of the self. Under such conditions, cleavages are mitigated by the fact that men who belong to different groups for most aspects of life may nevertheless find themselves part of the same interest group for some important purpose they both share.

In traditional society, by contrast, it is more normal for all major differences to coincide, for cleavages to be deepened because so many sides of one's life and self are encompassed by a single group, while so many other individuals are excluded. Regional, ethnic, and religious differences and contrasts in ways of life confirm each other. It is difficult for men of different languages to understand one another. Different religious practices frequently parallel language differences and further separate men of different faith and speech. If these differences coincide, as they often do, with neighborhood separateness and special economic activities defined by one's birth and ethnic group, the cleavages between man and man are likely to run deep. The art of empathy, of entering into the imaginative and subjective experience of another, is difficult, if not impossible. Differences are not moderated by the daily experience of interests shared.

These deep cleavages contribute to the major bane of political and social life in most emerging countries: to wit, the prevalence of mutual suspicion. One can trust only those within one's small group. Those outside it are to be suspected. Often, therefore, deep down in the innermost part of one's being, it is felt to be dangerous to reach out to people in other parts of the society. And this sense of suspicion toward others, and of the riskiness in dealing with any who are different from one's own group, tends to perpetuate the very diversity and mutual distance that must be overcome if an integrated national entity is to develop.

Where such marked differences and distrust exist, it is difficult for a sense of fellow feeling to emerge. Yet, fellow feeling is the basis of a sound state. If that necessary fellow feeling is to develop, many of these differences will have to be diminished. It is futile to hope that in a modern nation-state all differences will be overcome or eliminated. Our own country, for example, is a dramatic example of how certain differences persist and are the source of sharp and continuing argument. Still, the differences that do exist and seem inevitable are held within bounds by overarching agreement on fundamentals and by institutions that put a premium on moderating and compromising conflict.

Moreover, it should be clear that the lack of integration of new countries, their diversities and their deep-running differences are nothing new or unprecedented. Other states have faced analogous problems of integration before. For example, as western European states evolved out of their feudal diversity into dynastic states and subsequently into modern industrialized states, they had to overcome similar problems of fragmentation, mutual suspicion, and lack of a comprehensive sense of solidarity and fellow feeling.

What is new about the problem of integration in underdeveloped countries can be noted in two main points. First, it is probable that, in many instances, the diversity to be overcome is sharper than it was in those geographical areas in Europe that gradually evolved into Western states. Secondly, this diversity must be healed at a time when the tasks imposed on government are much greater than they were in the seventeenth, eighteenth, and nineteenth centuries, when national integration was taking place in Europe. Moreover, both the statesmen and the peoples of emerging countries have before them vivid examples of what they think an integrated, modern state should be. There is an impatience on the part of the leading strata of emerging countries to press forward toward this model.

On the other hand, the more rapidly the leadership attempts to create a modern, integrated state by pressing upon its many minority groups its own conceptions of what the state should be, the more likely is it to provoke resistance to the central government's desires.

The experience of eastern Europe following the establishment of new states after World War I is illustrative of this. Frontiers were drawn as nearly along ethnic lines as possible. But always important minorities speaking alien languages and living in the light of alien cultural ways were left within the new states. In each case, new national governments sought to hurry the integration of minority peoples into the nation by language legislation and enforced educational programs. In many instances, so much resentment was built up among these minorities under pressure from the central authority that they became all the more resistant. A natural integration was retarded by an overly impatient government.

There is, therefore, considerable experience in history to draw upon for clues as to how political and other leaders might promote national integration—and from the experience of eastern Europe, perhaps, a caution as how not to proceed.

It is possible to distinguish at least five different ways of approach to this problem. No one of them alone will suffice. Some combination of them may induce sufficient national integration to permit a state to deal with challenges from outside and to further necessary changes within.

The first concerns threats from abroad. There is little doubt that in the long sweep of history, challenges from beyond the border have been one of the most important forces working toward the integration of states. Regional, ethnic, and class differences and jealousy between professions, guilds, feudal dukes, and petty lords in Europe have been overcome and melded into a unity in the face of a common enemy. That fellow feeling we have mentioned—an awareness of mutual interests—is most rapidly promoted by the experience of facing an adversary together and jointly striving to overcome or hold him off.

To seek out a common foe, therefore, may be advantageous. Often it has the additional virtue of distracting one's people and the articulate and impatient rising groups from demanding opportunities at home as they direct their energies to dealing with a foreign threat, which may be very real—or which may, in fact, not exist.

But this course is not without risk. Sometimes an enemy may be real, and the divisions within the society, which the foreign adventure is designed to overcome, may be played upon by the foe, bringing the state to ruin. Moreover, resources and skills that may be required at home to assist social reform, economic development, or national improvement may be wasted in otherwise avoidable adventures.

Secondly, the political style of leaders makes a difference. It can, in fact, promote national integration or disintegration. Some leaders needlessly sharpen the anxieties of minorities. Yet, religious or cultural minorities can often be reassured and their precious peculiarity preserved while their energies, nevertheless, are won for the national enterprise.

Some leaders attempt to deal with diversity by posing as personifications of the nation itself. They often strive to draw around themselves the mantle of the country's distant tradition or the most recent unifying struggle—the struggle for independence. They will often try to combine their respect for the distant, traditional past with a vision of a heroic future of opposition to traditional neighbors or with a battle to modernize their societies. The emotional level will be high, and out of this very intensity may come a new sense of unity.

Moreover, if the symbolic head of the new nation shows interest in and due respect for all the diverse peoples in his realm, he may become a focus of affection for everyone and thus enhance the sense of fellow feeling.

In every community, there will be mediators—men who are much at home in both the modern world of the cities and the traditional world of the countryside. These are key human assets which any government wishing to integrate its people must nurture. The style of the leader should be such as to win these mediators to the leader's cause and to help them in their role of fusing the divisions in the nation.

Thirdly, certain political and administrative institutions can play a major role. It is usual to point out that the bureaucracy and the army are critical agencies in promoting national integration. A *national bureaucracy* attempts to establish as nearly uniform practices and procedures throughout the country as it can. This, in turn, encourages large numbers of individuals to respond in increasingly parallel ways. The national bureaucracy also opens opportunities to young men from many parts of the land. By assigning them to different regions and by promoting all according to merit, instead of region of origin, language, religion, or other inherited criteria, it begins to develop a corps of individuals who know the whole country, who see their task as apart from traditional differences, and who work on behalf of the total national entity.

But an overhasty bureaucracy, intent on ensuring that the letter of the one and only law is universally applied, will generate much antagonism against the central government. The areas of insolence will grow, rather than diminish; minorities will be resistant or sullen. Bureaucratic authority, therefore, must be nicely poised to respond to local differences as necessary, while still promoting a greater uniformity.

An *army* is one important nationalizing agent, pulling young men into a strenuous training in which differences of ethnic background, region, religion, and so on are minimized and men are infused with a patriotic zeal for the nation.

If, however, the army is not truly national, but is drawn only from certain elements of the society, it may sharpen envy and contradict unity. Promotion policies and service assignments, for instance, can either contribute to greater long-run social integration or reinforce or sharpen differences.

The *school system* and the whole network of public communications are of critical importance in inducing a growing sense of national identity. Perhaps no institutions have been the focus of greater tension than the schools. Understandably enough, parents do not want their children to be forced to reject their parents' ways. A school system that too urgently seeks to change the language of instruction or traditional values and aspirations will alienate parents and complicate the government's entire task. Yet, schools that do not hold up a vision of the nation of which all the diverse peoples are a part will indefinitely postpone arousing in the pupils a feeling of the nation's oneness. At the same time, however, the sense of personal peculiarity and of possessing special qualities, which marks each man's conception of himself, comes from his identification with his closest kin, region, or language group. To debase this in his eyes is to debase his source of self, to undermine his will and creative powers. This, therefore, must not be destroyed while the larger sense of oneness is being created. Here is a challenge to educators as great as teachers and administrators face anywhere.

Perhaps just as important to the integration of new states are the institutions of political organization, competition, and representation—the *political parties* and *legislative organs*. The temptation in many emerging countries, particularly in Africa, is to establish single parties that attempt to encompass all main political tendencies. Some countries have evolved political parties whose major purpose appears to be to moderate communal, ethnic, and similar conflicts, without insisting on a full monopoly of power. Certain overarching parties, such as the Alliance in Malaysia, the Congress Party in India, and the Party of Revolutionary Institutions in Mexico, consciously contribute to the integrative function. These political parties contain a large number of diverse and often competing groups. It is within the party that differences are negotiated, conflicts are compromised, half loaves are bargained over and shared. On the whole, national integration is likely to find its most congenial atmosphere where there are such political institutions consciously seeking, in as matter-of-fact a way as possible, to mediate competing claims and to find a sensible adjustment of differences.

And legislatures, if they are properly responsive to a variety of peoples in the country, can be powerful instruments for permitting minorities, marginal people, and diverse elements of the populace to meet with the majority, express their worries and disagreements, and work out a tolerable sharing of interests and advantages.

Unfortunately, however, increased popular participation in politics does raise a difficulty, sometimes acutely; for, as the populace becomes more active in politics, as educational opportunities expand and enhance group awareness of underlying social and economic differences, social tensions and group competition may increase. Learning the history of one's own ethnic or regional group sharpens awareness of past conflicts with neighboring communities. The differences in the way of life and in opportunity previously taken for granted are no longer tolerated. Politicians, seeking popular support, may aggravate the problem by appealing to parochial loyalties in efforts to gain or hold a following. Accordingly, in many countries, as the population becomes politically more active, one must expect a temporary increase in internal tension which works counter to national cohesion. But political institutions of parties and legislatures can be operated in a way to diminish these frictions, enhance a sense of fellow feeling, and meet in some measure the needs of the multitude of groups that make up these diverse fragmented societies.

Fourthly, one aspect of political and social reality that can encourage national integration might be called ideology. By this I mean a set of related ideas that define objectives for the society and provide some clues as to how they can be achieved. Ideologies must be plausible if they are to influence the men who lead opinion and who staff the bureaucracy and if they are to touch the mind and heart of the larger populace.

Ideology may define a foreign enemy and justify to the otherwise unconcerned populace how the state is threatened and what everyone must do to defend it. The wise political leader will use ideology in his efforts to suggest a goal that all can strive for to overcome antagonisms and conflicts. The political party will seek an ideology to mobilize the followers, win political backing, defeat opponents, and direct energies toward national objectives. Ideology, therefore, may find its place among the means of integration.

Many ideologies now being used for this purpose in emerging countries have their origins in nineteenth-century Europe. But those that are successful in answering the need among the leaders and peoples will amalgamate elements of ritual, traditional wisdom that evoke familiarity and trust with ideas from abroad better adapted to the practical tasks facing a modernizing society. Without indigenous roots, there can be no sound ideological growth. Familiar emotional chords will be struck from the independence struggle. Ancient enemies are likely to be reaffirmed. And an ideal society, part future, part nostalgia, will be evoked, suggesting a future of social harmony and happiness. There may be the promise of a national society of mutual respect, which men believe their fathers knew but which they feel they are losing as they seek to cope with the responsibilities of independence and the challenge of a changing and intruding world. In this way, common goals responsive to the aspirations of many groups in the society may be defined. Greater social integration may come from increasing the common stock of purpose and objective.

Finally, perhaps the most important single source of integrative forces is opportunity. Careers open to talent were Napoleon's promise, and he liberated men more rapidly from their parochial concerns than any other Frenchman up to that time. The cost was great; and in historical perspective, one might suppose that French political development might have been steadier and produced a deeper base for democratic practice without Napoleon. Economic growth and diversification provide another way in which opportunity can rapidly expand. A growing mesh of business activities or government responsibilities, transcending traditional communal and regional differences, will lead men away from local loyalties and make them citizens of the whole nation. If men see opportunities open to them beyond the confines of their narrow neighborhood or their limited traditional group, the old divisions appear irrelevant. In opening opportunities for interesting and fruitful activities, leaders may make the most creative contribution to the integration of their peoples.

Economic stagnation sharpens conflict and intensifies competition and social antagonism. On the other hand, economic development broadens opportunities and draws men into the wider, national entity. This is one reason why the economic development of emerging countries remains an important objective of the emerging and developed countries alike.

There are numerous ways to promote national integration. We have considered five: first, the effort to cope with foreign foes; second, the political style of leaders who play down differences and guide men forward together; third, the character of political institutions, such as the bureaucracy, the army, the school system, communications in general, and the political parties and legislature; fourth, the matter of a national ideology defining both goals and ways to achieve them; and, finally, the expansion of opportunity and broad economic growth. None of these comes automatically; all are the result of human effort and human choice.

It is my guess that those leaders will be remembered who move with energy and sense to pay respect to traditional differences as they draw their people into common effort for a future of greater opportunity and internal peace.

Chapter 14

Ideology and Political Development

Leonard Binder

In the past, the prerequisites of greatness never seemed so much a cause for concern as the conditions of decline. Today, a revolutionary and expansive optimism has replaced the conservative jeremiad. So many of us are convinced that no nation need be poor that few think it important to consider the virtues that preserve prosperity. Perhaps there is good reason for our greater concern with the progress of the developing nations; for the advanced nations of Europe, even after being reduced to scientific savagery and massive self-destruction from 1939 to 1945, still remain the advanced countries of the world. Who cares about the causes of decline if Germany can rise from the ashes in a decade? The more pressing problem is, how can the other countries, those of Africa, Asia, and Latin America, join the select group of the modernized and developed?

It seems evident and hardly arguable, in these days of the communications revolution, that ideology is one of the keys to development. At the outset, it is important to clarify what is meant by ideology. For most people, ideology represents a common tendency to confuse what is right with what is best for oneself. While this widely held view does not necessarily imply that ideology is a false conception of the truth, it allows that only one ideology can be correct; and there is some hint that we can discover which is true by being a bit more objective. But to this commonly held view we might counterpose an equally common view that there are two sides to every story. This second theory argues that there may be at least some truth in each of two (or more?) divergent perspectives of the same thing. The full complexity of the notion of ideology is brought out by adding a third problem, which may be summed up in the oft-repeated phrase "things are not what they seem." This third problem is concerned with the tenuous links between the world of our minds and what is out there in the real world.

The theory of ideology is primarily concerned with these three issues: (1) whether or how self or group interest distorts understanding; (2) whether the only validity any ideological view can have is relative to circumstances; and (3) whether empirical observation gives us any test of the validity of an ideology.

The inherent limitation on the validating capacity of empirical observation does not logically sustain the relativist position except in rendering it difficult, if not impossible, to prove which of two or more divergent views is true. It is part of the human condition, I suppose, always to be in doubt and ever to wonder lest our opponents have right on their side. As a consequence of this complicated theoretical situation, whereby ideological relativism is upheld either as simply valid or as the only practical assumption, we may ask whether perspectives or ideologies are relative to some static, unchanging characteristic of each group or whether they are relative to certain universal stages of development. Does one's notion of reality depend on one's social position, or does one's ability to get ahead in the world depend on one's view of the nature of reality? Are ideologies based on unique historical experiences and circumstances such that they are and must be radically heterogeneous; or are ideologies based on the level of rationality at which the world is seen?

Students of ideology and philosophy have disagreed rather

sharply over these issues, some leaning one way, some the other, and some hedging; but for our purposes it may be helpful to render the issue as a simple dichotomy. The two views may be loosely labeled as the romantic-nationalist and the rational-evolutionist. The rational-evolutionists have contributed a good deal to our understanding of the idea of development. The latter generally proposed three stages of ontological development that all peoples were destined to traverse, though there were some who wrote of a simple two-stage process. The three stages were animism, theological or metaphysical speculation, and scientific rationality—a trichotomy that reminds us of the ubiquitous and relatively uninformative use of the terms "tradition" and "modernity." The implication of the evolutionary doctrine is, of course, that at the ideological level all nations will pass through a rectilinear process of changing ideas and values. Presumably, development will be enhanced by stressing those elements of scientific-rational thought which are universally shared. Or, to put it in another way, the task of the propaganda bureaus of the developing nations is to foster ontological maturation.

In point of fact, however, it would appear that most of the governments of the developing countries are not thoroughgoing adherents of the rational-evolutionary school, but share certain views of the romantic-nationalist school. If they are not nationalists, at least they believe that ontology and ideology can be separated. They believe that a man who has learned how to be scientifically objective in many areas will nevertheless have no difficulty accepting nonrational justifications for the pursuit of self-interest on the part of his own government. The differences between modern rationality and romantic nationalism need not be seen as a contradiction. It is perhaps more correct, they would argue, to see these orientations as a dichotomy that is to be reconciled or synthesized in policy and in history. Truth is seen as though it had two natures, one unitary, hierarchical, and scientific and the other multilateral, segmentary, and existential. Nearly everyone agrees that development relies heavily on the first, that is, on scientific knowledge and its technological application. But the ideological problem is how to relate this sort of development to the multilateral, segmentary, and existential truth which is the only way in which man can know himself.

This is the problem faced by the leaders of the developing countries. Their proposed solutions have not yet been crowned with great success, nor have they earned great academic respect for their efforts. On the other hand, their position is made extremely difficult by the constraints of what we might call the ideological situation. The components of that situation defy easy specification, but we may simplify and say that it is composed of two elements. The first of these is the ideological heritage of the colonial era, and the second is the ideological character of the cold war.

The ideological heritage of the colonial era is the foundation of contemporary nationalism in the developing areas. Non-European nationalism has not been simply copied from Europe. Indeed, in most cases, non-European nationalism was a surprisingly isolated reaction to imperialism as an organized, ideological response. Our own analytical confusions have too often led us to generalizing all anti-Western or anti-imperialist responses as nationalistic. The ideological heritage of colonialism involved much more than a passive acceptance of certain Western standards. In the first instance, the intrusion of Western rulers had a direct and severe impact on the attitudinal characteristics of those colonized. An alien intrusion, and especially one that involves conquest, exploitation, or some form of superordination, must alter and intensify whole sets of attitudes regarding identity, social mores, integrity, openness to criticism, operational values, and the structure of social relationships. It is entirely incorrect to assume that a similar attitudinal set prevails throughout all the developing countries or even throughout all regions and among all classes within a single country. As a consequence, each of the variant attitudinal units has responded somewhat differently to the presence of alien rulers. One might rather say that the specific character of the hostility to the West was determined by the nature of the attitudinal subculture. In India, Mughals and Marathas reacted differently to British imperialism. In Syria, Druze mountaineers and Sunni effendis reacted differently to French imperialism. In Iran, the Bakhtiaris reacted differently from the Azeris. The same can be said for the Ibo and the Fulani, for the Baganda and the Busoga, for the Egyptian artisan and the Egyptian umdah.

The incorporation of the colonial experience into localized attitudinal subcultures does not exhaust the ideological consequences of European imperialism. While attitudinal subcultures were mostly self-regarding, the great, written, formalized cultural traditions of the colonial territories were for the most part aware of alternatives and to a degree insulated from the impact of European ideas. Not many persons were learned in the great traditions; hence few were capable of really stubborn intellectual resistance to the West. On the other hand, one of the more usual results of the localized attitudinal reactions was to turn more of the indigenous population toward a re-examination of their own formal culture. In many cases, conflict ensued as the new, westernized intelligentsia asserted that the traditional intellectuals had long misunderstood the nature of the great cultural tradition. It was often argued that traditional misunderstanding or even distortion of the written cultural heritage was the cause of defeat and subordination to Europe. Diverse interpretations of the great tradition may have been put forward, but it is characteristic of a great tradition that its written sources remain available for re-examination and ever more profound analysis. Thus, the great tradition exhibits a certain resiliency and a tenacity that belies the seemingly quick victory of Western ideas. Still, it must be remembered that the diverse and localized attitudinal subcultures limit the acceptance of the great tradition. High-school graduates approach this tradition differently from religious academy pupils, and the sons of farmers react differently from the sons of civil servants. Nevertheless, in the long run, the great, formalized tradition is the most effective unifying element in the culture, potentially capable of integrating into a single social and political unit all those who can identify with its language, its documents, and its history.

Then there is the segment of Western thought that has been intruded into the colonial areas. Not all of Western thought has been transmitted or even made available, and those segments that have been exported have been shorn of their social and historical contexts. It is a nice game to try to characterize the essential features of the Western cultural impact. Some hold that westernism or modernism is essentially rationality, others argue that it is essentially equality, others yet that it is specialization and the division of labor, others that it is impersonalism and an achievement orientation, and still others that it is politicization of the masses. I suppose it may be all these things in diverse measures at various times; but in discussing political ideology, it is probably more fruitful to leave aside such broadly analytical and indeterminate categories and to rely instead on the more readily recognized and specific challenges of the political institutions and formalized political ideologies or isms that the imperialists undoubtedly did export, and purposefully, too. Both institutions and isms were accepted by the intellectuals of the developing areas, and in that sequence. In the course of time, however, many of the adopted institutions have proved unworkable in most of the new countries, but the isms have remained as a sort of distillation of the contemporary political wisdom of the West. It is even possible to measure the political sophistication of would-be intellectuals by whether or not they are able to separate ideologies and institutions. The isms, then, are thought to transcend the historical and social contingencies of Europe and are adaptable to the circumstances of the new nations.

The three elements that we have combined to form the synthetic ideological heritage of the colonial period are (1) localized attitudinal subcultures, (2) the great written traditions, and (3) formalized European ideologies, or the isms. As we have seen, there were and are many other ideological tributaries to the anti-imperialist stream besides nationalism. While it is possible to discern some nationalist themes at a very early period, for the most part nationalism is very recent and quite distinctive. Nationalism comes late because it is a device for reconciling the universal with the particular when the universal has come to be defined as the isms and the particular in terms of the ways in which the localized subcultures and the great tradition have been linked. In many cases, intellectuals and political leaders of the new states have argued that the ideological basis of their policies of development is precisely an adaptation of a European ism—usually socialism. They do not so readily admit that they are changing or adapting the indigenous tradition. At any rate, the adaptation of a universalist theory or ism to special circumstances is the creation of an ideology, in the truest sense of the term.

But the ideological situation in which such a creation must prove its worth is not only composed of the heritage of colonialism; it is also composed of the consequences of the cold war. In referring here to the cold war, it is well to emphasize that we do not intend to imply that there has been no significant shift in the structure of world politics in the last decade. The loosening of the two major blocs, the emergence of both Gaullist France and Maoist China, and the increased activity of the developing nations themselves both within and without the United Nations have been significant events of these last years. There is now far more scope for a realistic attempt at the creation of a third force or, even more importantly, for the elaboration of a genuine third ideological way. But we note, despite these enormous changes, that all efforts of this sort are called "third." There may be fourth, fifth, and sixth nuclear powers, but there is only a third ideological way. In other words, the ideological situation, as opposed to the political situation, requires a confrontation with the two major ideological tendencies.

It is now clear to all that it is false to view ideological change in the developing countries as the consequence of a dilemma of choosing between East and West. However much both we and the Russians felt that ideological maturity meant choosing between us, the preference of the leaders of the developing nations for adapting a moderate Western ideology to their requirements is overwhelming evidence for the assumption that they did not see the challenge of East and West as that of choosing between the absolutes of American constitutionalism and Russian communism. I do not think that the intellectuals of the developing nations have ever seriously felt that they had to choose one way or the other. Instead, I believe they experienced the pressures of the two major ideological blocs as the confrontation with two dilemmas each posed by one of the great powers. In a sense, therefore, the ideological issues raised by the United States and the Soviet Union respectively were significant, but not necessary logical contradictories. The United States posed the issue of alternative paths to development: evolution or revolution? The Soviet Union posed the entirely different issue of whether the ideological justification of the development goal ought to be universal or particular.

The United States has not really argued that the developing nations ought to accept our laws and institutions, nor have we argued against change. Instead we have pressed for peaceful and gradual change. We have argued for the importance of stability and have decried attempts at violent revolution. There is no doubt that this American preference is deeply rooted in American thought, but the implication of our view in the context of the developing nations is quite different. Our emphasis on the rational and peaceful pursuit of self-interest, for evolutionary change, and for gradualism has been based on the argument that change thus achieved will be more firmly rooted. But to the leaders of revolutionary movements, the ideological content of our argument appears to be opposition to change and indirect support of the status quo.

While the Russians hold a revolutionary doctrine, they do not always argue the centrality of violent revolution. The Russian challenge to the new nations is in the assertion that ultimately there is only a single form of mature modernity. Soviet Communism represents the last and the universal stage of development. While the Russians know well how to flatter nationalist sentiment, the intellectual purport of Communism is that there is but one way for all.

In characterizing the ideological situation confronting the leaders of the new nations, it is of the utmost significance to note that there is no direct conflict between the United States and the Soviet Union on the issues as they face those leaders. The United States does not truly emphasize if she does subscribe to the idea of particularistic paths to modernity and development. The Soviet Union does not often emphasize violent revolution as the only valid way to development. But even more remarkable than this absence of a direct confrontation is the near-tacit agreement of both on what constitutes development. By our failure to give substance to the idea of a modern and yet diverse world of nations, we lend credence to the persistent notion—and a pre-Marxist one, at that—that all modernity is one. Furthermore, our programs of military, economic, and technical assistance are all based on the assumption that material changes will cause ideological change. In accepting this operational assumption, we are in essential agreement with the Russians.

The joint pressures of the ideological dimension of the cold war are most dissatisfying for the elites of the new nations. Most of them would prefer to be revolutionary and particularistic. Besides, what good is it to argue that ideological change will be the result of material change when the wherewithal to bring about material change is lacking? What the leaders of the new nations wish to prove is that by first bringing about ideological change they can accomplish material change. They are idealistic in the true sense of the term, even though the ideas by which they hope to reach material development are not quite the same that we hope to attain as a consequence of material development. While it is not at all clear that ideological change can bring about development, it is plain that ideological change can take place without modernization in a material sense. The problem is not thereby resolved, however, because we do not know from existing experience that no ideological change of any kind will be able to cause development. But the frustrations born of experience have caused the leaders of many new nations to compromise their idealistic predilections with the orientation of the great powers. This compromise has led to yet another kind of ideology—ideology as a contrivance for manipulating mass behavior.

In order to understand this particular area of ideology, it is important to remember that none of the issues of ideology have been settled. Specifically, if ideological change can produce modernity, we still do not know what kind of ideology is needed. In the view of the most advanced nations, nationality defines its own ends in terms of dilligence, planning, saving, co-operating, and in general using mature and reasonable means of achieving improved material welfare. But the problem of ideology calls into question this very notion of rationality by casting doubt on the value of material welfare itself. Hence, even if universal rationality is possible, it may not lead to development and modernization. It cannot be proved that rationality comprehends its own goals.

Even more compelling than these unsettling doubts about the inner meaning of modernity is the experience we have all had of people who say they desire development and are yet unwilling to act rationally in order to achieve it. They will not subordinate their private interests; they will not put off spending today in order to invest; they will not prefer the talented to the kinsman; and so on. Even in the best-situated of the developing nations, it is clear that appeals to reason are not enough. Appeals to nonrational values, such as nationalism or religion, have not brought better results. Wherever a measure of success has been achieved, the leaders of new nations have appealed to a broadly similar group of instrumental organizational and administrative values and symbols. National solidarity, the one-party system, state control over parts of the economy, popular mobilization, and the eradication of individualism are the intermediates between the ultimates of rationality and nationality. The purposes behind this choice of intermediates are manifest: the problem of the priority of either ideological or material advance has not been resolved; the practical solution is, therefore, not to seek to change behavior indirectly, but to direct behavior through organizational instrumentalities. In this manner, the leaders of new nations can be both revolutionary and particularistic. Their organizational instruments are revolutionary innovations, and their ideological justifications are specifically adapted to these organizations.

The thinking of the political elites of the developing nations is heavily influenced, therefore, in an instrumental and pragmatic direction. Moreover, their understanding of the significance of ideas is similarly influenced. They believe that ideas have consequences and try to tailor their ideas to the consequences they desire. Seen in this light, many of the ideas used by the political elites of the developing nations are doubly ideological. Of course, there is much variety and much superficial similarity among the official ideologies "employed" by non-Western political leaders.

There are highly differentiated and ethnocentric symbols like "Arabism," "Negritude," "Pyadawtha," or "Sarvodaya," and there are the many special socialisms: Arab Socialism, African Socialism, Destour Socialism, Islamic Socialism, and Syrian Socialism. At this level of verbal expression, it is difficult to be sure when we have found a persistent pattern or when not. Nevertheless, careful analysis will probably reveal three areas of great similarity that characterize the ideologies of development.

The first area is represented by the largely instrumental goals of the political elite. They seek, and not infrequently express, quite clearly what they are after: to unify their people and to create a solidarity, regardless of whatever social cleavages may have existed in the past. This unified society is then to be mobilized behind the development program. The mobilized, solidary society is then to be organized so as to carry out the tasks of development efficiently. The capacity to achieve specific goals is the result of the previous accomplishments; and, finally, with the acquisition of a generalized capacity, there is the crowning achievement of power.

The second area of similarity concerns the aspirations of all those who have been jarred out of their traditional orientations. Members of the political elite share the desire for the goals now to be described, but they are prone to see them only as the targets of organizational and instrumental policies: they are not assumed to influence the choice of means. Thus, those who are responsive to the modernized political elite are generally seeking a new dignity to overcome the sense of inferiority that has been the ubiquitous residue of colonialism. For a variety of reasons, independence and enhanced national dignity have come to be associated with improved material welfare. As a consequence of finding a new dignity and an improved material position, the third goal of equality can be realized. Equality is to have its most important manifestation, now that imperialism in its crudest form has been eliminated, in the new role of the developing nation in international affairs. As a final and perhaps culminating achievement, this new condition is to be expressed politically and culturally in such a way as to provide an affective identity resolution for all those whose sense of self has been disturbed by the need to adopt alien cultural ways.

The third area of similarity will be found in the devices employed by the political elite to move their clientele toward elite goals. The organizational devices of the one-party system and its mass line organizations are familiar enough among the new nations, but even where these obvious methods are not employed, we frequently find certain ideological devices. Among these devices of ideology-as-instrument or ideology-as-strategy we find the themes of populism; atavistic invocations of traditional symbols; attempts at indoctrination of cadres; press control, if not outright censorship; control over other media, over publishing, and over the import of books; and finally the often amusing, sometimes frightening, but rarely edifying device of government sponsorship of the arts (and particularly folklore).

These three components—elite goals, popular aspirations, and the widespread use of devices to control behavior—make up the present ideological situation in most of the developing nations. The outcome, however, is still uncertain, even as the nature of the ultimate goal remains obscure, for modernization is a backward-looking notion that remembers the superiority of the former imperial power. Modernization as an aspect of the future is not so clear. Still uncertain of the attainment of a clouded goal, the long-suffering but hopeful people of the "third world" will surely be mobilized, consolidated, organized, and moved in some direction. But which direction? I think the reason why the problem of direction is rarely treated with seriousness is because it is assumed that there is but one direction. If, however, there is more than one kind of modernity, effective modernization will demand a creative ideological effort on the part of existing or alternative leaders. Effective, successful modernization will then require an effort that differs immensely from the manipulative, instrumental, and anti-intellectual bent of existing ideological strategies.

Our own Western idea of development, including as it does the notions of rationality, gradualness, pragmatism, and objectivity, certainly points to sound values when placed in a meaningful cultural context. But these notions, when abstracted or when associated with the achievement of clouded objectives under conditions that do not permit open discussion, are the defensive weapons of those already in power. It is strange, but yet worth noting, that political debate is generally freer in those countries which have not tried to eliminate every vestige of genuine cultural tradition. Is it not also possible that, in the long run, these countries will be the ones to find new ways of achieving modernity, though some of them now seem less well mobilized for the task?

But, whether mobilized or not, it would seem that the precondition for the achievement of the kind of modernity of which we approve must be a condition of ideological integration between elite and mass. Rationality, pragmatism, gradualism, and objectivity are slogans that inspire fear of neocolonialism wherever there is less than a profound confidence in the political leadership. Ultimately, I do not think that even the peasants can be manipulated and fooled into becoming modern. If they are to be moved, they will be moved by exhortations that are expressed in the right way as well as pointing to the universally desired things such as power and wealth.

To organization, efficiency, instrumental-rationality, I therefore add another prerequisite of development, and that is ideological integration of leaders and followers. Modernity is not a fixed quantity, and development is the term for the diverse paths by which it may be attained. Probably it can be attained only by diverse paths, each suited to the conditions and the traditions of the people in question.

Chapter 15

Political Participation and Political Development

Myron Weiner

Is political participation compatible with economic growth
and national integration in the developing areas, or do both require centralized authority? There are few questions that excite
such controversy and are so central to the problems of modernization. To explore this question, I want to consider first whether in
fact there has been an increase in political participation in the
developing areas; secondly, whether the pressures on the part of
large numbers of people to take part in political life will increase;
and thirdly, what evidence is there, if any, to suggest that mass
political participation enhances or retards modernization.

I

Let us turn to the first question. Has there been an increase in
political participation in the developing areas? We are, of course,
all impressed with the ease with which the leaders of many new

205

nations can assemble mass audiences in the tens of thousands and mobilize large numbers of people to destroy a foreign embassy or march in a procession. But mobilization by the elite for *its* purposes should obviously not be confused with political participation, that is, the organized efforts of citizens to choose their leaders and to influence the formation and conduct of public policy. In spite of governmental claims to the contrary, the fact is that few newly independent countries encourage or even permit mass political participation. Only a handful of countries in the developing areas have free trade-unions capable of influencing labor policy, or peasant associations capable of influencing agricultural and pricing policy, or organizations of university professors or secondary-school teachers able to shape educational policies. Only a handful of countries tolerate opposition parties, and those that are under military rule often permit no parties at all. Some one-party governments restrict membership in an elitist party, and in many so-called mass parties, membership is often formal and without significance insofar as effective political participation is concerned. Moreover, in many developing areas, critics of the government speak or write cautiously or not at all for fear of being jailed, expelled from the country, or denied employment. The press, too, is often muzzled; and even when journalists are not jailed and newspapers not openly censored, publishers fear that they will be cut off from government advertising, newsprint, or sources of information. One could also prepare a long list of countries where intellectuals, either because they belong to a minority linguistic group, tribe, or religion or because they have dissenting opinions, are denied employment opportunities in universities, research organizations, newspapers, and government. Finally, we should note that few countries in the developing areas now permit free competitive national elections in which voters are given choices among opposing candidates.

It is easier to list the handful of exceptions to these generalizations than to catalogue the large number of countries that in one degree or another place major limitations on political participation. The notable exceptions include India, Nigeria, the Philippines, Malaysia, portions of East Africa, Chile, and Venezuela.

Why is it that governmental elites in the developing areas

who claim to speak for their people and who are populist and often socialist in ideology are so reluctant to share power and to permit organized criticism? There are essentially two reasons. One has to do with the *opportunities* available to governing elites to restrict participation, and the other has to do with their *goals*.

First of all, governments in the developing areas have the power to restrict political participation. So long as there is no well-established press and few well-organized voluntary associations or opposing political parties with mass support, it is relatively easy for a government that wishes to do so to restrict political participation. Even were the government of the United States or Great Britain, for example, inclined to outlaw opposition parties, the result would be mass organized opposition. Similarly, a military coup would be unlikely, not only because the military is committed to democratic civilian government but because a military dictatorship would be confronted with a sullen, restive population, a hostile press, and an organized opposition. In contrast, it has been remarkably easy for the military to overthrow civilian regimes in much of Asia and for a single governing party to outlaw opposition parties in much of Africa. These differences result not from any special virtues of Western leaders or defects in the character of politicians and military personnel in the developing areas, but rather in the kinds of commitment citizens, politicians, and the military have in their forms of government.

Moreover, when a military junta takes power or a civilian government establishes a one-party state in the developing areas, the amount of coercion needed is often very slight. Though we speak metaphorically of the revolution of rising expectations and of the great upheavals stirring Asia, Africa, and Latin America, in fact the number of people actively engaged in politics still remains quite small. It is, of course, true that in the colonial period the nationalist movements in many countries were large. In Algeria, for example, virtually every family had at least one male participate in the war, and in Indonesia and in India the nationalist movements were very large, indeed. But there were many countries, especially in parts of Africa, where the nationalist movement consisted of a small, educated middle class. Where the nationalist elite was small and relations with the colonial govern-

ment cordial—as in parts of French West Africa and in Ceylon—
the nationalist elite simply did not find it necessary to mobilize
large numbers of people. But even where the nationalist movement had been large, political participation often dwindled after
independence. Political elites often divided, as in Pakistan and
Burma, and failed to establish deep organizational roots in the
countryside. They were, therefore, readily replaced by the military with no violence, no popular public protest, and, indeed, a
certain amount of general relief.

A second major explanation for governmental efforts to limit
political participation is that the governing elites in newly independent countries often fear the destruction of their own values
and interests. First of all, it should be noted that few elites will
admit that they do in fact restrict popular participation. They will
typically argue that they permit, indeed welcome, mass political
participation insofar as such participation is consonant with *their*
values. Thus, mass participation in national economic development schemes is welcomed, but not efforts to resist taxes, demands
for higher wages in public sector industries, strikes against the
public sector, or demands for more consumer goods. Public support for the country's foreign policy is welcomed, of course, but
not movements that appear to threaten the national unity, such as
dissension over language policy.

Thus, military or one-party governments often outlaw opposition parties on the grounds that the nation cannot tolerate internal dissension that would threaten national unity, economic modernization, or political stability—three typical central values of the
new elites. In one new nation, for example, the dominant elite
fears that traditional tribal elites are so powerful that were they
allowed to organize freely, they would be able to rally support
from a traditional-minded public. In another nation, the elite insists that linguistic, tribal, or religious differences are so great that
were the populace permitted to participate freely, demagogic political leaders would inflame communal passions and destroy the
national government. The elite of another new nation points to
the fact that the population has not yet become accustomed to
obeying authority and that students, urban mobs, and impoverished peasants can easily be provoked into committing violence

and jeopardizing the order essential for national development. In still another nation, the elite claims that a public aroused by opposition parties may press for social welfare and increased consumption and be unwilling to sacrifice immediate economic gains for long-term economic development. Finally, the military elite governing one nation claims that politicians are unable to govern responsibly, that left alone the masses would support or tolerate incompetent, dishonest, and irresponsible politicians, and that only the military is sufficiently dedicated to orderly, honest modernizing government and capable of being trusted with the reins of authority.

In short, the justifications for limiting participation often appear to be quite plausible, if, for example, the consequence of free political participation is the disruption of a nation's territorial integrity or the eruption of internal violence. It should be noted, of course, that some democratic regimes in multiethnic societies—India, Canada, Switzerland, and Belgium, for example—have been no less successful than most authoritarian regimes at maintaining national unity. And it should also be pointed out that a democratic regime may prove to be more competent than authoritarian regimes in achieving that appropriate blend of coercion and consent on which any national government must rest. But there are clearly situations when it is hard to see how anything short of an authoritarian government could maintain an integrated state.

II

It is probably quite beside the point to ask whether it is right for so many new nations to restrict political participation; the fact is that most do and that each has found its own rationale. Looking to the future, it is more useful to turn to our second question: whether the pressures for political participation are likely to increase in the developing areas, and, if so, will it be possible for elites in the new nations to continue to resist political participation?

At present, the level of repression in most new nations is quite moderate, with only a handful of political dissenters in jail or in exile. The vast majority of the population simply accepts the government as it is. In short, so long as the efforts to participate are limited to small numbers, measures to resist participation can remain moderate. Few of the new regimes, therefore, could be accurately described as totalitarian, whatever their ideology may be.

How might this situation change? Or, to put the question another way, under what conditions is it likely that movements will develop for increased public participation in politics?

One possibility is the growth of an urban labor force. As industrialization produces a substantial labor force, it is quite likely that workers will begin to group together into trade-unions to protect their interests. Such a development is likely—and in fact has already occurred in the more industrialized developing areas— even if industry is under government control, for the desire for higher wages and improved working conditions is as natural in publically owned as in privately owned factories. Moreover, government bureaucrats must operate within much the same financial constraints as private entrepreneurs. Indeed, the constraints may be even greater; for while private entrepreneurs may pass on a higher wage bill to the public in the form of higher prices, government managers are accountable to national government leaders who must formulate national policies.

Unevenness in modernization is still another factor likely to precipitate political participation. Some regions of a country and some social classes and ethnic groups adapt more readily than others to educational and entrepreneurial opportunities, even in a planned economy. In India, for example, the state of the Punjab has doubled food grain production in a decade, while in the neighboring state of Uttar Pradesh, per capita income has declined during the same period, though both states are affected by the same national policies and both are governed by the Congress party. Similarly, in Indonesia, Nigeria, Pakistan, Tanzania, and Brazil—all large countries—rates of growth in different regions and among different ethnic groups have varied considerably in spite of the concern for equity on the part of virtually all these governments. Differential growth rates have been an incentive to political protest, no matter how equalitarian is the commitment of the government to regional and ethnic equity in development. The more prosperous regions and classes often object to government policies that use their taxes to finance what they often consider to be the less enterprising sections of the society, and in turn the retarded regions and classes typically demand more than their share of aid in order to accelerate their growth rate.

Still other contradictions confronting modernizing regimes, particularly in multiethnic societies, precipitate political participation and conflict. If the government declares that the state and nation are synonymous and that minority groups should accept the majority language and/or culture, ethnic groups are almost certain to organize in protest. On the other hand, if government believes in the preservation of a multiethnic society, invariably there are controversies over such issues as representation in government and the role of language in education and in administration and disputes over both taxation and investment policies.

More broadly, it can be argued that political participation is precipitated by the expansion of governmental activities affecting the lives of large numbers of citizens. So long as a government merely devotes its efforts to extracting taxes and engaging in minimum routine activities, such as the construction of dikes, canals, and granaries (as is typical in most traditional societies), only a handful of powerful and wealthy men affected by these projects will attempt to influence government. But, once a government engages in welfare activities, pursues distributive policies, and directly intervenes in the economy to maximize economic growth, vast numbers of people are affected and begin to group together to further their own interests. Thus, the attempt to pass land reform legislation in most societies often leads both landlords and peasants to organize. Similarly, the passage of industrial relations legislation is often an impetus to the organization of business chambers and trade-unions. And linguistic, tribal, and religious associations will often be stimulated by the establishment of adult suffrage or of a nationwide school system. In short, active governments provoke political opposition, while, paradoxically, passive governments are likely to have politically passive populations.

We see a similar pattern in the emotionally charged relationship between the state and organized religion. In most traditional societies, religious institutions are among the few organized institutions. The indifference and often hostility of modernizing governments to orthodox religion often provokes religious institutions to mobilize the peasantry for political action. Thus, post-Atatürk Turkey was confronted with counter measures by religious elements. Similarly, the contemporary governments of Indonesia, Pakistan, and Egypt have been challenged by ulema and by political parties of orthodox Moslems; and from Ceylon to Vietnam, a Buddhist resurgence has challenged secularized and often westernized governments. The fact that the demands of religious leaders are vague—that they are often more concerned with affecting the tone and symbolism of government than specific policies—makes them no less a challenge to modernizing regimes. Their strength lies, not in their program, but in their capacity to appeal emotionally to a traditional peasantry, to newly urbanized factory workers, to bazaar merchants, or to office clerks. It is in this arena that ideologies become important, not as guides to public policy, but because they present to a population entering the modern world contending world views that can provide some emotional continuity between the present and the past.

Another factor leading people to become more aware of politics is the growth of mass communications. There is considerable evidence that the spread of education, increased transportation, and communication between urban centers and the hinterland and the spread of newspapers and radio all serve to arouse a greater awareness of the effect of government policies on individual citizens. The number of people who feel they have the right to influence the affairs of government tends to multiply as societies modernize. In short, the process of modernization itself creates the conditions for increased political participation; and if modernization continues to take place in the developing areas, we can expect both representative governments and authoritarian regimes to be challenged by new participants who want to share power. The way in which regimes respond to these new demands will have profound consequences for all aspects of their development.

The modernization process is a disturbing one and is typically accompanied by more, not less, social conflict. It is striking, therefore, that in the midst of the modernization process, it is common

for utopian ideologies to emerge, emphasizing the dream of elimi-
nating conflict from society either by returning to some hypothetical preindustrial state or else by creating new industrial forms in
which the so-called "contradictions" between economic interests
can be eliminated. The opponents of industrialization were particularly articulate in late nineteenth-century England through the
voice of Ruskin, in Russia through Tolstoi, and in India in the
nineteen-twenties through Gandhi. Karl Marx and his followers
have, of course, been the major advocates of the position that it is
possible to eliminate conflict in modern industrial societies by
rooting out what they consider to be the internal contradictions of
capitalism, on the mistaken assumption that it is capitalism, and
not the modernization process itself, that is the source of societal
conflict. Both these positions are utopian: the one because, once
industrialization has begun, it is virtually impossible to move
backward voluntarily; the other because the elimination of private entrepreneurship does not by any means remove social conflict. The fact is that Communist regimes such as the Soviet Union
and China have been no less torn by internal dissension than
democratic capitalist regimes.

Let us be clear on this issue. All modern societies are characterized by internal conflict. The more complex an economy becomes, the more the economic interests are differentiated. The
more decisions government makes, the more controversy there is.
Policy making in modern societies involves the making of choices,
that is, of choosing between alternative conflicting possibilities.
Modern political systems differ not so much in the type and degree of conflict—it is remarkable, for example, how many political
controversies are shared by both the United States and the Soviet
Union—but in the mechanisms through which conflicts are resolved.

III

What I have described here as some of the conditions likely to
result in increased political participation have, in fact, already begun to take place in many new nations in one form or another. As

these trends continue and, as we have suggested, are accelerated in just those societies which are modernizing most rapidly, the new nations will be confronted by even more powerful demands for political participation. And this leads to our last major question. What will be the consequences for modernization if the new regimes do become more willing to tolerate large-scale political participation? Will increased political participation weaken national unity and retard economic growth?

We have already noted that central coercive authority is often all that has held some new nations intact, but we have also noted that many countries have moved toward national integration even though a national democratic government has tolerated organized dissent. But what of the claims that large-scale political participation may be an impediment to economic growth? Here the issue is even more clouded. One school of thought contends that economic planning must be performed by experts, that current consumption must be sacrificed in the interest of long-term capital investment, and that such policies can best be pursued by an authoritarian but progressive government—a benevolent dictatorship, if you will—free from public pressures. Those who take this position argue that there must be participation, not in the sense in which we have used this term, but participation—or better, mobilization—in the country's development program. Thus, several new governments exhort the population to participate in rural development schemes, but do not permit them to organize to make demands upon government.

A recent variation on this approach has been to encourage local popular government so as to foster participation in the government's rural development program at that level, but to maintain a ban on national political parties. Pakistan has pursued this strategy, and it will be interesting to see whether it is possible to encourage local political participation while restricting national party politics. It will also be interesting to see whether this limited form of political participation has any significant effect on rural economic development.

In this connection, it should be pointed out that the most authoritarian regimes in the developing countries are eager to win popular support even while they restrict popular participation in government. In the absence of opinion polls or national elections, it is, of course, most difficult to judge how successful authoritarian governments are at winning popular support. Unfortunately, we tend to assume that those authoritarian governments which speak in a radical and revolutionary language have popular support, while conservative authoritarian regimes do not. All too often we also naïvely assume that a revolutionary regime is more capable of carrying through social and economic reforms, facilitating national economic growth, and maximizing economic equality than is either a conservative authoritarian government or a democratic regime. It is essential, however, not to confuse the symbols of revolutionaries with the performance of governments. Some regimes that stress the symbols of revolution—such as the present Egyptian government—have commendable records of honesty and progressiveness; but one can also cite many instances of so-called revolutionary regimes in north Africa, west Africa, or southeast Asia bordering on economic chaos but giving the appearance—to the outside world, at least—that they are popular. But how do we know? Can we simply accept the claims of revolutionary regimes? How do we know how popular Algeria's Ben Bella was?

Surely governments must have some support to remain in power, but how much support and how much mobilization are essential to carry on a program of economic development? In the industrial sector, probably very little, since the most oligarchical government can build a steel mill and recruit a labor force. But in the realm of agriculture and small-scale industries, where even in the most socialist-minded systems thousands and millions of private decisions are necessary, coercion alone is not sufficient. One option is mobilization without participation, and this is the strategy pursued by ideologically oriented authoritarian governments. Here the effort is to exhort the citizenry to contribute their labor to national development in the interest of some higher national ideals without regard for their personal improvement and without seeking to influence the course of policy. The other option is to allow full-scale political participation, which means that people are permitted to protest and to demand higher wages, better working conditions, and more government aid in the hope that as individuals seek to improve their personal well-being and to influence national policy they will, in fact, be playing a role in the nation's development. Let us be concrete. How does a government stir a passive peasantry to adopt new agricultural methods when efforts to introduce new techniques by government extension officers have not succeeded? One possibility is to permit and even encourage peasants to express their complaints against local government officers and landlords and make demands upon government in hopes that this will be followed by rural efforts to avail themselves of the new technologies offered by government officials. How a government handles protest during this formative stage of development may be critical for subsequent economic and political behavior by the citizenry. If government represses protest, it may set the stage for alienating the peasantry; while, on the other hand, a responsive government may establish the foundations for public trust and build a relationship under which the governed and the governors work together for common goals.

As modernization proceeds, protest and the desire for political participation will mount in the authoritarian and semiauthoritarian governments now existing in much of the developing world. When this takes place, the governing elites will be forced to choose either to exercise stiffer coercion or to share power and tolerate greater opposition.

It is unfortunate that so much international attention is given to the accomplishments of totalitarian regimes and so little to their failures. We do not have the time here to present what is known about rates of economic development in authoritarian and in democratic regimes. Suffice it to say that no causal relationship and, indeed, no significant correlations exist between forms of regimes and rates of growth. Many authoritarian and totalitarian regimes have had low rates of growth, and so, too, have many democratic regimes; but one can also point to both authoritarian and democratic regimes that have done well. The attitudes and behavior of the population and the policies pursued by governments appear to be more important than the forms of government. It is only in the extreme situation where no sense of community exists, where proclivities toward violence are extreme— where, in short, only coercive authority seems capable of sustaining order—that one can readily claim that an authoritarian regime is a precondition to national integration and economic development. But, barring these extreme situations, we can say that whether a country achieves national integration or economic development is not simply a matter of whether it has an authoritarian or democratic form of government, for the historical record shows that both have the capacity to succeed, depending in the final analysis on how their leaders behave. If this is so, then much of the current debate over the merits or demerits of military, one-party, or competitive party regimes is beside the point. It comes down to the simple issue of whether a governing elite values in its citizens obedience or independence; whether an elite is willing to admit that there is a wide variety of alternative acceptable policies, not simply a single correct way to integrate or to modernize; and, in the final analysis, whether a governing elite is willing to see itself lose office.

Chapter **16**

Distribution
and Development

Joseph LaPalombara

The twentieth century's dominant theme is surely the quest for modernity. No period since the dawn of history has witnessed so many men restlessly in search of change. The process of modernization, which began in Italy in the fifteenth century and spread to most of the West over the following five hundred years, is now world-wide. Whether we describe this contemporary process as the "breaking down of tradition" or as the "revolution of rising expectation," it is apparent that people demand and are experiencing change at a pace and of a magnitude for which there are few, if any, historical parallels.

Many of the changes now under way center on the nation-state and are often described as "nation building." Their range is, of course, immense: the desire for material improvement clearly points to profound transformation in agriculture and industrial production; the skills demanded by industry, as well as the ideologies of equality, require major attention to education; the introduction of science and technology and the urbanization of many countries create problems of innovation and management that severely test the capacities of the very best human resources available to a country.

To think of nation building or modernization without regard to the central role in this process that government and politics must play is to ignore how closely related are transformations in the social, psychological, economic, and political spheres. Economic development, for example, does not occur in a vacuum; at the very least, it compels us to ask how one is to provide the savings, the financial and commercial arrangements and institutions, the infrastructure such as roads and communications and power, and the educational systems that will make economic change more than an abstract hope. As I conceive of the term, then, a "developed" political system is one that permits the political leadership of a country to manage with reasonable efficiency (and without undue violence or upheaval) the kinds of "crises" for a nation that rapid changes—and the demands that go with them—usually entail.

One of the crises that confronts all political systems sooner or later is that of *distribution.* By this I mean demands on the rulers to modify in some way the prevailing distribution in society of goods, services, and related values. Such modification may simply involve *new* formulas for distributing existing goods and services among the population. "Share the wealth" (or, more often, poverty) campaigns are basically of this variety. Increasingly, however, distributive demands on political leaders imply or openly require the provision of goods and services traditionally not included among the so-called "normal" activities of government. Time was when people saw government as essentially that particular form of social organization created to provide for internal order and defense against foreign invasion. All other activities were considered to be "outside" the proper sphere of government. In the West, advocates of such narrowly defined spheres of governmental activity found their philosophical spokesmen in persons like Herbert Spencer. Even Thomas Jefferson, democratic advocate that he was, cautioned that the best government is one that governs least.

That age of political innocence—if innocence it was—vanished forever with increased demands for political participation and the growth of distributive ideologies. It is commonplace today to associate the latter with the writings of Karl Marx and the growth of socialist thought during that last half of the nineteenth century. But the taproots of such thought lie much deeper in human history. In a sense, one can say that the crisis of distribution first occurred at the dawn of civilized society, when a tribal chieftain or nomadic leader found that in order to continue to rule or govern, he needed support from allies. These latter, in turn, extracted for their services more than an average share of whatever goods and services such early political systems could produce. Premodern eras also provide examples of tribal or other political organization where a sense of sharing—or widely distributing—existing goods and services was deeply ingrained. One might say that such political systems were already highly developed, in the sense that I have been using the concept of political development.

But the crisis of distribution referred to here occurred rather late in the evolution of the older nation-states, although clearly well in advance of the nineteenth century. The crisis is apparent in the debates at Putney, England, in the seventeenth century, and particularly in the demands of the Levellers. It is evident in peasant uprisings and forced occupation of farmlands in places like seventeenth-century Russia and eighteenth-century Italy and France. It is apparent, too, in at least two centuries of philosophical writing that preceded Karl Marx in the West. These writings stressed the idea that, as a matter of right, citizens of a nation-state were entitled to as much of the amenities of human existence as the resources and the inventive capacity of the nation would allow. During a period stretching over several centuries, Western man succeeded in expanding the functions of government to cover everything from military defense to health insurance, from economic development to universal education, from agricultural modernization to urban renewal, from care for the aged to protection of natural resources, from control of disease to the conquest of outer space.

Demands such as these were generalized and fortified not merely by distributive ideologies but also by the human quest for knowledge, spiritual enlightenment, and private material gain.

Economic development requires roads, ships, railroads, and ports, and governments have historically been deeply involved in the creation of these facilities. The management of industrial enterprise demands new skills, and governments have been called on to provide them through systems of mass education. The quest for knowledge, itself, becomes so complex that governments are inevitably drafted—as entrepreneurs or regulators—in the development of communications, science, and technology.

Thus, the demands for distribution require more than a better sharing of the economic pie. They require as well that government discover new and satisfying ways to meet the growing and varied appetites of those whom it serves.

The crisis of distribution, then, challenges political capacities along two important and related dimensions. The first of these is essentially ideological: it involves the question of how widely existing goods and services are to be shared within the nation. The second dimension is essentially technical; it asks the question, what is the ability of government to organize itself and society in such a way as to maximize the amount of goods and services available to the nation as a whole?

That these two dimensions are intimately interrelated is demonstrated both by the histories of all relatively modern countries and increasingly by the many newer nations that now seek to take the leap to modernity. A few examples will serve as illustrations.

Whether the economy is managed by private or public sectors, it is obvious that economic development requires savings: the accumulation of capital. Political leadership the world over, therefore, faces the dilemma of how much of what is available should be distributed as consumer goods and how much allocated to capital formation. The plight of the British worker in England's urban centers, described by Karl Marx in *Das Kapital*, was at least in part a requirement of industrialization. Similarly, the decades over which Soviet citizens were—and to a considerable extent still are—deprived of many of life's amenities have been justified by Soviet political leaders as the necessary cost of economic modernity. In many of the newer nations, the dilemma is much more desperate and poignant, because total resources are so limited and because gains tend to be obliterated by population increases.

A second illustration involves economic planning. Planned economic growth, whether publicly or privately managed, requires striking amounts of information, managerial skill, and complex human organization. If government is to be involved at all in this process, as it surely must be, it must play a part in such varied activities as improving educational facilities, building roads and power lines, organizing statistical gathering services, providing a stable financial and credit apparatus, and extending efficient public administrative organization from the capital to many far-flung local centers within the nation. In addition, the government must provide law and order, enforce contracts, protect workers, temper the disruption of village life, and generally co-ordinate the millions and millions of human actions that go into a successful economic plan. That such challenges to governments are not easily met is strikingly communicated by crises in places like India, Pakistan, Egypt, and China. But the immense complexities of the problem are also to be seen in failures of planning in countries like the Soviet Union and Great Britain, which have had more experience—and certainly have more human and physical resources—than most of the world's nations.

To summarize our illustrations, then: on the one hand, distributive demands tend to challenge prevailing ideologies about who in society should get what and how much. On the other hand, such demands gravely test the technical, organizational, administrative, and innovative capabilities of the government.

We should add one further dimension: namely, that a political system's increased capacity to meet distributive demands is closely related to how flexible and creative it is in the matter of anticipating them. If demands imply industrial capacity, and the latter requires skilled literate workers, universal public education (another distributive demand) must be advanced as quickly as possible. In this regard, Japan's experience—even that of the Philippines, on a more modest scale—is quite instructive. Similarly, if demands grow for better health, improved agricultural production, and greater output in technological products, then universities, either at home or abroad, must produce fewer lawyers and philologists and more doctors, agronomists, agricultural economists, scientists, and engineers. Such observations seem self-evident, but the great lack of such professional talent (even in so-called modern societies) is proof that the relationship is rarely plain enough to give rise to purposeful public policy. Without implying either the inevitability of progress or a single end state of development, we can certainly see why governmental capability to handle increased and changing distributive demands is circular. Only the satisfaction of certain and perhaps prior distributive demands makes possible government's and society's ability to handle others.

As we have noted, large-scale distributive demands occupied the older nation-states relatively late, or at least sometime after such nations had confronted earlier crises, such as legitimacy and integration. Consider the case of Great Britain, which, while not entirely typical, suggests the sequence of crises that rulers of European states experienced. Demands for greatly broadened political participation did not occur in Britain until the eighteenth and nineteenth centuries, long, long after there was any real question about national identity and integration and at least a century after the issue of legitimacy of monarchical institutions had been relatively well settled. Electoral reforms, spread over the nineteenth and twentieth centuries, eventually and inevitably generated strong distributive demands. We know that the political leadership of Britain proved sufficiently flexible ideologically and creative technically to respond to these demands without extraordinary upheaval. To be sure, the transition did not take place without some violence, coercion, and other forms of human suffering. The enclosure movement, antilabor legislation, general strikes—even rebellion—support the axiom that privilege does not readily yield to efforts to broaden its base. Yet, as we reflect on British political history, it is evident that what the British call "muddling through" is typically an Anglo-Saxon understatement. Few nations display similar capacity to adapt to radical changes in the socio-economic and political environments. Even the British capacity has its limitations, however, and they are suggested by lingering problems of distribution (for example, the debate on educational reform or the problem of British industrial obsolescence) that continue to plague British political leadership.

A somewhat similar story might be told for Scandinavia,

Canada, Australia, New Zealand, Switzerland, and the United States. On the European continent, however, the picture is not nearly so encouraging. In some places, such as Czarist Russia and eighteenth-century France, resistances to participation and distribution demands were blindly rigid and led to revolutionary violence. In Italy and France, great instabilities in government represent in large measure the failure of political and governmental leadership to respond to the insistent requirements of distributive ideologies, ranging from liberal democracy to orthodox Marxism. In countries such as these, we might say that apparent technical governmental capacity is not matched by ideological flexibility. The result is almost always political imbalance and frequently downright governmental paralysis. Advanced countries like Germany and Japan must also face this dilemma. There, it is not self-evident that the mere general increase in material well-being will obliterate the ideologically conditioned dimension of the distribution crisis. To put this somewhat unfairly, perhaps, it is far from certain that a commitment to the ideology of socialism will inevitably be buried under an avalanche of washing machines, automobiles, and transistor radios.

Nevertheless, by comparison with the developing nations, those farther along the path to modernity are enormously advantaged. The most striking thing about the developing nations is that those who govern them are confronted with simultaneous crises. Hundreds of millions of Asians, Africans, and Latin Americans want greater political participation and more goods and services, more equitably distributed. Where nation-states have existed for some decades, such "loads" on political leadership are quite serious. But they are somewhat less burdensome than the load of simultaneous crises that weighs on places in Africa and Asia, where the nation itself is of recent origin and the resolution of crises of identity and national integration is still problematical.

In such places of heavy crisis loads, the distribution crisis is greatly magnified. How, one might ask, can the Congo cope with such demands when the issue of national boundaries is still undecided? How will Nigeria, Ghana, and a host of other African political systems manage planned economic development when, on the one hand, the popular clamor for consumer goods is deafening and, on the other hand, such governments are faced with a frightening scarcity of economic, human, and organizational resources? How can Indian economic planners—immensely capable as they are professionally—respond effectively to demands for more and better schools, hospitals, food, housing, and industry when population growth rates more than cancel economic increments? How can they foment greater political development along distributive lines when the issue of a national language continues to threaten to break the nation apart at the seams? How can Bolivia or Peru, Egypt or Afghanistan, Indonesia or Tanzania, hope to respond to distributive demands when a lack of material resources is magnified geometrically by a scarcity of organizational and administrative talent? It is this gap between demand and governmental capability that tends to transform favorable expectations into disintegrative frustration. It is this gap, too, that leads many political leaders to elect repressive measures and other dictatorial governmental practices as a means of containing the unstable and centrifugal forces that grow out of unsatisfied popular demands.

As a temporary expedient, tight governmental control may well have its justification. In both human and technical terms, however, there are reasons to doubt that such patterns, if they persist over time, will facilitate political development, in the sense of responding to the impulses toward equality, differentiation, and capacity. Stringent controls, repressed demands, one-party systems, and other devices instituted in the name of achieving national integration have a way of becoming self-justifying. When this occurs, as it already has in a number of countries, rulers are not subjected to the important influence of policy criticism and constructive opposition. While they may for a time increase capacity through police or military methods, the use of this technique itself tends to inhibit the growth of administrative innovation and other creative governmental activities essential to the satisfaction of distributive demands.

The one-party systems provide a good illustration of this last point. Where they exist, their leaders claim that they are justified for reasons such as these: First, a new nation cannot permit party competition because demands will be excessive and opposition destructive to national integrity. There is considerable truth in

this, except that neither repressive measures nor bread and cir-
cuses will long contain opposition. For such regimes, the ability
both to maximize material development and, more important, to
provide for peaceful political succession remains doubtful. Second, one-party patterns are said to be the logical structure in
countries that are classless. Such a formulation assumes either that
the only basis for political party organization is social class (which
is empirically false) and/or that classes do not exist in one-party
countries (which is empirically questionable). Third, one-party
leaders often claim that the party can and does provide a context
for genuine policy debate and constructive opposition. Presumably, some variant of democratic centralism exists, wherein all
major points of view—or demands and proposed solutions—are
expressed and where, once a decision is reached, it is binding on
all participants. Mexico, under the Party of Revolutionary Institutions, is an often-cited example of such a system, as is India, although the latter country, despite dominance of the Congress
party, certainly does not have a one-party system. Others will
refer to the writings of Lenin and the operation of the Communist
Party of the Soviet Union, although it is particularly that country
(certainly under Stalin, but even since his death) that points to
the many irrationalities and instabilities inherent in single-party
arrangements. In any event, one can be skeptical about the ability
or willingness of single-party political leaders to allow for full and
open debate or about the courage of party and bureaucratic and
trade-union opponents to provide honest criticism of policy. And,
finally, one can doubt the validity or efficacy of the myth that
divisions in human society can be managed within a single overriding party organizational framework. Considerable evidence suggests that the price paid for such delayed modernity is enormous.

In short, there is very little reason to believe that one-party
leaders are somehow exempted from Lord Acton's surmise that
"power tends to corrupt and absolute power corrupts absolutely."
Without insisting on the precise meaning of corruption, we can
suggest that absolute power is not the most promising way to confront the problems of increased equality and governmental capacity that are implicit in the crisis of distribution.

I recognize, of course, that these comments create an enormous dilemma for developing nation-states. But the truth is that the problems of modernization usually involve genuine dilemmas. As such, they cannot be attacked through single, unchanging solutions. Were this the case, they would no longer be problems or dilemmas. Thus, while the experiences of the more developed countries may offer suggestions regarding what may work or what may prove disastrous, no one would urge—and surely no responsible leader of the younger nations would accept—a slavish aping of older-nation experiences. This is true whether the older nations be democratic systems such as Britain, where the management of crises of political development spans centuries, or less democratic systems, where the lack of democracy itself reveals previous incapacity of these nations to manage the crises of participation, and particularly of distribution.

What this means today is that all governments, regardless of where they may be placed on a scale of modernity, are under considerable pressure to meet the challenges of further political development. Pakistan's need to make a viable nation out of a West and East physically separated by over one thousand miles has its counterpart in American attempts to make the Negro a full-fledged member of the American community. Soviet efforts to create the kind of technical and bureaucratic capacity that can resolve the nagging problem of agriculture is mirrored in programs to develop southern Italy and in the many nations, old and new, striving for effective economic planning. Egypt's attempt to translate the revolution of the nineteen-fifties into more effective satisfaction of mass distributive demands can be multiplied many times, in countries like Cuba and Brazil, China and Vietnam, Israel and Iraq.

In all these and other places, the demand for distribution is omnipresent, stridently articulated by political parties, trade-unions, communal groups, and the like, or rumbling just below the deceptively calm surface of one-party systems.

Exactly what role the government will, should, or must play in this process remains only in part an open question; most persons agree that it must be prominent, on a scale not experienced by most of the more developed nations.

If this is the case, I would urge that the following observations are worth considerable attention. First, it is vital that we learn to make important distinctions between public administration that is of the "law-and-order" variety and "development administration." Many of the ex-colonial countries, such as Malaya, India, Pakistan, Nigeria, and Ghana, to name but a few, are either adequately or superbly served by administrators deeply influenced by colonial structures and practices. Where such administrative elites are strong, they are certainly able to provide the stable legal and political framework that is a prerequisite of economic modernization. Their central role in meeting the crisis of distribution would be in part that of extending existing bureaucratic mechanisms to encompass the legal, commercial, financial, and budgetary needs of an economically developing society. Additionally, such bureaucratic elites—if they are expert generalists with a strong identification with the nation and a genuine sense of the broad problems of development—can serve vitally important co-ordinating roles.

However, the developmental tasks to which a nation commits itself will often require new kinds of administrators and administrative organization, some of which will be alien to and unwanted by traditional bureaucrats. Such newer administrative organizations have appeared in both some developed Western and less-developed non-Western societies. It is vital that greater information be secured regarding how well or badly such agencies have functioned in meeting the crisis of distribution and why. It is also essential to draw from such experiences whatever lessons are to be learned about the viability of the public sector as a means of producing the kinds of administrators that development requires. To put this sharply, how well suited are such new administrative structures as public corporations or ministries of community development to the tasks of economic innovation and management and social transformation that such organizations are created to handle?

Second, I would suggest that meeting the crisis of distribution implies for most countries forms and degrees of public participation in decisions and their implementation that are not easily encouraged when the public sector strives toward a monopoly of control. Not many public bureaucracies, no matter how flexible or competent, can manage the crisis of distribution acting alone. They desperately need the help of their own people, not in the mass sense, but rather in a context of purposeful organization that includes trade-unions, co-operatives, professional associations, youth groups, student organizations, and the like. The critical test of development administration therefore extends beyond internal bureaucratic considerations; it points to the skill with which a political system can organize and co-ordinate all those segments of society without whose co-operation the desire for greater and more equitable distribution of goods, services, and welfare values will never be transformed into reality.

IV

THE
MODERNIZATION
OF THE
ECONOMY

Chapter 17

The Modernization
of Technology

Stanislaw H. Wellisz

The economic well-being of a country hinges on its ability to transform resources into goods that satisfy human wants. The natural resources a country possesses are a factor in development: it is easier to develop a country that has plentiful and fertile land, economically useful minerals, and abundant sources of power than a resource-poor area. There are many richly endowed countries, however, with low living standards, while Switzerland, Holland, and Denmark rank among the world's wealthiest nations despite the poverty of their natural resources.

The amount of man-produced capital and the rate of capital formation play a more important role in development than the primary resources. A worker with adequate tools can produce more goods than one who is ill equipped. Yet, technology imposes limits on the usefulness of capital. Before the great Industrial Revolution, which started in western Europe in the eighteenth century, the entire world was poor and stagnant as measured by the standards of the mid-twentieth century; it was not so much the shortage of capital as the lack of investment opportunities that put a brake on economic growth.

If we look at the economic development that took place in the United States between the eighteen-seventies and the nineteen-sixties, we observe not only a great increase in capital and a more modest one in the supply of labor, but also—indeed, primarily—immense technological progress. Most of the products of everyday use were not available eighty or ninety years ago, and even those that existed at the earlier time are now produced by vastly different methods. In fact, more than two-thirds of the increase in national income that occurred in the United States over the last ninety years is attributed to technological change and only one-third to the increase in capital and in labor.

With the help of new technology, a resource-poor country can overcome its natural handicaps. On the other hand, a country that relies on the richness of its own resources may fall victim to progress in other parts of the world. Exporters of natural rubber, natural fertilizers, or natural fibers have already been deeply hurt through the invention of synthetics that permit the resource-poor countries to do without costly imports. Even the supremacy of petroleum—the "liquid gold"—might be threatened in the not-too-distant future by nuclear energy.

Technological progress is the prime mover of economic development, but, unfortunately, it is not a miracle drug. To develop, the economically backward countries must modernize, but a simple injection of modernization does not cure poverty.

It is clear, first of all, that modernization is not a substitute for investment. Obsolete equipment must be replaced, new factories built, and new machines installed to embody the new techniques.

Investment in human beings is also needed if a country is to modernize. Artisans who work superbly well with primitive tools may not be able to become efficient operators of modern machinery. It is not that modern machines require more skills than old methods; they require different skills. An artisan must understand the uses to which his product will be put. He must have a good knowledge of materials and much manual dexterity. In many branches of production, an artisan must also be endowed with an aesthetic feeling. Most of the knowledge of the artisan is not required of an operator of a modern machine. The operator must work with regularity, which is not required of an artisan, and he must be able to follow with precision both written and verbal instructions. He must be something of a technician and a mechanic, but not an artist. The artisan often becomes a victim of technological progress, for the demand for his skills is likely to decline. To take up his place and to provide for lower-cost goods destined for the large masses of people, rather than just for the chosen few, it is necessary to invest in training and education in order to produce the necessary skills.

Modernization of management must keep pace with modernization of production techniques. With mass production, there arises a need for quality control, which is almost nonexistent in a small enterprise. If each piece is produced separately, the production method can take into account variations in raw materials, and each unit that is produced can be tested. The high quality of a product can be maintained in spite of, or rather because of, variability of the product. When large quantities of materials are fed into mass-production machines, there must be absolute uniformity in the input, lest the product be defective. Likewise, the product must be subject to testing if it, in turn, is to be used on a mass scale. The lack of adequate quality control is one of the main reasons why many of the newly developing nations, known for the excellence of their traditional wares, find it difficult to sell their mass-produced goods on world markets.

With mass production, it is also essential to formalize methods of supervision and accounting. The head of a small establishment can make all the major decisions, supervise his workers, and keep all the figures in his head. A large-scale factory requires a complex division of decision making, supervision, financial control, and accounting. Just as a skilled artisan cannot be turned overnight into a skilled operator of modern machinery, so a manager of a traditional enterprise may be incapable of managing a large-scale modern firm.

The modern mass-production firm must maintain extensive and formalized relations with other parts of the economy. It cannot rely on personal contacts of the manager to locate raw-material sources or to find the customers. Unlike a small business, it must have a purchasing and selling network and engage in market research to be sure that its product satisfies the changing needs of the customers. The high salaries commanded by marketing personnel in the major industrial countries show that the marketing functions are no less important and no easier than the functions of a technician or a manager.

As factories and farms are modernized, changes are required in the service sector. A transport system adequate to serve the needs of small-scale manufacturing may become overtaxed by the demands of modern industry. Need may arise for new types of facility, such as refrigerated transport and cold storage. Even the retail network may not be adequate. For example, in many countries the distribution, and not the production, of artificial fertilizers is the most serious bottleneck in farm modernization.

Let us sum up these preliminary remarks. Technological modernization requires the introduction of new machines and new production methods. To operate the new machines, new skills must be taught, and, what is even more difficult, new managerial methods must be adopted. The modernization of the production processes must be accompanied by the modernization of transport, storage, wholesaling, and retailing. This is a long series of requirements, and the question is how to meet them most efficiently.

There are two basically different approaches to the technical modernization of a country. One is to utilize the newest available techniques, and the other to modernize gradually. Both approaches have their weaknesses and their strengths. Let us consider them in turn before attempting to arrive at a synthesis.

The use of the newest available techniques has a strong emotional appeal as well as real merit. In applying the latest methods, one bridges the gap between the primitive economies and the most advanced economies of the world. The new methods now used in the advanced countries have proved their viability. Other methods have been shown by experience to be less advantageous or have become obsolete. It makes little sense to fail to take advantage of developments in the field of traction by building steam locomotives where diesel will provide more service for the same amount of investment.

With the application of the newest technology, an underdeveloped country may find an opportunity of forging ahead of the more advanced nations, instead of trailing behind them. Once the new technique is well mastered, the next step, that of developing even newer techniques and products, is not so difficult.

Last, but not least, the introduction of the newest and the best has a profound psychological effect. It is a symbol of a new order, of victory over agelong economic inferiority which all too often was accompanied by political subjugation.

Experience with the introduction of the most advanced techniques shows, however, that the strategy has serious drawbacks. The most immediate and obvious of these is that investment in the latest methods usually produces very small increases in employment. Most of the economically backward nations face the problem of creating jobs for rapidly rising populations. If the bulk of new investment is embodied in the newest capital-intensive processes, the task of providing jobs falls on the traditional, nonmodernizing sectors of the economy. The new techniques deepen the gulf between the industrial sector employing the chosen few and the ever-growing masses of people who are forced into the already overcrowded agriculture and petty trade.

Modern techniques involve production on a vast scale. It is impossible to build a small-scale petro-chemical complex or a small-scale iron and steel complex incorporating the newest techniques. The construction of a major modern plant may strain technical and financial resources of a country and delay the modernization of other sectors.

Finally, highly capital-intensive modern techniques provide training for a small number of skilled workers and have little effect on the traditional ways of the masses of people. Where the modernization of the attitudes toward work is at stake, the most modern techniques are not a good general training ground.

Let us look at the root of the difficulties. The latest techniques come from western Europe and the United States, that is, from regions where machines are cheap and finance is readily available. Labor, by contrast, is very expensive compared with the less-developed countries, but the high cost of labor is compensated, to some extent, by high skills. Indeed, with the general rise in educational standards, there has been a steady narrowing of the gap between skilled and unskilled labor. In Holland, for instance, skilled workers earn only 20 per cent more than the unskilled workers, whereas in the less-developed areas, skilled workers command wages two or three times as high as unskilled manual labor.

Confronted with high and rising wages, the European or American businessman attempts to cut costs by replacing manual work with machines. The problem of finding skilled operatives for complex machines does not stem the process because of the vast pool of skills.

The technique chosen by the Western businessman is clearly inappropriate for an underdeveloped country where the cost structure is vastly different. It would stand to reason, therefore, that in setting up a plant in such a country, it would be preferable not to push mechanization as far as in the West and to use less capital and more workers. Unfortunately, in the strategy that calls for the use of the latest available methods, the substitution of labor for capital is rarely possible. Technical progress responds to needs. In countries where there is urgent need to cut down on labor costs, the newest techniques are also likely to be the least labor-using ones. Labor-intensive techniques in western Europe and the United States are obsolete techniques.

Modern techniques require the use of "factor proportions" that are inappropriate for the newly developing countries, and they also require managerial skills of a type that is very scarce outside the most-developed lands. What is needed is a mixture of daring and innovation with the ability to run a vast bureaucracy. Few businessmen in the less-developed nations have the ability or knowledge to lead vast administrative teams, and the tendency is, therefore, to use government administration as a blueprint for the organization of large business and to staff such enterprises with civil servants or former government officials.

Despite the similarities between the formal organization of a state bureaucracy and a modern corporation, the civil service is a very inadequate tool for business administration. The essence of civil administration lies in the enforcement of rules and regulations and in the routinism of procedures. The essence of adminis-tration of an enterprise lies in the ability to take advantage of unforeseen opportunities and to avoid unforeseen dangers, in the ability to take risks, and in the ability to innovate. To maintain economic efficiency, the advanced mixed-enterprise countries such as France put great emphasis on the separation of the state administrative functions from those of the publicly owned enterprise. Even the eastern European nations are making prodigious efforts to imbue economic activities with a spirit of independence and flexibility foreign to state administrative behavior.

The use of the latest technique does not guarantee, therefore, the fastest economic progress. What is most appropriate for France, Holland, or the United States may prove to be worse than the old, traditional ways in India or Nigeria. The use of the latest technique, without regard to the background in which it was developed and the conditions of the country that uses it, is transplantation, not modernization; and transplantation usually fails.

The second approach consists of retracing, at an accelerated pace, the path toward industrialization pursued in an earlier period by the countries that are now economically advanced.

At the start of industrialization, the conditions in western Europe resembled in many ways the current conditions of the less-developed nations. Unskilled labor was cheap and plentiful. The few skilled workers commanded high wages, and machinery was expensive. The markets were limited in size. Compared with the newest methods, the earlier industrial techniques are more intensive, rely less on labor skills, and can be operated efficiently on a smaller scale. Typically, the older techniques generate much more employment per unit investment than the newest ones, and they require much less efficiency on the part of the co-operating sectors, such as transport.

The advocates of gradual modernization claim that, by developing industries that grew in western Europe at an early stage and by relying on the older techniques, the less-developed nations will be able to modernize and industrialize with greater efficiency. They will be able to build on what is already available, instead of scrapping old equipment and discarding old skills. Moreover, the tempo of modernization can be quite fast because it will not be necessary to remake technical discoveries. The techniques are all there, to be adapted at the right time.

The weaknesses of the gradual modernization approach are so obvious that it is all too easy to reject the entire line of reasoning, including the valid and valuable points.

It is clear that there are industries that were once of great importance, but are now receding. Coal mining is an obvious case in point. Though coal still has many important uses, it is being displaced by other fuels, and it is by no means clear that the development of coal mines (which is, by the way, a rather capital-intensive operation) should receive a high priority. Secondly, though the older techniques almost invariably employ less capital per worker than the newer ones, very often they require more capital per unit output. To use an extreme example, bullock carts are a very capital-intensive mode of transport, if one considers the amount of investment per ton-mile of goods carried. The statement that the older techniques are simpler than the newer ones is also incorrect, for technological research often leads to the discovery of simpler methods of doing things. As a training ground for labor, the older techniques also leave much to be desired, for it is difficult to see the rationale of imparting obsolete technological knowledge which will soon have to be replaced by newer knowledge.

The gradual modernization approach must also face a number of serious practical obstacles. Much of the capital equipment required for modernization must be imported from the highly developed countries, which no longer manufacture old types of machinery. Western European and American experts who provide the technical aid are not familiar with older production methods. The old equipment was meant to manufacture products that are obsolete by today's standards. The products might still be satisfactory for internal use, but they would not be likely to find favor on the international markets. Thus, the gradualist approach would force the underdeveloped countries to forgo the advantages of international technical co-operation and international division of labor.

Now for the residual elements of truth in the argument for gradual modernization. The argument correctly states that the techniques that are introduced should utilize existing skills and take into account current scarcity relations. Clearly, it makes little sense to disregard the large pools of available unskilled labor and introduce methods that require a small number of highly skilled workers. Likewise, it makes little sense to try to muster extremely intricate tasks before learning simple ones, for the greater the step, the larger the chances of failure. The possibility that an underdeveloped country will turn overnight into a leader in technology in competition with the advanced countries is remote, for the latter have immense technical and financial resources. Leadership brings high rewards, but it also has high costs. If the leader takes the right move, he will soon be imitated by other countries; and if the rivals are ecomically stronger, most of the rewards may go to them.

Thus, both of the extreme strategies of modernization can be seen to be unsatisfactory, for neither really comes to grips with the essence of modernization. One approach advocates the transplantation of ready-made techniques and neglects the local conditions. The other recommends the transplantation of a path to progress and fails to consider the changes that have taken place in the world since the start of industrialization.

To modernize means to find ways of making better use of the resources at hand. It means the application of the latest knowledge to the problem, and it also means the solution of the problem at hand and not of the problem of another country or another era. To use old methods is to abdicate the use of new knowledge. To transplant latest techniques is to solve problems that often have no relation to the problems at hand.

The first step toward modernization ought to consist of the removal of barriers that impede the search for new solutions and the use of new techniques. Many underdeveloped countries have an institutional framework that is a mixture of laws passed in the preindustrial period and of regulations copied from advanced industrial nations. The premature introduction of the latter are as much of an impediment to technical change as the excessively long retention of the former. A few examples will illustrate this point.

The collection of octroi taxes—that is, of taxes on the transhipment of goods—discourages efficient concentration of manufacturing and the adoption of mass-production methods and induces small-scale local production that avoids the tax. Octroi taxes have been discarded by the industrial nations, but they are still collected in some of the less-developed lands. While retaining harmful and obsolete taxes, these countries emulate the West in the use of corporate profit taxes and stiffly progressive income taxes. The purpose of these taxes is income equalization, which is a laudable social goal. However, such taxes discourage investment in readily identifiable projects, such as new equipment and machinery, and direct it into more easily concealed areas, such as trade. Usury laws are another legacy of the past. Their purpose was to protect the debtor from exploitation by the moneylenders. Yet, if usury laws are enforced, the potential borrowers, some of whom need money to modernize their enterprises, are cut off from sources of finance. The establishment of official investment banking institutions is no substitute for the moneylender. The banks (which, in imitation of conditions in advanced industrial countries, lend at very low interest) cannot grant credit to risky, innovating small enterprises, but largely confine themselves to safe loans, from fear of turning into charity-dispensing institutions. Or take factory legislation. The laws protect factory workers, fix minimum wages, add social security payments to the cost of labor, limit the enterprise's ability to hire and dismiss workers. The objectives are again admirable, but the effect is to reduce the profitability of modern enterprise and to encourage the persistence of small, antiquated shops that are exempt from the legislation. Many of the social laws have important objectives that cannot be neglected, but these objectives must be pursued by means that are not inimical to technological and economic progress, lest they be self-defeating.

The removal of barriers to innovation and to development releases local forces of entrepreneurship and progress. All too often we blame the indolence and ignorance of the inhabitants of a region for its stagnation. It is only by looking at the careers of the migrants from the stagnating region that we realize there was a great potential for progress and development which was frustrated by the institutional framework.

The removal of institutional barriers leads to better use of local knowledge for purposes of local enterprise. Local opportunities tend to be neglected by high-level officials and by high-level advisers who, naturally enough, concentrate on large-scale projects. Yet local projects, humble as they may look compared with mass-production facilities, may make great contributions toward the modernization of an economy. Even in fields where there are economies of scale, it may pay to start with small units. What is lost in purely technical efficiency may be gained in flexibility, ready access to the market, and ease of management. The small, scattered units provide, moreover, a laboratory that no large enterprise can reproduce. Failure of a small unit is not a great loss, while success leads to expansion and to imitation. An experiment on a small scale, if successful, can be reproduced in a more ambitious form. On the other hand, an initial experiment on a gigantic scale is too dangerous to be undertaken. Thus, innovation is much more likely to come from below than from above, and encouragement given to "grass root" development is one of the surest ways of promoting modernization.

There is no need, of course, to confine policy action to removal of barriers to progress. There is room, first of all, for the dissemination of knowledge. Information and advice on industrial sites, materials, and techniques is bound to speed up development. It may be appropriate to engage in pilot planning, in order to show what changes are likely to occur in the future, and to permit the evolution of better enterprise plans.

There is also room for large-scale enterprise in selected branches of industry. Even here, however, care should be taken to adapt rather than to copy. It may be possible, for instance, to combine automated fabricating operations with hand transport, instead of using conveyors as would be done in the West. Possibly not all the fabricating operations need be fully automated. For instance, transistors can be made by machine or largely by hand methods. The problem of the appropriate techniques must be rethought and reanalyzed in each case. This means that the local technician or engineer must learn the new Western methods. It also means that the Western technician and engineer who works in the less-developed country must get rid of the all-pervasive idea that the way things are done back home is the best way. Instead, he must rethink the problem in terms of local conditions.

He should not copy what he has learned and done in his home country, but he must become an innovator.

The application of new knowledge to the solution of problems of underdeveloped countries is the most effective means of overcoming economic backwardness. Instead of competing on unequal terms with advanced countries, the newly developing countries should build on the areas of their own strength. New ways must be discovered to utilize the materials that are not available in the West and to take advantage of the vast labor resources. Some progress is already being made in these fields, as, for instance, in the new uses now being found for coir and jute; but much remains to be done.

The general strategy of modernization helps solve the vexing problem of striking a balance between the satisfaction of existing needs and provision for the future. In broadest terms, the question is whether to modernize the consumer goods sector and increase immediate consumption or to modernize the producer goods sector and invest so as to produce more consumer goods in the future.

Many of the newly developing nations have a policy of building the economy from the base up, where "the base" means the heavy industry sector. Technical knowledge and investment go into the base, while consumer goods sectors and services remain relatively backward, with the idea that their turn will come, once the base is built.

The strategy of building from the base up results, more often than not, in serious economic losses, for most of the less-developed countries have neither the co-operating industries nor the demand necessary to maintain heavy industries at an efficient level. The advocates of heavy industrialization justify the sacrifices in terms of the benefits that will come in the future.

While the sacrifices made to modernize the heavy industrial sector are all too evident, it is by no means so clear that the future benefits are equally great. Heavy industry of the type prevailing in the United States or western Europe serves today's needs, but no one knows whether the needs will be the same twenty years from now. For instance, though steel is still the backbone of modern industry, nonferrous metals and plastics are moving to the fore. Sacrifices made today to build a steel industry might, therefore, be much greater than needed to provide the future steel requirements.

The entire concept of "basic industry" rests, moreover, on a misunderstanding of the changes that have occurred in the world economy since the eighteenth century. Eighteenth-century England had to start by developing coal mines and an iron industry because it could not purchase coal or iron from abroad, just as it had to develop its own technology because it could not import technical knowledge from abroad. Today, primary steel and other products of heavy industry are very easy to obtain from abroad. Highly industrialized countries such as Japan can prosper while relying on primary imports, and there is no reason why the industrialization process should start from the so-called base.

The real base of economic progress is neither the steel industry nor the automobile industry, for steel and automobiles, like technical knowledge, can be imported. One thing cannot be imported, and that is the institutional framework that is conducive to technical progress. The institutional framework yields immediate results, for it improves the use of the resources at hand, and it also lays the foundations of future growth.

Once the foundations of progress are laid, it is best to invest in new techniques where they are likely to yield the greatest returns. In one country this may mean roads, in another steel, in yet another light consumer durables, textiles, or food products. One must, of course, avoid bottlenecks; but the bottlenecks show us urgently felt needs. An economy that encourages and rewards the use of knowledge at all levels—from the humble local entrepreneur to the high-level planner of national transportation networks—can dispense with a rigid blueprint and a rigid prescription for technological progress. For progress, in the last analysis, consists of the discovery of new, betters ways of combining the elements at hand, and discovery is something that can be encouraged and nurtured, but cannot be prescribed for.

Chapter 18

The Modernization
of Entrepreneurship

Alexander Gerschenkron

Most people will agree that the emergence of modern entrepreneurs has been an integral part of the great economic transformation known as the historical process of industrialization. The
question I wish to consider is twofold: (1) What were some of the
distinguishing "modern" features of industrial entrepreneurs, particularly in the early stages of that transformation? (2) How did
those characteristics come about? In dealing with these questions,
I shall be thinking mostly of the area of European industrializations, which should give us sufficient scope both for generalization
and differentiation.

There are many ways to define an entrepreneur, and scholars
have been arguing for a long time, often heatedly and confus-
ingly, about the relative merits of this or that definition. For our
purposes, it is sufficient to say that (entrepreneurs are people
whose task it is to make economic decisions) Naturally, there is
hardly any economic activity that does not involve decisions. The
man who spends his working day sorting out big and small or-
anges is involved in a continual process of decision making. But
there are big and small decisions. The big decisions refer, for in-

stance, to what shall be produced and how it shall be produced; what goods should be bought and sold, where and when, and at what price; whether output shall be kept constant, or whether it should be increased or reduced; and so on. All such decisions are entrepreneurial decisions.

There have been entrepreneurs in this sense at all levels in all periods of economic history. A peasant in a backward agrarian country who decides when to start plowing, what to sow, and when to reap makes entrepreneurial decisions. So did a Venetian merchant in the sixteenth century who decided what kinds of spice he should buy in the East and then carry across the Alps and whether Augsburg in Germany or Lyons in France was the most promising market for his wares. Very broadly speaking, such decisions are not different from those of an executive or group of executives in a modern American plant—say, in Wilmington, Delaware—who has decided to concentrate on the production of a new vibration-absorbing material or from those of an automobile factory in Detroit that has decided to add a small car to its list for the next fall.

But, despite a certain similarity of all entrepreneurial decisions performed in all times and climes, we all know intuitively that the differences among the cases just mentioned are enormous. Entrepreneurship on a medieval farm or in a craft-guild dominated artisan shop in Perth or Strassburg of the fifteenth century, or even in a large wool-processing mill in Flanders of the same period, was, in many important respects, not comparable to the entrepreneurial activities in the modern age, from the eighteenth century onward, when rapid industrial progress, spreading from one country to another, became the characteristic feature of economic life, primarily in Europe and North America. Let us try to make some of those differences explicit.

For one, modern industry requires large amounts of fixed capital. In other words, it demands construction of buildings and acquisition of machinery whose contribution to output must be utilized over a considerable period of time. This means that an industrial entrepreneur must look far ahead into the future. His time horizon must be high. To be sure, even in preindustrial times, there were merchants who loaded and dispatched ships on

long sea voyages, waiting for many months, perhaps a year, for
the reappearance of the vessel and the sale of the return cargo.
But neither was even such a relatively long stretch of time, during
which the merchant's capital was tied up in his risky venture,
comparable with the average life span of modern machinery nor
did transactions of this sort ever begin to assume, within the total
volume of goods and services produced, a significance even re-
motely comparable to the share of industrial output in the national income of a modern industrial country.

With the heightening of the time horizon, also, something
else happened that was at least indirectly related to it. Industrial
entrepreneurship became a lifetime occupation. A merchant in
preindustrial days who had accumulated a sizable fortune would
be strongly tempted to say farewell to his mercantile pursuits, acquire a landed estate, and attempt to elevate himself into the
ranks of the gentry. A modern industrial entrepreneur in Germany or England often liked to see his children marry into
a noble family; he was sensitive to the social prestige and the
amenities of a country house, but in valuing those things he did
not cease to be what he was, that is to say, a modern industrialist.

Connected with what has been just said and partly following
from it, there were other differences. The connections between a
merchant and his customers were often fleeting affairs, once-over
transactions. Hence the urge was strong, indeed, to deceive the
buyer as to the quantity and quality of what he purchased. *Caveat
emptor*—it is the buyer's lookout—warned the Roman law, and
the idea of dishonesty became fully associated in the popular
mind with trade and traders. Various etymologies reflect the connection. In German, for instance, the verb for exchange is "tau-
schen," but if two little dots are put over the "a," the word becomes "täuschen" and means to deceive. In French, the similarity
between "truc" and "troque"—trick and barter—reflects the same
connection; and the etymological origins of the very term "barter"
in English, as in several Romance languages (whence the word
came), point to cheating and deception. In Russian, an often
quoted popular proverb used to advise: "If you do not cheat, you
will not sell," which only repeated in a pithy form something that
had been said time and again since the days of Ecclesiasticus.

It is not claimed, of course, that the modern industrial entrepreneur was at all times a paragon of impeccable probity. He was not. But it is fair to say that the permanence of his activities, the closeness of relations with the customer established by installation of equipment and delivery of spare parts, the very fact that so much of modern industrial output was sold, not to an amorphous mass of anonymous buyers, but to other industrial entrepreneurs —all these factors necessitated a much more scrupulous attitude toward the buyer. Furthermore, and no less importantly, modern industry was largely based on a well-developed credit system. The price at which a modern entrepreneur got his capital disposition— that is, the interest rate—had to be relatively low, which it could not be if the service of the debt included high risk premiums. If there was to be an industrial entrepreneurship, its standards of commercial honesty perforce had to be high.

And, finally, modern industry was inseparable from technological and organizational progress. New ways of doing things were continually emerging. Very few modern industrial entrepreneurs were truly great innovators, in the sense of being the first to apply a revolutionary, unprecedented technique. Most of them were imitators, a part of what Professor Schumpeter called the "secondary wave," which spread a new signal innovation over broad segments of the industrial economy. But, as everyone who ever worked inside a modern enterprise knows, the distinction between the innovator and the imitator is a very uncertain one. Every imitation requires a great deal of energy to overcome the inertia, to abandon the accustomed way of doing things. It raises a million technical and economic problems that must be solved. And they will not be solved unless there are alert minds to welcome the new and to see the solutions and strong wills to carry the tasks to successful termination. No comparable problems, no comparable pressures to tackle them had existed before the advent of modern industry.

Thus, modern industrial entrepreneurship has specific features that could not have been easily discovered to any similar extent and in any similar intensity in the preindustrial periods. We can now turn to an attempt to deal with the second question we asked earlier. How did these features come about? What is the historical process in the course of which entrepreneurship became modernized so that the proper functioning of modern industrial enterprises could be assured? This is a question that used to exercise—and still does exercise—very many scholars, and a considerable literature of the subject has been created. As I see it, the most interesting problem in this discussion is related to the broader problem of prerequisites of modern industrialization. This calls for a brief digression.

According to a widespread view, which has been particularly popularized and dramatized by Professor Rostow, the times of rapid industrial progress—the great spurts of industrialization— were preceded, country by country, by a more or less protracted period during which the "preconditions" of modern industrialization were created. Such "preconditions" or "prerequisites" are taken then so seriously that some scholars are willing to speak of "necessary and sufficient" preconditions, just as in a logical definition one speaks of conditions that are necessary and sufficient in order to define a given object. Thus, it would be argued, certain agrarian reforms involving a change in the system of land tenure, abolition of restrictions on the personal freedom of the peasantry, and increase in the productivity of agriculture were a necessary prerequisite for the subsequent industrialization.

Or, it would be asserted, particularly by Marxian writers, that a previous accumulation of wealth over considerable historical periods was a necessary precondition for financing the capital investment of entrepreneurs during great industrial spurts. In either case, the inference is that where such preconditions were not established, no industrialization could take place. But such arguments and assertions, presented as propositions of ubiquitous validity, do not stand up under the test of confrontation with the empirical material, even within the relatively restricted area of Europe of the nineteenth century. In important cases, considerable industrial development took place despite the absence of the allegedly necessary prerequisites, however logical the sequence of events scheduled in an abstract scheme may appear to the ear of an uncritical listener. For, analytically speaking, the attempt to convert logical conditions into historical preconditions is hardly more than a sleight of hand, a coarse analogy that insinuates into the argument the concept of historical necessity, which is something that lies on the other side of the line separating scientific pursuits from metaphysical speculation and political propaganda. And, historically speaking, the concept of necessary prerequisites fails because economic life is pregnant with many alternative solutions, so that in countries where the so-called necessary prerequisites were not present, various substitutions for them have been developed in the very course of industrial development. This was true of the lack of proper agrarian reforms, as it was true of the lack of preindustrial accumulations of wealth, even though Soviet scholars are still busy trying to find the "original accumulation of capital" in every country that ever went through the process of industrialization.

This brief discussion of prerequisites of modern industrialization has a direct bearing on the problem of creation of modern entrepreneurship with which we are concerned. Is creation of modern entrepreneurship a prerequisite of modern industrial development? And is this creation itself a protracted historical process, in the course of which the prerequisites for modern entrepreneurship are created? The first of these questions is very often based on a misunderstanding. When people say, "Of course entrepreneurs are a prerequisite of industrialization. How else could you industrialize without them?" they are again confusing preconditions with conditions. Entrepreneurs use capital and hire labor in order to produce industrial goods, but this is the very stuff industrialization is made of; these are the very conditions of any reasonable definition of industrialization. But what we are talking about is not a definition or a description of industrialization, but a historical process, more or less lengthy, in the course of which the prerequisites of modern entrepreneurship are created. And this, indeed, is a real problem that calls for some more extended discussion.

It is not difficult to argue that in *some* countries, things may be discovered that make us think that certain features of modern entrepreneurship have roots in a fairly remote historical past of those countries. Take, for instance, the experience of master artisans in towns dominated by the craft guilds in the late Middle Ages. There is no doubt that in many cases the institutional framework of the craft guilds—their rules and regulations and their ideology—served to inform the guilds' membership with the instinct of workmanship, with the pride of the quality of their work, and, by the same token, with the idea of honesty in dealing with their customers; that is to say, with a characteristic that we found before to be very germane to modern industrial entrepreneurship. All this began centuries before the year 1517, in which Martin Luther started the Reformation by nailing his theses on the door of a church at Wittenberg.

But there is no reason for us to deny that Protestantism, particularly in its Calvinist branch, tended to promote the attitudes of honesty and thrift, lifetime dedication to one's work, and interest in innovation, even though it remains entirely a moot question to what extent it was the doctrines of Protestant churches rather than the adherence to a penalized minority, be it the Huguenots in France or the Nonconformists in England, that determined the attitudes. Nor is it clear that people did not tend to espouse Protestant persuasions *because* they had certain attitudes. Still, it is quite reasonable to say that in *some* countries, in the course of their preindustrial history, certain habits of thinking originated from several sources that provided a propitious climate for the exercise of modern entrepreneurial attitudes. There is nothing wrong in considering, therefore, those habits of thinking *where they actually occurred* as prerequisites for the emergence of modern entrepreneurship in the countries concerned. Yet we must be very wary of generalizing such findings and regarding them in any way as *necessary* prerequisites.

It is precisely this, however, that is done by several sociologists and psychologists who are trying to develop general theories of modern industrialization with particular stress on the entrepreneurial element therein. One body of such theories tends to emphasize the dominant value system of the society within which modern industrial development takes place. It is argued that unless the social value system that prevails is such as to bestow social approval upon the role played by the entrepreneurs, they cannot succeed, and a modern industrial development will not occur or at the very best will be hopelessly retarded. Thus, a change in the values of the society as a whole is regarded as a necessary prerequisite for the deployment of modern entrepreneurial activities and, by the same token, for industrialization. Generalizations of this sort are in obvious conflict with the facts.

Economic history, within the European framework, provides sufficient cases where magnificent entrepreneurial activities were conducted in the face of a dominant value system that was violently opposed to such activities and continued regarding the working of the land that brought forth the blessing of its fruit as the only economic activity that was pleasing in the eyes of the Lord. Theories of this sort are wrong, but they are not entirely useless because they do help to raise the interesting question of how the lack of social approval was overcome or, to put it differently, what substitutions, if any, were found for the absence of social approval as a prerequisite of modern entrepreneurship.

There is an even more comprehensive theory for the emergence of modern entrepreneurship, which combines social and psychological factors and tries to establish the necessary prerequisites in a grandiose historical scheme comprising many centuries. It is argued that modern entrepreneurship requires replacement of the "authoritarian personality" of the "traditional society" by the "innovational personality" of the modern society. In either case, the personality is said to be the product of the methods of child raising in the four or five years after birth. It is further claimed that the change is brought about by the withdrawal at some point of status respect from the "common folk" by an upper group. Thereby the traditional society is disrupted, and the common folk spend many hundreds of years in a state of "retreatism." During that period, the parent-child relationship experiences profound changes and the methods of child rearing are fundamentally altered so that in the end—in the very long end—the innovational entrepreneurial personalities emerge from the lap of the society, and modern economic growth can begin.

It is easy to see the difference between the two theories just sketched. While the former considers that what the enterpreneurs need is just approval of their activities by the dominant value system of the society, the latter envisages a thoroughgoing transformation of personality formation in the society at large as a prerequisite for the emergence of entrepreneurs. But this is not the only difference. Theories that center on "social approval" can be criticized, because, in many societies, stratified and complex as they are, approval by some groups is paralleled by disapproval by others; and a single system of dominant social values is hardly more than a fiction. Still, the historical record shows societies where the traditional agrarian beliefs have survived fairly unchanged into the modern period and are accepted, at least superficially, by groups that are rather far removed from the tillage of the land. Russia in the late nineteenth century may serve as an important example of such a society.

But the point is that with respect to this theory, it is still possible to get some empirical data in order to see how well or how badly it squares with the facts. On the other hand, the theory claiming basic changes in the methods of infant rearing and in parent-child relations over long centuries defies any empirical testing, which would require, within the meaning of the theory, psychoanalyzing huge samples of dead men who are unable to tell their tales on an analyst's couch. All we can say is that by looking at the treatment of infants and very young children in a number of countries that had gone through very successful periods of industrialization and have produced considerable entrepreneurial figures (such as Germany or Sweden before World War I), it is very difficult to discover any striking progress in this respect. Thus, the theory is little more than a figment of speculative imagination, and this particular attempt to view the emergence of modern entrepreneurship as a very prolonged process requiring creation of certain definite necessary prerequisites may be shelved as altogether unconvincing.

When general theories fail us, we must return to a more modest, but also more effective and more enlightening way of looking at the creation of modern entrepreneurship. What has been said before about substitutions in other areas of industrial development for missing prerequisites should give us some guidance also with respect to the problem of entrepreneurship. As we take a closer look at those substitutions, we are able to say that the need for them and also their complexity were not randomly distributed about the map of nineteenth-century Europe. On the contrary, there was a rather clear relationship: The more backward a country was on the eve of its big industrial spurt, the fewer in it were those elements that might be reasonably regarded as prerequisites of industrialization and the more widespread and intensive was the use of substitutes for such prerequisites. Another way of putting it is to say that in the more advanced countries, their preindustrial history presented a rich and colorful picture, while their industrial history was relatively simple. By contrast, the preindustrial landscape of backward countries was rather barren, but the history of their industrializations much more complex and variegated, precisely because it was shot through and dominated by substitutions of many kinds.

Let us apply this generalization to the field of modern industrial entrepreneurship. A backward country such as, say, Russia in the last decades of the nineteenth century no doubt suffered from many disabilities in this respect, as it did in others. The number of able entrepreneurs was relatively small, their time horizon limited, their standards of commercial honesty deplorably low; and entrepreneurial activities were viewed with suspicion by both the mass of the populace and the intelligentsia. In a less backward country, such as, for instance, Germany in the middle of the last century, most of those negative features were present (even though in an attenuated form, and, in particular, the tradition for honesty in commercial dealings was fairly high, probably as a result of the craft-guild experience in the past centuries).

One cannot go amiss, therefore, in saying that in either country the prerequisites for modern entrepreneurship were either nonexistent or present to a quite insufficient extent. And yet Germany in the second half of the century went through a magnificent industrial upsurge that brought her abreast of England, the "workshop of the world." Russia before 1914 did less well than Germany in absolute terms, but its great spurt of industrial development in the eighteen-eighties and particularly the eighteen-nineties is a matter of historical record, and the rate of industrial growth it achieved in those years was far above anything ever attained by Germany. How could that happen in the face of the disabilities just mentioned? The answer is that in either country men succeeded in developing specific substitutions.

The inadequacy in the numbers of available entrepreneurs

could be remedied or substituted for by increasing the size of plant and enterprise above what otherwise would have been its optimal size. In Germany, the various incompetencies of the individual entrepreneurs were offset by the device of splitting the entrepreneurial function: the German investment banks—a powerful invention, comparable in its economic effects to that of the steam engine—were in their capital-supplying functions a substitute for the insufficiency of the previously created wealth willingly placed at the disposal of entrepreneurs. But they were also a substitute for entrepreneurial deficiencies. From their central vantage points of control, the banks participated actively in shaping the major—and sometimes even not so major—decisions of the individual enterprises. It was they who very often mapped out a firm's paths of growth, conceived farsighted plans, decided on major technological and locational innovations, and arranged for mergers and capital increases. To some extent, although less effectively, similar pressures were brought to bear upon Russian entrepreneurs by the Imperial bureaucracy—that is to say, first and foremost, the ministry of finance, which also in other respects provided substitutions similar to those incarnated in the German banks and altogether pursued very similar policies of industrial expansion. In Russia, of course, the quantitative and qualitative deficiencies of entrepreneurs were also alleviated by importation from abroad of foreign entrepreneurial talent, although the overall extent thereof should not be exaggerated.

And, finally, also the lack of social approval of entrepreneurs, the existence of sentiments and values unfavorable to them, was overcome to a considerable extent by the fact that the power of the state—the judicial machinery as well as the police and the army—were used to protect the entrepreneurs and their interests from social forces that were hostile to them, to say nothing of many statutory provisions that pursued the same purpose.

The conclusion, therefore, must be that the processes of modern industrialization are much too variegated to allow of simple generalizations. Those processes in general vary with the degree of backwardness of the countries concerned. And this is as true of modern entrepreneurship as of other factors of industrial progress. It is simply factually incorrect to hold that in countries in which the historical roots of modern entrepreneurship were weak or even nonexistent, no industrial development could take place. It could, and did, in fact, occur because human ingenuity discovered a number of ways to substitute for the missing and allegedly necessary prerequisites.

But something else is of great importance. With the spurt of industrialization also begins a rapid process of transformation of entrepreneurs while their ranks are speedily increasing. For, more important than all historical prerequisites of modern entrepreneurship is the effect on entrepreneurs of being passed through the great training school of industrialization. Few things are more surprising than the great change in values, attitudes, and standards experienced by the Russian entrepreneurs over just one generation between the eighteen-eighties and the years preceding World War I. An astonishing process of modernization took place, not before, but in the very course—and as a consequence—of a spurt of modern industrialization.

These two conclusions, taken together, do help us understand the historical record of European industrializations in its graduated diversity. But, in addition, they also contain a message of some encouragement for the currently underdeveloped countries. In their case, too, the lack of entrepreneurial talents and the absence of historical roots of modern entrepreneurship need not be an obstacle that cannot be overcome by ingenuity, dedication, and, above all, a reasonably short passage of time after a serious industrialization effort has been launched. There is, of course, no such thing as "industrialization gratis." Industrialization always was and will remain a costly business. Still, one may perhaps express the hope that in the currently underdeveloped countries, "substitutions" will be discovered that may prove less unpleasant and more equitable than were some of the devices applied in the formerly backward countries of Europe in the nineteenth century.

Chapter 19

Modernizing
Subsistence Agriculture

Clifton R. Wharton, Jr.

A most critical problem facing the developing world is how
to modernize its agriculture, for it is on subsistence agriculture
that a majority of mankind depends.

Much of the developing world faces a severe crisis in the pursuit of its goals of adequacy, if not modest affluence, over the next
twenty-five years due to the race between population and food
production. Let me repeat the recent figures of John D. Rockefeller, 3d, President of The Agricultural Development Council,
Inc., and the Population Council: In 1840 the world's population
reached one billion; less than a hundred years later, it was two
billion; thirty years later, it was three billion; and ten years from
now, it will increase to four billion.

Most of the developing nations are experiencing population
growth rates in excess of 2 per cent per year; some, as high as 3
per cent. Every month China adds a Costa Rica, and every year
India adds a Taiwan: economists have estimated that just to keep
every man, woman, and child with their *present* levels of food,
clothing, and shelter, output must grow at least as fast as popula-

tion—2 to 3 per cent per year. But a growth rate for agricultural output at 2 to 3 per cent makes no provision for higher levels of income and improved nutrition. Most developing nations also seek to achieve a growth in per capita income of about 3 per cent per year. If these nations are successful, part of the additional income will cause an increased demand for food, since this is the commodity that takes up the largest proportion of income increases at low levels. If per capital incomes in the developing nations rise at a rate of 3 per cent per year, about two-thirds of this increase will be transferred to the food-producing sector. Thus, about a 2 per cent increase in the demand for food due to growing incomes must be added to the 2 to 3 per cent increase due to population growth. These two elements imply that the developing nations must have their agriculture grow at a compound rate of 4 to 5 per cent per year. Therefore, some of the strongest pressures for developmental performance will fall upon agriculture. Yet agriculture in its traditional and subsistence form has proved to be a most resistant and technologically stagnant sector.

THE CHARACTERISTICS OF AGRICULTURE IN THE DEVELOPING WORLD

The present state of agriculture in the developing world is usually described as "traditional," "subsistence," "static," "backward," and "primitive." The desired state is described as "modern," "commercial," "dynamic," "progressive," and "advanced."

Each pair of contrasting terms involves some comparative or relative standard that is elusive when applied internationally or cross-culturally or temporally. We tend to forget or to ignore the fundamental temporality, culturality, and nationality of our ideas of "modernity." The "modern" farmer of the Punjab in India would be considered "traditional" if his farm were located in Iowa. The practices of a "progressive" farmer of Minas Gerais, Brazil, in 1955 would be judged "backward" in 1965. A 1 per cent rate of growth in annual output in Indonesia would be considered "dynamic," but in Taiwain it would be considered "static."

Some Fallacies about Modernizing Agriculture

Many past difficulties in modernizing subsistence agriculture have been due to fallacies regarding subsistence agriculture and subsistence farmers. A common fallacy is the belief that agriculture is synonymous with "primitive" and that industry is synonymous with "modern." While most agriculture in the nonindustrialized nations must be classified as technologically primitive, we fail to recognize that many sectors of agriculture use the latest, most modern techniques. A quick comparison between rubber estates and rubber small holdings in southeast Asia would quickly reveal the fallacy. Technological dualism is as true in agriculture as in industry. Another closely related fallacy is the belief that agriculture is inherently backward technologically. Yet, a strong argument could easily be made that the United States dairy, poultry, and rice industries are among the most automated (as one index of modernization) in the world. A third fallacy is the belief that, because so much of subsistence agriculture is technologically primitive and the levels of living provided are so low, the production process is economically inefficient. But, as Professor Theodore Schultz has ably pointed out, poverty is an inadequate index of economic efficiency.

These fallacies often form the basis for similarly fallacious policies and programs: (1) "If you wish to become modern, you must develop industry (which is modern) and ignore agriculture (which is primitive)." (2) "Only industry is capable of fully exploiting the rewards of new technology because agriculture is inherently primitive." (3) "Agriculture can never be as efficient economically as industry."

Such fallacies have frequently resulted in policies and programs that either ignore subsistence agriculture or prevent its contributing to the process of general economic development. Today, there is growing awareness that subsistence agriculture, instead of proving a brake on economic growth, is a major untapped developmental potential, provided it is properly and skillfully exploited.

THE DESIRABILITY OF MODERNIZING
SUBSISTENCE AGRICULTURE

There are several reasons why agricultural modernization is important for the total development process.

First, agriculture "employs" the largest number of people in the world. More people are directly dependent on the food and fibers of agriculture than on any other industry. And the largest human component in agriculture will be found in subsistence and semisubsistence agriculture.

Second, agricultural growth is an important, linked partner in the over-all process of economic growth and cannot be ignored without serious damage. The food for the industrial workers and the fibers for industrial products come from agriculture. The largest potential market for industrial products lies in agriculture, since the majority of people in the early stages of development are agriculturists. The industrial equipment required for industrialization almost invariably must be imported and paid for by agricultural exports.

A third reason commonly given is the potential role of agriculture in the process of capital accumulation for growth. Despite the relative poverty of agriculture, many experts believe that the agriculture of today's advanced nations was a major source of the investment capital that contributed to economic growth.

THE PROCESS OF MODERNIZATION AND ECONOMIC GROWTH

The development of subsistence agriculture is synonymous with modernization. And modernization inevitably involves a greater and greater introduction of economic factors.

Subsistence agriculture, where the farmer and his family plant to eat and eat to plant, involves economic choices, even though none of the product is sold and none of the required inputs are bought. The subsistence farmer faces a number of economic choices without the usual monetary standards; but an implicit price or value of some kind still exists to enable him to choose among crop/animal mixes, labor-time allocations, and labor use devoted to enterprise combinations. A pure subsistence farmer is still influenced by economic factors. Once the subsistence farmer enters the market, economic influences on production, consumption, saving, and so on are accelerated. Marketing some production creates a greater degree of dependence on outside forces and a heightened interdependence between the constituent parts of the society. Entry into the market also exposes the individual farm to the many impersonal, harsh, subtle, and arbitrary influences of economic forces which are often beyond the control of the individual farmer. Greater commercialization means an increasing vulnerability to forces that are beyond the farmer's control. These forces may be either favorable or unfavorable to the farmer's well-being. The price of what he produces may rise, and his income may go up as well, increasing his ability to buy the materials of better health and life and raising his general level of living. But the prices could also fall, sweeping before them all the greater output due to new varieties, improved practices, and higher yields.

The increased importance of economic factors, as development proceeds, raises the question of their usefulness in *promoting* more rapid agricultural development. Can economic factors be used to speed up the process of agricultural modernization? Can one manipulate economic factors to stimulate more rapid progress in the agricultural sector?

Agricultural development is a process involving the interaction of a large number of variables, both economic and noneconomic. A great deal of the difficulty in prescribing a successful developmental program for agriculture in a specific region or country hinges on the very high degree of specificity, complexity, and interaction involved. Some variables are highly specific to the locale where the agricultural production takes place. Some variables are absolutely essential to growth; without them, growth is virtually impossible. Others aid the process by speeding it up, but are not absolutely essential. Moreover, the great variability between countries or regions and through times makes today's prescription invalid tomorrow and the East's prescription invalid in the West.

In an attempt to unravel these complexities and to reduce them to a basic, simplified level, The Agricultural Development Council has sought to determine what are the universal *essentials* for agricultural development. In the forthcoming book *Getting Agriculture Moving*, Dr. A. T. Mosher has identified five essentials: (1) transportation, (2) markets for products, (3) new farm technology, (4) availability of purchasable inputs, and (5) incentives. The stage of development or adequacy of these five determine, we believe, the possibilities of agricultural development. One or more may be crucial in any given situation or at any given time, but all are equally important determinants in that they are interrelated with each other in making growth possible.

Dr. Mosher has also identified five *accelerators:* those factors which, while not absolutely essential for agricultural growth, can make a contribution to speeding up the rate of growth, once the essentials are met. The five accelerators are: (1) education, (2) production credit, (3) farmer associations, (4) improving or expanding the land base, and (5) planning.

Only two of the essentials involve traditional economic variables: markets for products and incentives; also only two of the accelerators: production credit and planning. All four cannot be properly treated in a single paper; therefore, let me discuss briefly only one economic aspect of "incentives"—prices.

The major, all-pervasive economic factor affecting farmers is price—the prices of what farmers buy and of what they sell. But prices must always be multiplied by quantities to produce gross figures of income, expenditure, and personal income. Except for weather, pests, diseases, and so forth, production quantities are subject to the control of the farmer, but the prices (or costs) are usually outside his control.

It makes no difference whether the prices and costs are determined by the "invisible hand"—the impersonal forces in the market—or by the "all-seeing wisdom" of the collective forces of the state—whether democratic/free enterprise, autocratic/dictatorial, or socialistic. In all cases, the farmer rarely has anything to say regarding the prices of what he buys and sells.

Price/cost signals are still the most rapid socioeconomic communication device at the disposal of man for controlled and planned development. They transmit their information more swiftly, more efficiently, and more pervasively than any other system yet developed. Price/cost signals carry information regarding what is wanted and what is not wanted; who wants it and who is ready to pay for it or to sell it; what is precious and what is not. They reach down to the most remote village, touching even the farmer who sells only a small fraction of his output.

The determination and adequacy of the price/cost signals, however, are the source of considerable disagreement among econonomists and planners.

First, there is the question of the extent to which the subsistence farmer or peasant producer is or is not an "economic man." Do such people really respond to economic incentives, like their urban cousins? The arguments on this issue have a long history. There is a rapidly growing body of irrefutable evidence that peasant and subsistence farmers *are* indeed "economic men" who respond positively and negatively to economic stimuli as quickly as the most commercialized farmers in the modern world. The evidence is quite clear that subsistence man is fully as responsive to the opportunity for a larger income (higher gain beyond costs and effort spent) as the next man. Such responsiveness takes a variety of forms, ranging from the introduction of new crops to the adoption of new practices—even those at odds with existing cultural methods. We often fail to realize that some of today's staple food crops in the developing world were not indigenous to these areas; for example, white potatoes are not indigenous to western China, but they are grown there. Rubber is not indigeneous to Southeast Asia; yet in Malaysia, Thailand, and Indonesia, small peasant farmers adopted the crop and produce it, even though they had to wait six to seven years before they could expect any financial reward for their efforts. Certainly this is not the behavior of an indolent, tradition-bound peasant with a short-time horizon. The explosion of corn production in Thailand for export to Japan is another recent example.

One can find many other examples to show that the peasant producer does respond; and one can also find cases where he does not. Careful study of the latter reveals the second and third areas of doubt regarding the effectiveness of price signals. They have usually occurred where either (1) the signal was frustrated by intervening barriers such as isolation (nonexistent transport facilities) or price distortion (a monopolist) or (2) the signal lost its strength by being overwhelmed by noneconomic forces such as cultural values.

Most developing nations have a form of economic organization that is closer to free competition or private enterprise than to state direction. But, the closer one gets to the producer, the greater the likelihood of imperfection or distortion in the price/cost signal. There is too much "static," "jamming," or interference. In some cases, the interference is by merchants who exploit their monopoly powers through their control of credit or limited markets. There are equally important, all-pervasive social-cultural-political forces that can interfere with the operation of the price/cost signaling process. These factors are at work, regardless of whether the price is determined by a competitive market or by government decree.

Noneconomic factors do have an influence on the process of total economic development, and they also affect economic factors. One example can be seen in the case of "agrarian reform." In many countries, the existing pattern of landownership and the associated distribution of production can frustrate attempts at change. The price signal may be effective, but the actual cultivator's share of any improved income may be such that he has no incentive to respond. Or the tenurial arrangements may be such that the subsistence farmer feels he has limited control—economically, politically, or both—over his own future. Therefore, why invest in the present for someone else's future gain—not yours or your heirs'?

THE PROBLEMS ENCOUNTERED IN USING ECONOMIC TOOLS

The "cultural static" with price signals is only one example of the interference that can occur in the deliberate use of economic factors to promote economic development.

Two other factors deserve special emphasis, since they tend

to be most frequently ignored or misunderstood by planners and developers. The first is that agricultural development is a "systems problem." The second is that there is a "specialness" to agriculture as a productive process, differentiating it from other forms of production.

The process of agricultural development has been best described by Professor Max Millikan as a "complex systems problem." There are actually two complexities involved: (1) the very large number of interrelated factors and (2) the unique importance of any one factor or series of factors in any given situation. We can reasonably identify almost all the relevant factors and variables that affect agricultural development, but the relative importance of any one or any set varies through time and from location to location. Consequently, the first *skill* in the economic development of agriculture is the ability to identify successfully (1) the key factors that will stimulate more rapid growth and on which one can operate—the policy and program variables; and (2) the major inhibitors or obstacles, some of which may be amenable to action and others of which are not amenable to change, but all of which must be taken account of in any program of directed change; and (3) the correct sequence and combination of steps to be taken.

Many slogans and panaceas have been promoted in the past and are being propagandized today, such as co-operatives, community development, and agrarian reform. A fascinating chapter in the history of agricultural development could be written on the rise and fall of "success stories" in programs of agricultural development: SCIPA (Servicio Cooperativo Interamericano de Produceión de Alimentos) in Peru, ACAR (Associação de Credito e Assitência Rural) in Brazil, the Rockefeller Foundation in Mexico, Etawah in India, Gezira in the Sudan. Today's magic programs are: JCRR (Joint Commission on Rural Reconstruction) in Taiwan, Comilla in East Pakistan, and the Red Book Rural Development scheme in Malaysia.

The real downfall in agricultural development programs to date has been the failure to recognize that agricultural development must be analyzed in its complex totality, focusing on the key interacting facets, each of which must be studied in a particular context and in a continuing ongoing fashion. Univariate solutions that concentrate on a single factor to the exclusion of all others are rarely successful. Moreover, the critical problems in any one country or region need not be the same as in another. Even where a program attacks successfully a combination of critical factors, we must recognize that there is very limited transferability to another problem situation. Finally, any successful program of directed change will alter the original problem situation so that adjustments in the program itself will be required through time. Such changes will be facilitated by continuing evaluation and analysis of the program and its focus while the program is under way.

Planners and policy makers in the developing world are also coming to recognize a second difficulty not fully appreciated in their earlier work: the special characteristics of agriculture. Agriculture is characterized by heterogeneity in its physical inputs and climatic factors. Not only does the quality of labor and management ability vary among farm people but, more important, soil, rainfall, humidity, hours of sunshine, and so on also vary considerably, sometimes even within the same farm. These differences are the "givens" within which the farm operator or manager's decisions must take place. National plans that ignore the basic heterogeneity of the inputs in agriculture can only result in failures. As a biological process, agriculture is far more subject to environmental factors. Bananas do not grow in Alaska (except, perhaps, in a hothouse), but a shoe factory in Tokyo need not be different from one in São Paulo. Through improved technology, man has been able to reduce considerably the influence of climate and environment, but he is still very much subject to the factors associated with the particular location where the biological process takes place.

Two other special characteristics of agriculture recognized as important for programs of change are the large number of decision makers and the large number of different kinds of decisions made throughout the agricultural production process. In a typical developing country, agricultural production is carried out by thousands or millions of farm operators who are widely dispersed. Attempts to plan or control the activities of such a large number of individuals over so wide an area are faced with extreme difficulty. The time span required in agricultural production involves a large number and wide variety of decisions. Most agricultural products involve a crop cycle or time lag between initiation (planting) and conclusion (harvest). The production decisions of the cultivator throughout the crop cycle are of many kinds and require different skills and knowledge: which crops to choose, which variety, when to plant, when to weed, when to fertilize, when to harvest. Decisions at each point in time are capable of influencing the final outcome.

CONCLUSION

In the developing world, the agriculture that most requires modernization is subsistence and semisubsistence agriculture. Of these, the former is the more primitive technologically. The modernization of agriculture in the advanced, industrialized nations is of relatively minor importance when viewed in a world context. The Louisiana rice farmer who plants, fertilizes, and sprays by airplane can hardly be considered backward. His foreign brother whose back is bent daily in the paddy fields of southeast Asia or the corn plots on the steep slopes of the Andes in Latin America is the crucial problem facing world development. How to modernize his production?

Several recent works have emphasized that the economic growth of agriculture requires *modern* factors of production and *modern* attitudes, values, motivations, and skills. Modernization involves the conversion of a subsistence agriculture, with traditional techniques and with its primary orientation to production of food and fiber for the farm family, into one where modern techniques predominate and the primary orientation is not to the direct physical sustenance of the farm family, but where the same goal is met indirectly by the skillful manipulation of the farm resources to maximize the net revenue derived from them. But the knowledge that this is so does not take us far toward the more important answer of how to bring it about.

Despite all the experience with programs of directed agricultural change, especially since the end of World War II, the sad fact is that we *still* do not have a universally applicable solution, technique, or program. Here is exactly where the major flaw in past efforts and present approaches seems to be: we should *not* try to find a universally applicable solution. There is none and can be none. There *are* key, identifiable factors that are essential to agricultural growth and will accelerate it. But while we believe that these factors are universal, the relative importance of one or all must be based on the *unique* problem situation. And, most important, each problem situation must be studied in its *totality*.

Recognition that uniqueness and totality are the essential preconditions to the formulation of successful programs may go far toward assisting the developing nations in modernizing their subsistence agriculture.

Chapter **20**

The Modernization
of Industry

Paul N. Rosenstein-Rodan

Economic Growth: Past and Present

Modernization of industry is the most significant symptom of economic growth in the last 150 years. Economic growth itself—and certainly sustained economic growth—is also a relatively recent phenomenon, having emerged less than two centuries ago. Until the eighteenth century, national income increased yearly at a rate of less than 1 per cent, and income per head remained almost stationary. In the eighteenth century, there was an acceleration of growth to between 1 and 1½ per cent per annum; it was the horse-and-buggy speed of economic development. Following the Industrial Revolution throughout the nineteenth century and, in fact, until the outbreak of World War II, a marked acceleration took place both in industrialization and in economic growth, reaching the classical rate of around 3 per cent per annum; that was the railway speed of economic development. After World War II and in the nineteen-fifties in many—but primarily the rich—parts of the world economy (for instance, the European Common Market), a further marked acceleration took place and the rate of growth reached 5 per cent per annum; it was the airplane speed of economic development.

Can the underdeveloped countries achieve the same acceleration of economic growth? This is, indeed, the most important task of our generation. If it is not fulfilled, poverty in midst of plenty will go on. The development decade of the United Nations proclaims it as a target. Is it a feasible target? The record of the past would seem to say *no;* the feeling and knowledge of the present say *yes!*

The Widening Gap between the Haves and the Have-nots in the Past

Modernization of industry was most unequally spread among various nations of the world economy. A lion's share of the tremendous increase in income between the Napoleonic wars and World War II accrued to less than 30 per cent of the world population. The others had to run fast in order to stand still. The international distribution of income seemed to proceed according to the principle, "To him who hath shall be given."

This was contrary to the expectations of classical economic theory. Underdeveloped countries with plentiful labor and scarce capital had naturally low wages. Low-wage products should be exported advantageously, and low wages should attract foreign capital flows through international investment, which should gradually raise employment wages and reduce the inequality in international income distribution. But the advantages of plentiful and cheap labor were more than compensated by the disadvantages of lacking organization and deficiency of basic auxiliary industries like transport and power, which are commonly referred to as "social overhead capital." In consequence, even the very high amount of international investment was not sufficient to prevent a growing inequality in international income distribution.

This is not as surprising as it would seem at first. For a long time, the same process was taking place on a national level in the rich countries. Their development was largely industrialization, and industrialization meant urbanization. Towns are areas of high wages (higher than in rural zones). Nonetheless, capital was invested in areas of high wages (towns)—not because of but in spite of high wages—because the advantages of urban concentration more than compensated for the disadvantage of high labor costs. Towns were "growing points"; they had a higher rate of growth. The inequality between the urban and rural zones was increasing for a long time before the feedback effect of urban wealth reached the rural zones. The road to greater eventual equality led through a long phase of rising inequality.

The growing inequality between urban and rural zones on the national level was reproduced on the international level. The developed countries represented, so to speak, the "towns" in the world economy; the underdeveloped countries represented the more slowly growing rural zones of the world economy. The gap between the rich and the poor countries was widening until the outbreak of World War II.

In the nineteen-fifties, however, even the underdeveloped countries realized on the whole a 4 per cent per annum rate of growth. The very rich countries (United States and United Kingdom) had only a 3 per cent rate of growth; the rich, but not very rich, had a 5 per cent rate—while some, like Japan and the Iron Curtain countries, had an even higher rate. The average rate of growth of the rich countries was around 4 per cent. For the first time in 150 years, the *relative* gap between the "haves" and the "have-nots" has stopped growing. The growth of the underdeveloped countries is by no means steady, sustained, or assured; the absolute gap is still growing. More is needed. But the success in raising the rate of growth of underdeveloped countries to a rate at which the relative gap stopped widening is a good augury that it need not widen any more and that even better results can perhaps be achieved in the future.

History Does Not Repeat Itself

Economic growth and modernization of industry were not only more widespread during the last fifteen years but also proceeding at a higher speed. Many of the variegated causes of growth in the past are still operating, but some new ones have emerged. Today, not only do we start on a much higher level of technology but we also have a better knowledge of economic and social mechanisms and techniques. By using technological, economic, and social progress, not only can we repeat the past performance of those countries which are developed today and transplant it more widely to the underdeveloped countries; we can also achieve a considerable acceleration in modernization. We have, accordingly, not only to describe the process of getting growth started as it happened in the past, in order to learn from it, but also to examine new ways now possible to accelerate this process.

In describing economic development, we shall examine, not ultimate, but only proximate, causes. Economists have always realized that their aggregative concepts represent, as it were, the mechanism through which more basic cultural or psychological forces operate, and they know also that the decision-making processes in a country and politics in general are highly relevant. Most of these processes are described elsewhere in this book. They are reflected, however, in economic aggregates that can be handled as over-all proximate causes.

How Economic Growth Began

Before 1800

When income increases, people do not increase proportionately their consumption of the same goods they were consuming before. They demand at first somewhat more of the same foodstuffs, but then other types of foodstuffs: meat on Sundays—not only rice, bread, or potatoes; then textiles, household goods, and later (on a higher income level) other durable consumer goods. These additional goods are then either produced or imported. A division of labor enhances acquisition of varied skills in producing assorted goods. Artisans and handicraftsmen, first on the farms and then in towns, receive foodstuffs for their products. Savings, in the form of a food-subsistence fund, pay for setting them up in towns and for building up merchandise for trade. The tools of the artisans are relatively simple and do not require much capital. More than four-fifths of the people are engaged in agriculture. Overseas trade, on the other hand, has long turnover periods and is the most capital-intensive occupation. Savings increase slowly, perhaps because incentives for them in the form of investment opportunities are lacking. Mostly the increase takes the form not so much of tightening of belts as of not consuming so high a proportion as formerly of an *increase* in income. This form, when marginal savings are higher than average savings, is to play a preponderant part in the modernization of industry and economy later on. Increase in income occurs from technical progress (new methods of land reclamation, three-field system of cultivation, sheep enclosures, and so on), from improvement in terms of trade, and from piracy and booty. International capital movements, another most important source of an increase in income, only came later in the nineteenth century.

After 1800

A vast increase in scientific knowledge put to practical application led to a vast technological progress, resulting in a substantial reduction in overseas transport costs and mechanization of industry. Reduction of transport costs by over 60 per cent made possible a much larger international division of labor. New machines made necessary a greater concentration of resources. Greater demand for man power could be met by mechanization of industry. Technological modernization introduced new production and management methods and new skills and led at the same time toward the building up of basic and auxiliary industries of social overhead capital (transport, power, and communications) as well as more efficient techniques in trading. A growing proportion of man power was absorbed into industry and trade in towns. The restructuring of the economy took the form of a growing production, first of consumer goods and then of capital goods.

The vast and continuing process of industrialization was made possible by a flow of savings that was enhanced and enlarged by the incentive of new investment opportunities. At the same time, both research and working experience led to a flow of technical improvements, so that technological progress became a built-in part of the industrial system.

THE ROLE OF INTERNATIONAL TRADE

The lowering of transport costs and the growth of international trade led to a larger industrialization in Europe and in the developed countries than would have otherwise been possible and to a larger production of primary produce in underdeveloped countries. The expansion of markets made it possible to take advantage of economies of scale and a better division of labor. Both sides benefited from this exchange, although the indirect benefits of acquiring better skills of labor on the job (the so-called learning functions or external economies) may have been greater in the developed countries, since external economies may be greater in industry than in agriculture. Each dose of improvement in productivity—as a once-for-all change—transmits its benefits in the form of lower prices, but a chain process of continuing changes does not necessarily propagate its effects equally between adjacent and peripheral territories.

Trade in the nineteenth century was not only a device for an optimum allocation of resources of the world economy; it was also an "engine of growth." Western Europe's demand for imports of primary produce was increasing proportionately with her growth and thus induced and propagated growth in countries exporting primary produce. Economic growth thus induced in underdeveloped countries sometimes led to a lopsided pattern of growth in which production of primary produce for exports was built up by modern methods, while the rest of the economy remained less developed. This lack of complementarity and propagation created sometimes a "dual economy"—isolated enclaves of modern economy without radiation in a sea of primitive economy. In spite of these drawbacks, the opening up of trade brought great gains to underdeveloped economies. Their growth was, however, more a commercialization than industrialization; it was largely a horizontal expansion process, a widening rather than a deepening of methods of production—a process of agglutination, rather than concentration.

Technological progress, economizing on use of raw materials, producing synthetic products, and making some mechanized agriculture competitive, as well as policies of agricultural protectionism, reduce nowadays the forces making for transmission of growth from developed to underdeveloped countries. Expansion in the center no longer leads to a proportional increase in demand for imports from the periphery. International trade, while advantageous and useful, is not now a sufficient "engine of growth." Expanded production of the home market is needed. The stage is set for a modernization of industry as an essential part of balanced agricultural and industrial development in developing countries.

Can they modernize faster, realizing economic progress in a different modern way, or must they retrace the steps of the developed economies in the past?

MODERNIZATION OF INDUSTRY IN UNDERDEVELOPED COUNTRIES TODAY

Such modernization can proceed better and faster than in the past for several reasons:

1. Technology is very much richer today. There is a greater choice of machinery. Some of the new means of production, like the assembly-line method, require less skills than former methods. A great deal of equipment can be bought jointly with installation services.

2. Access to and communication of technological knowledge are widespread and easier and cheaper than in the past.

3. No price in money and time has to be paid for technological research. Imitation, rather than invention, is needed in many or most sectors of industry. It is true that simple imitation will not suffice, for it has to be adapted to different local conditions (see below). But adaptation, which implies minor innovations, is easier than new technological research and invention. Imitation with adaptation to local conditions is easier in industry than in

agriculture because differences in technology between developed and underdeveloped countries are smaller in industry than in agriculture.

4. There is progress not only in technology but also in economics, notably in conveying and using relevant information. The so-called economic planning or programing is only a new term for a co-ordinated and consistent economic policy. But knowing what investments are intended makes it possible to calculate and anticipate their indirect effects and requirements and to provide for them in time. The building up of complementary transport and power (social overhead capital) can be thus synchronized with industrialization. In the past, lack of transport or power often prevented the creation of industrial establishments, while lack of industrial demand for transport and power inhibited investment in those sectors. At best, there were long intervals between investments in industry and social overhead capital; at worst, the lack of synchronization prevented investment in both. The synchronization of those investments can shorten the interval between the two and lead to new investment which was formerly impossible.

5. Synchronization of different industrial establishments may make a complex (or bundle) of industries succeed when each single one might not have made the grade. A pattern of mutually supporting investments in different lines of production can enlarge the size of the market, reduce risks, and accelerate the tempo.

> Isolated advance is not impossible. A solitary process of investment and increased productivity in one industry alone will have favourable repercussion elsewhere in the economy. There is no denying that through the normal incentives of the price mechanism other industries will be induced to advance also. But this may be a snail's pace of progress. The price mechanism works but, in the conditions prevailing in many backward economies it may work too slowly. . . . Within the domestic economy advance in one direction A, say in the machine industry, tends to induce advance in B, say steel industry as well. But if it is only a passive reaction to the stimulus coming from A, the induced advance of B may be slow and uncertain; and B's slowness and passiveness will in turn slow down and discourage the initial advance in A.

The application of capital to one industry alone will be subject to
more sharply diminishing returns.[1]

Better economic policy may nowadays bring about an autonomous (or occasionally induced) advance in a number of mutually
supporting lines of production.

6. Import substitution vastly increases the range of investment
opportunities. Where trade statistics show that products are imported which could be domestically produced at costs not higher
or not markedly higher than abroad, market research is not required, since at proper costs domestic demand is known and assured. A whole series of products that can be manufactured by
simple production processes offer relatively easy investment opportunities. Those are at first mostly consumer goods, but gradually a range of intermediate products and simple capital goods
considerably widen the range. It is naturally important that imports be substituted by domestic production in an efficient way.
To produce bananas on the North Pole in hothouses is technically
possible, but it not an efficient allocation of economic resources.
Experience shows, however, that a vast and growing list of imports can be efficiently produced in underdeveloped countries.

7. Finally, better knowledge and technique of money and
credit policy may reduce the ups and downs of cyclical fluctuations and, with them, risks and uncertainty.

DIFFICULTIES IN MODERNIZING INDUSTRY IN UNDERDEVELOPED COUNTRIES

The problems of modernizing industry are smaller today than
they were a century ago, but they are considerable, nonetheless,
and should not be underrated. Although imitation is easier than
invention, it cannot be applied automatically, but requires adaptation.

1. First, the simple imitation of Western methods is typically
impossible. Perhaps the most obvious problem is that the avail-

[1] Ragnar Nurkse, *Problems of Capital Formation in Underdeveloped
Countries* (New York: Oxford University Press, 1953).

able labour force differs greatly. In the West the mass of men are literate and able to read instructions and information. Moreover, they have an understanding of the functioning of machinery, and thereby of its care and handling, which they have absorbed through their pores, so to speak, as they grew up in a mechanized civilization. Among them are many with varying degrees of training in engineering, scientific, financial, accounting, and managerial knowledge and techniques—and the elements of this knowledge acquired unconsciously from the entire world around one are as important as the elements learned in formal education. It is impossible to man an enterprise in an underdeveloped economy with corresponding individuals. Men anywhere can be trained rapidly in skills, for men everywhere are intelligent, but the broad background of other individual characteristics cannot be duplicated. A Western-type enterprise must be adapted to the human differences; indeed, a perceptive observer of an efficient industrial enterprise in a low-income society will note in how many ways both conspicuous and seemingly insignificant its operation differs from that of an enterprise in the West.

2. Equally important, every Western industry depends for its efficiency on other industries. It assumes the ready availability of materials, components, and tools. It depends also on auxiliary enterprises which can provide technical, financial, and managerial services on demand; on a complex network of communication and transportation facilities; and on an intricate system of business practices. A Western economy is a technical (and cultural) complex, not a set of isolated pieces of technology. In an underdeveloped society the auxiliary industries are missing and the framework of business practices is different. One piece cannot be detached from the complex and used efficiently elsewhere without skillful adaptation.[2]

The adaptation to the human differences described under (1) above is possible, but it takes ingenuity, time, and money. Some parts of machines will be badly used; replacement will be faulty and more costly. In part, these are unavoidable costs of training industrial man power on the job and represent the teething pains of infant industry. The dependence on complementary components and other services described under (2) above will

[2] Everett E. Hagen, *On the Theory of Social Change: How Economic Growth Begins* (Homewood, Illinois: Dorsey Press, 1962), p. 31.

invariably lead to longer gestation periods (a steel mill will take five years instead of three for its completion), to lower efficiency, and, over a sometimes long infant-industry period, to higher costs in spite of lower wages. But many success stories—not only in Israel but also in south Italy, Greece, Spain, Yugoslavia, Mexico, Taiwan, and others—can be considered to be representative, rather than exceptional, cases and to point the way to the future.

3. A specific difficulty consists in the fact that the existing technology is adapted to Western needs and is capital-intensive and labor-saving, while underdeveloped countries would require labor-intensive and capital-saving methods. In many cases, the existing technology simply does not provide efficient labor-intensive methods of production. Some adaptation is possible; for instance, using capital-intensive equipment and old-fashioned methods of handling raw materials to machines and of packaging their products. In some cases, last-but-one methods of production can be applied when they not only are more labor-intensive but also require less special skills than the most modern machinery. In many other sectors, on the other hand, the most modern technology may save on skilled labor even more than on labor in general: and here the last-but-one technology—even if it were available at lower secondhand prices of machinery—is not appropriate.

Undoubtedly, research both in underdeveloped and (let us hope also) in developed countries will in time produce capital-saving inventions. But it would not make sense to tell the underdeveloped countries to wait until such new technology is invented. On the basis of existing technology—with intelligent adaptation—a vast modernization of industry is possible and is taking place. If agriculture, which is lagging behind progress in industry, can catch up, the goals of the decade of development can be reached.

Chapter 21

The Modernization
of the Labor Force

Richard D. Lambert

Historically, the styles in which countries have industrialized
have been many and diverse. So, too, have been the ancillary patterns of recruiting, training, disciplining, and retaining workers.
To the extent that modernization has been a unitary process at all,
it has encouraged the disappearance of certain industrial styles
and the substitution of others. A proper treatment of our general
topic—modernization of the labor force—would attempt at least
to enumerate the many industrial styles and, allowing for the differences in cultural setting in which they are found, to speak of
the labor-market phenomena that seem to be commonly present
within each style. I must here limit myself to only three broad
styles, chosen because they encompass what seem to be the principal historical forms in which the work force in the newly developing countries has been reorganized. The first style may be illustrated by the plantation, although it will be found in mining and
other raw-material producing industries as well. The second has
as its prototype a factory or mill where the agricultural raw materials are first processed, although it is really identified by its way
of organizing labor and the relationship between the workers and

machinery. The earliest form of the third style is the artisan shop, but it is the most omnibus category and includes a wide range of manufacturing styles, as we shall see.

THE PLANTATION AND ITS LABOR FORCE

Let us start with the industrial form least removed from the traditional agrarian society—in fact, one that, since it does not involve a factory, is not usually thought of as industrialization at all. However, this is the first and in many cases still the most prevalent style of Western economic organization that was introduced into the underdeveloped, particularly colonial, countries. Needless to say, the phenomenon of landless labor engaging in agriculture principally for someone else's benefit is not new. The most common form of agriculture, however, was some type of peasant cultivation in which a kin group tilled lands on which they had some durable claim; they consumed a large part of their own product, and it made up most of what they consumed. Even where the agricultural style placed ownership, control, and disposition of the product in the hands of others, it usually took the form of sharecropping. If not, the inducements, internal organization, discipline, and control of workers usually lay in some other not strictly economic institution, usually of a quasi-political nature, such as an aristocrat and the workers on his own lands. Or it had a religious base, as in lands attached to a church, a temple, or a mosque. Most often the rewards to the workers were in kind, and recruitment rarely depended on the attraction of workers in an open market. Rather, an agricultural worker was usually a socially distinct type of person, often of low status, whose range of job choices was very limited. In Western society, one of the most important changes accompanying industrialization was the transformation of labor into a commodity, being available for purchase (in theory, at any rate), being offered on the market to the highest bidder, withdrawable at the discretion of the worker, and paid for in money which the worker could use for any desired commodity, not just his own products. Roughly speaking, the transformation from labor as an outflow of a status to labor as a commodity was one of the early contributions to modernization of the plantation system.

It is true that status still determined the likelihood that a man would be available for recruitment, and the ability of the laborer to choose among a number of bidders was very limited, the right to withdraw from plantation employment was sharply circumscribed, and indebtedness and "company stores" reduced the distinction between payment in cash and in kind; but, nonetheless, it was and is a break with the past.

This is particularly so if we look at it from the viewpoint of a plantation and its approach to securing and retaining its labor.

How great a problem the recruitment of workers was and is seems to depend on, first, the density of the population in the area where the plantation is established and, secondly, how well the local populace can meet their subsistence needs from the traditional economy. Needless to say, these two factors tend to be interrelated, but not entirely so. There are a number of cases, for instance in many parts of southeast Asia, where the number of people in the local labor force should be sufficient; but they are unwilling to undertake plantation wage work in sufficient numbers, and they have alternative means of making nearly equivalent livelihoods through traditional agriculture. Hence the importation of Indian labor into plantation economies such as Ceylon's or Malaya's.

More often, plantations are established in places which, because of inaccessibility or unpleasantness of climate, are sparsely populated. Here, the recruitment and stabilization of the work force is a primary problem for the management. If the area in which the plantation is located has a large available surplus population, the plantation has little difficulty finding workers. If the plantation has been long established and is large, many members of the local labor force will have worked there at one time or another, and older members of a newcomer's family can be depended on to break him in. Moreover, the level of skill required is usually not very great, and most of the local population is already familiar with agricultural work. A core staff of full-time workers can provide for continuing services. For peak demand periods, workers can be drawn in on piece or daily rates. A preference for known workers and experienced hands builds up a core of semi-employees who can usually count on some work on most days but who have no claim on employment on days when there is no demand.

In this way, the plantation becomes just one more competitor for agricultural labor, particularly at the planting and harvesting time, and is usually in a good bargaining position since the pay is in cash and often slightly above the going rate for agricultural labor on a family farm. The plantation's impress on the community depends on its size relative to other economic units. If it is big enough, it will tend to eclipse other farms or make them subsidiary. There is little attempt to control turnover; in fact, a daily hiring procedure is often adopted. Applicants appear on the site, and some are selected then and there. Both the hiring and disciplining of workers are usually done for the management through various types of intermediaries. There is usually a gang boss of some sort who often selects his own workers, has power of dismissal or other disciplinary measures, and is responsible for seeing that the work rules are followed. The gap in the status between plantation managers and workers is typically so great that this intermediary has a great deal of power concentrated in his hands; thus the system has almost always led to abuses, including all sorts of petty extortions for securing and retaining jobs.

Where the plantation is located in an inhospitable climate or terrain or where it is far from the main centers of population, the problems of recruitment and retention are quite different. In the first place, while demand by the very nature of the agricultural cycle is variable, the plantation must maintain a full complement of employees often throughout the year and moreover make a sizable initial investment in each one. There is, first, the inducement that must be offered to get the worker to migrate. Then, the transportation costs typically are paid by the plantation. If the company can manage it, this will be treated as a loan chargeable against wages. The length of time required for repayment is one means of lowering turnover. These initial costs represent sufficient investment in the workers on the part of the company so that the easy ebb and flow of employees through a plantation more fortunately situated cannot be tolerated. Hence, most companies are concerned with retention as well as recruitment of workers. Typically, this concern expresses itself in an indenture or contract. The severity of punishment for breach of contract and the extent to which the facilities of law enforcement are available for their support vary from country to country. In general, the more modern the economy, the less the element of compulsion, ranging from the extremes of slavery where a man and his labor were a form of private property down to the elaborate bonus systems, graduated remittances to the family at home, and all-expenses-paid, off-season visits to the home territory. In fact, in many of the under-developed countries, the first laws protecting workers from abuses tend to be those concerned with plantation labor.

In the out-of-the-way plantations, the employees are most often year-round. But since all the additional amenities of life typical of the larger society, such as housing, medical care, educational institutions, churches, markets, entertainment, tend to be left behind by the emigrant employees, if they are to be supplied at all, it is often the company that must provide them. The available cash surplus in workers' wages is rarely great enough even to make a start. Hence, a substantial part of the labor costs for a distant plantation is the provision of general amenities. They represent a constant source of friction between management and the workers, although sometimes these amenities even surpass those found elsewhere in the society. The company usually looks upon them as a paternal distribution of benefits above and beyond the wage contract and expects the workers to return a due measure of loyalty and gratitude. This expectation is often disappointed.

Often when plantations recruit from great distances, they do so from narrow little pools of surplus labor, which are their traditional recruiting grounds—a set of families or villages with the custom of sending out sons or splinter families. These manpower pools often have well-worn pathways for the flow of people, money, and goods. The recruiting and supervisory intermediaries commonly have roots in the same area or set of families. This symbiotic relationship between a residential base and a faraway area where principal livelihoods are earned is just one of the limits to the modernizing effect of plantations. In fact, the plantation, in general, has very little modernizing effect on its own labor force or that of the surrounding countryside. Where males alone are drawn away from their traditional homestead, as is usually the case in the early stages of plantation settlement, its effects on the recruitment area and the recruits alike may be disruptive. Gradually family settlements tend to get established and reflect with some distortion the pattern of the home region. The durability of home-area culture traits among emigrants is remarkable, especially when the number of like people is large. If anything, the plantation can serve as an enclave of resistance to modernization, although it may indirectly contribute by dislodging the older forms of agricultural organization. Just as often, however, even the neighboring farms follow the old ways.

THE GANG-OPERATED MACHINE

The second industrial style to be discussed follows closely on the change from peasant subsistence to market, cash-crop agriculture. So long as an economy is still a peasant economy, a great deal of the processing of agricultural produce is done in the home or in very small units, such as a village mill for grinding grain or oilseed. With the industrialization of agriculture, some degree of mechanization becomes imperative. The chief advantage of the machines, which are rarely complex, is that they can handle considerable bulk in a relatively short time. Hence, the machines tend to be large and to have attached to them gangs of men who feed them, maintain them, and cart away their end products. Within the work gang, the only "skill" resides in the gang boss who is responsible both for the operation and maintenance of the machine and the workings of the whole crew. Such an organizational form is relatively simple and grafts rather easily onto the rural economy, and the mill or factory rarely has difficulty in finding its labor since the level of skills required is very low and its connections with agriculture give it immediate access to any surpluses there. Turnover is slight. Wage levels tend to be low; and if the mill is seasonal in its operation, it can use the labor market as it pleases, much like the plantation in an area of abundant labor described above. Since the supervisory span of control and the hierarchy are very small, problems of discipline of workers and maintaining work norms are very few. Such units, once the initial capital investment has been made in machinery, tend to be extremely resistant to change. When this industrial style is the predominant one in an economy, it may no longer be strictly agrarian, but it is still very far, indeed, from modernization.

FROM ARTISAN TO AUTOMATION

Nonagricultural manufacturing in preindustrial societies has generally been done by artisans in family or familylike groups. In the more complex among these societies, superstructure organizations like guilds regulated relations among the small production units and between them and the outside world. Sometimes they provided some minimal standardization of product, set entrance and training requirements, and occasionally even met credit, transport, and marketing needs. Sometimes groups of artisan families were more or less permanently attached to courts or religious institutions. On other occasions, artisan families with their supporting complement of manual workers were gathered for a great work such as a cathedral, a tomb, a road, or an irrigation canal. Nonetheless, the basic units in the nonagricultural sector of the economy were the small artisan families who characteristically managed to produce or secure the necessary raw materials, own and maintain the tools and equipment, and manufacture and market the product. The beginnings of the modern factory system can be traced to the removal of one or more of these processes from the hands of the artisan. Although the process historically was not quite so simple as I am about to describe it, the esssence of the transformation can be illustrated by the case of textiles. The weaver family may or may not have raised its own cotton or wool or silk, but it usually spun it into yarn or thread, loomed it, and either for cash or kind marketed any surplus it did not use. Usually fluctuations or difficulties in the market, either for supplies of raw materials or the distribution of finished goods, forced the family producer into dependence on a middleman with more command of the market and greater capitalization. Soon the craftsman found himself working on raw materials owned by the middleman and receiving a percentage return for his craftwork. It is only a step from this to the ownership of the household loom or other means of production by the former middleman, who perhaps now pays a straight time or piece rate, and only another short step, usually with some increase in mechanization, to the gathering of a number of artisans together under the same roof for better quality control and supervision, where they work on machines owned by the employer. At this point, the labor force may and often is recruited from families with little or no craft experience, since their discipline and control are more important than their previous skill.

From here, what kind of factory and organization of the labor force develops depends on where the factory comes to rest on each of three interrelated evolutionary dimensions: first, the number and complexity of the operational steps required in the manufacturing process; second, the number and complexity of the operations assigned to each man-*cum*-machine; and third, the extent to which the skill requirements are transferred from the man to the machine. As each of these three dimensions changes, the nature of the work force—that is, its recruitment, organization, training, and retention—tends to change.[1] In general, it can be said that the trend toward modernization involves the development of an increasing number of steps in the manufacturing process, a greater and greater subdivision of these steps so that the span of operations carried out by any one man is very narrow, and the transfer of the control of as many of those operations as possible from the man to the machine.

To illustrate the different types of factory and their accompanying work forces, let us take a number of examples at various points along the modernization continuum that represent differing resting points on the three dimensions mentioned above.

Let us start beyond the level of the artisan shop, but still at the lower end of the modernization continuum. Let us take a fac-

[1] I use the words "tends to change" to avoid a common technological determinism that seems to argue that the prime determinant of change is always the machine. If there were space, I would discuss the differences in factory styles in, say, India and Japan. Here, I can only enter the warning that what I am saying is an unavoidable oversimplification.

tory where there are only a few simple manufacturing operations performed; hence, the span of skills exercised by the operative is narrow, and the crudeness of the machines calls for operator attention and agility, but little accumulated skill. Such factories tend to be what in India are called "the sweated industries" such as carpetmaking, coir making, cigar and handmade cigarette rolling, embroidering, basketmaking, even armature winding. Such industries tend to have low-paid workers, frequently women, working on piece rates for wages that are sufficient only as a supplementary family income. Their earnings often provide the subsistence margin for their family; thus, the workers can be retained or retrenched at the owners' will, and job applicants are usually abundant. From the employer's viewpoint, his labor costs cover nothing beyond wages actually paid for production. It is for the protection of this class of workers that minimum wage and working condition legislation is usually passed.

In the second example, we move a little further along the modernization continuum; the production process is complex, each employee tends to perform a wide span of tasks within it, and the operation of the machine is fully dependent on the skill of the operator. Typical of this style is the small metalworking shop. For instance, in Howrah, across the river from Calcutta, there is a huge maze of shops, in each of which a half-dozen workers will do a variety of metalworking tasks: minor foundry work, turning, grinding, boring, milling, filing, making their own tools. I have even seen one worker making his own crude lathe in his spare time off other jobs. In an old-established settlement of such artisans, there are a constant recruiting of apprentices and long years of training at relatively low and constant wages. The organizational style is familial, and the owner is usually a fellow worker who probably for many years was a skilled operator in a similar establishment before he came by a little capital, some old machinery, and a few contracts to start his own shop. In time, one or more of his employees will try the same route. The aggregate production and number of this mass of shops are relatively constant, with some turnover of personnel and ownership of individual units. Except for the type of machines used, in organizational style the type is not very different from, say, the silk-screen industry in Kyoto. Few of the units ever get beyond a dozen workers, because success above that point requires a managerial style different from the family and calls for greater specialization of labor, more rational production flows, and greater capitalization to tide over market fluctuations. Hence, there is a noticeable absence of units between ten or less employees and fifty or more. As for the labor market, once such a cluster of small shops is established, the most surprising thing is how rarely they seem to experience a genuine labor shortage, although inflationary trends can induce considerable turnover among units. This is so even in the face of the existence nearby of large-scale, more rationalized factories producing similar products. The transformation from the artisanlike generalist to the single-operation specialist is in one sense a skill loss; but in the large-scale factory, the only ones using these generalist skills sit at the apex of the skill structure: in the toolroom, doing patternmaking, or assembling the final product. While such people are usually in short supply, the graduate of the small machine shop usually does not have the requisite familiarity with sophisticated machines and is too prone to rough handicraft substitutes to do the job.

Here, then, are two contrasting examples, both relatively far removed from modern industry: the collection of low-skilled attendants of simple operation machines and the cluster of highly skilled artisans.

Let me now present two other factory styles much further along on the modernization continuum with correspondingly different relationships to the labor market and internal organization.

For our third example, the production process has many steps, but they have been broken down into numerous simplified tasks; thus the range of tasks within each job is relatively small. Once the machine is set, the operator does not manipulate it, but tends it, although this requires a fair degree of skill. The bulk of the operators are semiskilled, and the number of differently defined jobs is considerable. A classic example is the textile mill on whose daily muster several hundred occupational titles will be found, each with its differentiated, and for the most part semiskilled, task. The textile mill is, of course, the prototype large-scale factory for the early stages of industrialization in many of the underdeveloped countries, and its nomenclature and organizational style have been taken over almost intact from their nineteenth- or early twentieth-century form in the West. Often they were frozen at this stage and have thus fallen behind the continuously innovating industries in the metropolitan countries or the new producers, like Hong Kong. This stagnation of the technology and form of work-force organization gives the occupational titles in this industry the sanctity of artisan designations, and the labor market becomes strictly craft-organized.

Internally, the textile mill resembles a bank of pigeonholes in which there is movement in or out of each slot through departures and replacements, but almost no movement between them through job changes or promotions. Turnover and absenteeism tend to run high and are usually caused by factors beyond the control of the factory. Thus, a textile mill must surround itself with a considerable amount of surplus labor to normalize the daily work force. The fragmentation of that market makes the demand for an abundant supply even more pressing. Fortunately, when the expansion in the number of mills is slight, workers tend to be abundant because the skill level of the quasi crafts needed for the mill is low, the apprenticeship period is short, and thus a substantial supply is available from past turnover in their own and similar units.

Modernization is these factories usually means the substitution of machines for workers, an increase in the number of machines per worker, or the replacement of hand-tended by automatic machinery. In all these cases, the size of the labor force is reduced. Another modernizing trend is the creation of multistage machines, thus confusing the well-entrenched craft designations of the operators. In either case, worker opposition is likely to be fierce; and, aside from resisting modernization in general it will take the form of pressures for decasualization and transfer of some of the costs of variable demand to the company instead of the employee and semiemployee.

The fourth and final example is the factory where the production process is complex and the within-job range of tasks may be either slight or great, but the bulk of the control has been transferred to the machine and away from the operator. Higher-skill categories are reserved for those who just set machines or maintain them or make the tools and jigs to guide them, or those who man complicated machinery where the tending takes considerable experience, or those who work from drawings and retain a craft-like style of using the machine as a tool, instead of just tending it. This type of factory tends to recruit at the bottom and to fill its upper-skill and supervisory jobs through in-plant training and internal promotions. The factory is largely self-contained, and added to wage incentives for satisfactory job performance are the workers' own aspirations for upward mobility, which is absent in the other styles discussed. The primary internal strain in this type of factory is the workers' desire to give mobility a ratchet effect— that is, to move up, but not down—and to gain property rights in a job. To this end, the worker again seeks a craftlike occupational title with a limited work load, thus pushing the company in the direction of the craftlike organization of example number three. The company, on the other hand, wants maximal flexibility. I know of one factory where occupational titles, though used in managerial planning, are never given to employees so that changes in the tasks assigned to a worker will encounter the least resistance.

We have now discussed six different industrial styles: the plantation, the agricultural produce processing factory, and four types of strictly manufacturing enterprises that vary according to the complexity of their production process, the range of tasks performed by each worker, and the extent to which the control lies in the machine or the worker. In each case, we have scanned the way in which the unit faces its labor market, the level of skills required, the internal organization of the work force, and the degree of modernization implicit in each style. Many more types could be discussed. Moreover, the emphasis has been almost entirely on the structure of the factory. Equally important in the modernization process are the development of attitudes and the work habits of the workers, no matter in what form of enterprise they find themselves. They must, for instance, really come to believe that the company should treat them according to their productivity, and not a large set of extraneous factors, no matter how complicated the debate about productivity. There must be some elementary transfer of loyalty to and identification with the abstract company on some model other than the paternalistic, familial one. On the company's side, the most fundamental change is in coming to believe that the quality of the work force is genuinely important and is to be ensured not just through disciplinary measures or keeping out unions, something that is a rare attitude in managers in the nonmodern industrial styles. But these matters, equally important to those discussed earlier, must be taken up elsewhere.

In closing, let me say that one of the characteristics of newly developing economies is that in almost every industrial category, the production units are strewn out along the entire length of the modernization continuum from artisan handicraft production to the most glass-encased, rationalized, modern enterprise. It is by no means clear that the substitution of later for earlier forms is uniformly proceeding; in many countries, the current equilibrium points seems to be midway along the evolutionary path, and more advanced styles are pulled back toward it. But this may merely mean that a non-Western style of modernization will emerge.

Chapter 22

The Role
of the State in
Economic Development

Eugene Staley

The role of the state in economic development is a topic beset with controversy and emotion. Discussions of it are often doctrinaire. But let us explore the topic in a pragmatic, practical spirit. There has been enough experience by now with different kinds of relations between the state and economic life so that we know a good deal about concrete problems and results; this is tending to soften doctrinaire positions.

CONVERGING TENDENCIES
IN ECONOMIC SYSTEMS—"MIXED" ECONOMIES

In fact, it may not be going too far to speak of tendencies toward convergence of economic systems that were formerly poles apart.

On the one hand, the so-called capitalist systems all over the world, including North America, have for a long time been moving in a socialist direction—free state-supported education for everybody, steeply progressive income taxes, social insurance for such needs as health care, and target setting for national economic growth.

On the other hand, socialist systems and socialist parties are nowadays recognizing that there are some virtues in decentralized types of economic management, in mixtures of collective and private ownership, and in limited use of profit incentives. This is certainly true where the socialist doctrine is evolutionary and politically democratic, as, for example, in the case of the British Labor party. Even in countries where the more totalitarian types of socialism have been installed by Communist parties, there are indications of loosening in economic orthodoxy. Yugoslavia is an obvious example, and other Communist countries of eastern Europe, like Poland and Czechoslovakia, are somewhat pragmatic and experimental. The Soviet Union itself is now experimenting with the idea that the slipshod performance of some of its consumer-goods factories might be improved by allowing the managers to manage in accordance with market demands, without so many directives from the central planners, almost as though the firm were a private enterprise.

Of course, the Soviet manager will not be a capitalist owner, in the sense of being entitled to keep whatever profits the firm may make. But in comparison with the so-called capitalist countries today—which really have "mixed" economic systems, no longer like nineteenth-century capitalism—this difference is not so huge as it might seem at first glance. In the United States of America, supposedly the archexponent of the private profit system, management is more and more professional, with interests not always identical with those of the owners (the stockholders). Also, the federal government taxes away nearly half of a business corporation's profits. Of the remainder, part is generally plowed back into the enterprise, and what does go to the owners is assailed again by federal and state income taxes. Furthermore, many of the profit-receiving stockholders are themselves collective entities, like insurance companies, universities, and investment funds held by thousands of stockholders, large and small, including workers and their organizations.

It is inaccurate, then, to talk nowadays in the old-fashioned vocabulary that made clear-cut distinctions between "capitalism" and "socialism." The reality today is more like a spectrum, a rainbow. Nearly all economies today—except, perhaps, the Chinese Communist economy—are really mixed systems. There are different sorts of mixtures, some with more and some with less emphasis on state economic activity, some with more, some with less, of a role for private enterprise.

THEMES TO BE EXPLORED

Let us turn now to the central question: How can the leaders of a modernizing, developing country reach wise decisions as to the kind of mixture between government economic activity and private economic activity that is best for their country? What should the government itself do? What should it encourage private individuals, firms, co-operatives, and associations to do?

In discussing these questions, I propose to develop three themes.

First, there are no universally right answers to these questions. There is more than one feasible road to development, and what is best in the circumstances of one country is not necessarily best in the circumstances of another.

Second, there are certain functions essential to economic development that the state must perform; there are others that it can either perform itself or stimulate private enterprise to perform.

Third, there are weighty social and political advantages in pluralism, that is, in a system so arranged that economic, social, and political power are not all concentrated in the same individuals or families or organizations.

Diverse Paths to Development

History shows that modern economic development can be achieved under a great variety of relationships between the state and the economy.

Great Britain, the firstcomer to modern industry, made its initial break-through with little or no deliberately developmental effort by the government—more, in fact, as a consequence of freeing private enterprise from medieval and mercantilistic restrictions. But, as the new industrial economy took shape in the nineteenth century, the British government found it increasingly necessary to intervene to check abuses and to cope with new problems. By the middle of the twentieth century, the concept of the welfare state had become firmly established in Britain. Britain's economy was a mixture of private enterprise and socialism. The profits of private enterprise were tempered by stiff income and inheritance taxes. The socialism was a liberal socialism, that is, one associated with personal and political freedom under laws adopted by a government responsive to the people in free elections.

On the continent of Europe—in Germany, for example—the state played a more active role in the early stages of economic modernization than had been the case in Britain. The state was more often an industrial promoter or an entrepreneur, though private enterprise carried out most of the actual operations of commercial and industrial expansion.

The United States of America relied principally on private, profit-motivated initiative to develop its modern economy. But the role of the state should not be underrated. The American government in the nineteenth century opened extensive new land areas to settlement, especially by building or subsidizing canals and railways. It also shaped the course of development by important policy decisions. One of the most significant was the Homestead Act, which made land in the nonsettled Western regions available free to anyone who would settle on it and cultivate it. Another was the establishment throughout the country of land-grant colleges and universities, so named because the federal government provided grants of public land to help the various states establish institutions of higher education devoted to improvement of agriculture and the mechanical arts. These universities, with funds provided jointly by federal and state governments, set up agricultural experiment stations and spread the results of research to farmers through agricultural extension services. The Homestead Act, the land-grant universities, and the publicly financed agricultural research and extension services represented crucial decisions in what would nowadays be called development policy. It was in no small measure due to these decisions that the United States not only achieved one of the most productive agricultural systems in the world and integrated it with modern industry but also avoided the creation of those great landed estates—latifundia—which were created in Latin America, where there was also nonsettled land, and which had such a harmful influence on Latin American economic, social, and political development.

Another highly significant aspect of the role of government in American economic development is the free, universal, public education that very early became American policy. A tremendous public investment was made in education. This has paid handsome dividends; it is one of the key factors in explaining why the American economy has a higher productivity than any other major economy and also why it continues to show a high degree of adaptability, innovation, and progress. Characteristically, this public investment in education has been made, not through the federal government, but almost entirely by state and local governments. The education industry is largely run by locally elected boards, made up of citizens who contribute their time. In some countries, universal educational opportunity at public expense is put forward as a socialist aim. But Americans do not think of their universal, publicly financed educational system as socialism. Rather, they view it as a means of promoting individual opportunity and responsible self-government. This is one more example of how meaningless labels like socialism, capitalism, or free enterprise can be in relation to practical realities.

Japan was the first Asian country to develop a modern economy. Following the Meiji restoration of 1868, the government vigorously promoted economic modernization by sending many Japanese abroad for training and by importing technical assistance. With great energy, it built up a public educational system. The government served as midwife to important industrial projects, sometimes directly through state investments that were later turned over to private enterprise, sometimes through assistance and subsidies. The initiative of the government was supplemented by that of great private combines owned by powerful families, whose widespread interests and close ties with the political rulers gave them an outlook on economic development almost as broad as that of the state. In addition, there were tens of thousands of small private enterprises, which contributed in the aggregate an important part of Japan's growing production and exports. They were generally linked in subordinate relationships, through sub-contracts, to larger manufacturers or trading firms.

In terms of economic development, Japan's system worked. But there were grave social and political defects in it, such as excessive influence of the military and perpetuation of an oligarchic, almost feudal, type of control over the national life, which set the stage for a policy of aggressive expansion and for the disastrous defeat in World War II. Following the war and the measures of democratization imposed by the Allied occupation—for example, in such fields as land reform and education—Japan has again shown great capacity for economic development. The role of the state in setting targets, directing, and co-ordinating is very important, while private enterprise receives encouragement and has responded with initiative and innovative vigor.

In the Soviet Union, as we all know, development has gone forward for nearly fifty years now, under a system in which the role of the state, dominated by the Party, is absolute. There is a highly centralized system of over-all planning. State monopolies operate all large-scale commerce, finance, and industry, while the collectives or co-operatives that function in agriculture and small-scale commerce and artisan activities are fundamentally state-directed. Since Marxist dogma holds that anyone who employs labor and produces at a profit must be an exploiter, no private economic enterprise of even moderate size is permitted. The system is monolithic rather than pluralistic; that is, economic power, political power, and social power are concentrated in the hands of the all-powerful state-Party apparatus. Under Stalin, it was a totalitarian system in the sense that someone has defined, with only slight exaggeration, as a system where everything is either prohibited or compulsory. Since Stalin, there have been some evidences of loosening. This illiberal type of socialism—that is, socialism combined with political dictatorship—has in the Soviet Union achieved a rapid pace of industrial growth. It has put great emphasis on scientific and technological development, education, and provision of medical care and similar welfare measures for the masses. Its weaknesses have been in agriculture, the production and distribution of consumer goods, and the lack of personal freedom.

Thus, in Great Britain, continental Europe, America, Japan, and the Soviet Union, we see countries that have modernized and developed their economies, but the historical paths they have traveled toward economic development have been very diverse, especially with respect to the role of the state in development. There is every reason to suppose that in the future, too, a multiplicity of patterns will continue.

Look at today's newly developing countries. Among those that have achieved fairly rapid economic modernization and growth during the last decade or two, we might list Mexico, Puerto Rico, Greece, Israel, and the Republic of China on Taiwan. All these represent mixed economies, with substantial government initiative in development and also substantial private enterprise. But there is a fairly wide diversity among them as to specific development methods used by the governments and as to the interrelations of the public and private sectors. If we take avowedly Communist countries—for example, Bulgaria, Yugoslavia, Hungary, and mainland China—here, too, along with the basic similarity of a much greater role for the state, we find a considerable diversity in specific methods.

Diversity is natural, for the situation of every country is unique. Even if this were not so, experiments with different methods would be justified. Despite what the doctrinaires and dogmatists of the extreme left or the extreme right say, there is no single right way to develop a country, no "correct line" from which all departures are wrongheaded deviations.

I can assure you that this point is much better appreciated nowadays than formerly by serious American students of the development process and by responsible policy makers. It is now recognized as naïve to think that the economic and political institutions that Americans have selected and molded over a century and a half to suit their conditions and temperaments could be transplanted to very different economic and cultural backgrounds without substantial modifications or that they would work the way they do in America. The same principle of nontransferability applies also to the political and economic institutions and development formulas of other countries, including those that are Communist.

Therefore, leaders in newly developing countries and advisers who assist them will be wise to study the good and bad experiences of many countries, not to imitate any one exactly. It is better to adapt (not simply adopt) ideas and practices from several sources, to invent a new combination of policies and methods particularly designed for the circumstances and aspirations of the country concerned.

To repeat: There is more than one feasible road to economic development. But this does *not* mean that all roads are equally good. Some policies and methods are likely to be more effective than others in achieving economic advance. Some have social and political advantages or drawbacks. Let us explore these issues further.

Tasks of Government in Economic Development

What are the crucial tasks of government in a country striving to make the great transition from a traditional, preindustrial economy to a modern, industrial one? They can be divided conveniently into three major groups: (1) creating the physical and social foundations for development; (2) over-all planning and integration of development; and (3) bringing about larger and more efficient production and distribution of goods and services.

Physical and Social Foundations of Development A modernizing economy requires large investments in new physical facilities: roads, dams, irrigation canals, power systems, telephone and telegraph networks, school buildings, and urban facilities such as paved streets, water supply, and sewage disposal. Usually these requirements must be met by public authority.

Besides physical facilities, however, governments of developing countries have to build some very important social foundations of development. Most important is provision for education. This means not only primary and secondary schools and higher

education but also several types of adult education that are
particularly important and rewarding from the standpoint of
economic development. Among these are agricultural extension
services; community development work involving education for
literacy, health, and local self-government; industrial extension
services; and inservice training to modernize and upgrade the
skills of managers and workers in industry, commerce, and other
fields, including the government's own civil service.

To create adequate social foundations for development, it is
often necessary to carry through agrarian and social reforms.
These are needed to open the way for more effective participation
in national development by hitherto underprivileged groups and
to release potential sources of human energy and initiative.

Planning and Integration of Development　　The government
must take responsibility for analyzing the country's economic position and its development potentials, determining feasible and
mutually consistent development goals, and devising ways to
move the economy toward those goals as rapidly and smoothly as
possible. This requires (1) analysis of resources, (2) setting of
short-range and long-range targets for economic advance, sector
by sector and so far as feasible industry by industry, and (3)
spelling out for the information of all concerned what the attainment of the proposed targets will mean in increased production
and in increased requirements for materials and equipment,
trained man power, capital, and foreign exchange. This process, if
it is realistic and followed up by positive measures of implementation, creates well-founded expectations that enable all economic
agencies, governmental and private, to base their own plans and
decisions on a common general plan and thus to work together for
economic expansion. Such planning also makes it possible to foresee where resource shortages are likely to develop—for example, a
shortage of foreign exchange or of certain types of highly trained
man power—and to take steps to remedy the deficiencies or, if
this is not possible, to readjust the targets.

It is desirable to bring into the planning process representatives of the important operating agencies of the government and
of the various private economic interests and groups whose team-

work is needed if plans are to become realities. This participation and involvement are especially important in mixed economies, for the private sector can make a significant contribution to the attainment of national goals, provided it is stimulated and encouraged to do so.

Achieving Larger and More Efficient Production and Distribution The tasks of actually establishing and operating productive economic enterprises—farms and factories, trade, and finance—are, of course, differently handled under different politico-economic systems. The possible methods include: (1) direct government or quasi-government operation, (2) provision of the legal framework and the physical and social foundations that encourage private individuals and firms to produce and sell goods and services, their incentive being business profits, or (3) a combination of these methods. An additional possibility, often a part of the combination, is production and distribution by various kinds of co-operatives or by special corporate bodies in which the public sector and the private sector participate jointly.

In practice, as we have noted, nearly all countries today use some type of mixed system. Governments presiding over mixed systems have many ways of influencing the private sector: by taxes and subsidies, by providing sound marketing information, by training programs, by regulations and allocations, and by manipulating market prices. The term "managed market economy" has been used to characterize systems in which the government gives considerable stimulus and direction to the private sector, but largely by influencing the market mechanism rather than by direct commands.

I have watched and sometimes participated in the development efforts of governments in a number of newly developing countries in Asia, Africa, and Latin America. Based on this experience, it is my opinion that most governments could do a much better job than they are now doing at managing the market economy. They could harness the private sector much more effectively and helpfully to the national development plan if they consciously set about it and skillfully employed a suitable combination of methods. Among these methods would be:

1. Economic studies and marketing surveys to reveal new opportunities for constructive private enterprise in industry, agriculture, and commerce, taking into account the planned economic growth of the country.

2. Wide dissemination of information about these new opportunities, together with offers of various kinds of help to innovating entrepreneurs, through agricultural and industrial advisory services, development of financing agencies, applied research centers, and institutes for imparting new or improved skills to managers, technicians, and workers.

3. Price incentives and disincentives to make it more profitable to produce the things most helpful to national development and less profitable to produce wasteful or harmful items, this price manipulation to be achieved through a variety of methods such as subsidies, taxes, and regulation of imports.

Unfortunately, governments all too often resort to direct administrative regulation (by means of licenses, allocations, quotas, and the like) or even undertake the management of industrial and commercial operations, when indirect manipulation through the market-price system and the other devices just mentioned would be more effective in achieving the desired results.

For example, industrial growth in a certain country was being seriously hampered by shortages of a number of important raw materials. The government established administrative controls for the allocation of these materials to manufacturers at low fixed prices. The results? (1) High rewards to pseudo manufacturers who by influence or bribery could obtain allotments at the official price and then sell in the black market that quickly developed. (2) Administrative breakdown and corruption of public officials. (3) Disincentives to efficient, growing firms, for allotments were based on production data several years old, and to expand, a manufacturer would have to buy in the black market at higher prices than those paid by nonexpanding and probably less efficient competitors.

These were not at all the results the government sought. It would probably have been better to allow the prices of the scarce materials to rise somewhat, thus encouraging substitution of other materials where possible, and also to dampen the demand for the scarce materials by stiff taxes on the nonessential end products embodying important amounts of them. These measures for making the market mechanism work in favor of the government's developmental purposes, rather than against them, would also have had the advantage of being administratively feasible, whereas the much more ambitious effort to allocate and control every ton of the scarce materials imposed an impossible task on the already overloaded administrative personnel and produced an administrative breakdown.

I wish someone would write a practical, down-to-earth treatise for government officials of developing countries on how to use the market mechanism instead of fighting it, how to enlist incentives of private gain to support the economic development plan instead of creating situations in which these powerful and pervasive forces are made to work against the government's aims.

To enlist the private sector effectively in support of the development plan, it is, of course, essential to persuade the private sector that its constructive efforts are wanted and that rewards can be won by efficiency and expansion of production. In one country that I know, the government successively nationalized certain foreign firms, then all foreign firms, then all large industrial and business operations, each time alleging that this was the end of nationalization. A friend of mine who was working with this government in a technical assistance program designed to improve the managerial efficiency and productivity of smaller manufacturers told me his troubles. In the shoe industry, for example, there were nationalized units run as so-called co-operatives by government officials and also small private manufacturers. When my friend tried to interest the government-designated managers in technical improvements and better business methods, he found little interest; they had no incentive to try something new that might be risky and get them into trouble. When, on the other hand, he offered his help to the small private manufacturers, they, too, were unreceptive; they feared that if they became conspicuous by being efficient and growing, they would be nationalized. So a segment of industry that, by better state policies, could have been stimulated to modernize and produce more shoes at lower costs was working very inefficiently and showing little progress, either in the state sector or the private sector.

Developing a Pluralistic Society

Finally, and very briefly, the third theme: Wise decisions about the role of the state in economic life and about the role of the private sector will take into account not only economic considerations—that is, how to achieve a rapid increase in production, income, and living levels—but also the social and political consequences of alternative approaches. What may be the repercussions of different patterns of government economic activity and of different attitudes toward private enterprise on growth in freedom, individual initiative, and ability of more people to participate effectively in self-government? On advancement of personal liberty and human dignity?

Development leaders who aim at true democracy will be wise to develop a pluralistic society—one in which economic power and political power and social power are not concentrated in the same hands. This means developing *different*, though overlapping, leadership groups or elites in the major areas of national life—economic, political, educational, religious, artistic, and so on. Those who control the wealth should not also have uninhibited control of the government and the educational system, and vice versa. Those who direct the police should not also direct the farms and factories and the artistic life of the country. Such a "separation of powers" distinguishes a healthy democratic society from despotisms and oligarchies in which too many privileges and powers are held by relatively few families or in which a single-party elite controls everything.

Chapter 23

Equity versus Productivity in Economic Development

Max F. Millikan

The conditions in which the presently underdeveloped countries are seeking to expand their productivity, modernize their economies, and launch a process of self-sustaining growth of per capita national income and product differ in many ways from the circumstances obtaining during the nineteenth century, when most of the presently developed countries got themselves started on a path of growth. Not the least of these differences is that in eighteenth-century England or nineteenth-century France, Germany, and America, the idea of devoting governmental policy to the promotion of social justice and an equitable distribution of the fruits of progress to the various sectors of the community was still very much in its infancy.

While the consciences of a few Westerners were troubled at the time by the injustices created by the Industrial Revolution, and there was some pressure for reforms in child labor, imprisonment of debtors, and the like, it was not until the twentieth century that the West saw the flowering of the concept of the welfare state and the invention of the principal public instruments currently employed in the pursuit of economic equity, like the progressive income tax and social security legislation.

In contrast, the underdeveloped countries of today are entering on the development process in a climate of world-wide concern for distributive justice that makes it impossible for any modern democratic state, whatever its stage of development, to neglect considerations of equity in the formulation of its development policy.

There are two reasons why the statesman or politician of today must concern himself with social justice. The first is that today's moral climate requires that a politician responsive to public opinion should be able to demonstrate that social justice is one of his central concerns. From this point of view, what matters, of course, is less the substance of real social justice than the symbolic evidences of an apparent concern with it. As we shall see presently, measures taken in the name of social justice may frequently inhibit rather than promote it in reality. From this standpoint, the language in terms of which policies are described may be more important to the politician than their actual consequences.

The second reason for concern is a pragmatic one. Increasingly in the underdeveloped countries, aspirations for modernization and development are not limited to one group or class, but spread throughout the whole social structure. Unless opportunities to participate both in the fruits of development and in the activities that bring it about are widely distributed throughout the society, there may be serious frustration and social unrest, imperiling the minimum degree of political stability essential for effective development programs. Thus, a set of policies that produces in the short run a rapid rise in such national aggregates as gross national product, but concentrates the fruits of this progress on a limited range, sector, or social class, may in time produce strains in the society that will bring development to a halt. Here the pragmatic concern is with genuine equity, and not with the symbolic language used to describe national policy.

It may be helpful, to begin with, to outline the various senses in which the word "equity" is applied to the development process. The first has to do with the contrast between the rich and the poor, or with what the economist calls the distribution of income by income class. Income is unquestionably more unequally distributed in underdeveloped than in developed societies, in the sense that traditional societies exhibit a dramatic contrast between the mass of the population, existing at income levels barely sufficient for subsistence, and a tiny elite, enjoying a level of affluence in many cases beyond that achieved even by the captains of industry in a Western state.

A second inequity present in most underdeveloped countries is the disparity in average living standards among the different regions in the country. Most countries, developed or underdeveloped, have backward regions like the Northeast in Brazil, the Andean highlands in Peru, or the south of Italy, where the average level of income is but a fraction of that in the more prosperous areas.

A third and somewhat related type of disparity is that between the rural areas and the urban centers. While there is tragic poverty in most big cities, average incomes there turn out to be two or three times those of rural communities, even when the desperately poor are included in the urban averages. This injects a dimension of equity in the problem of the relative priority to be given to agriculture as against industry in development programs; but, as we shall see presently, apparent equity is a poor basis on which to make the ultimate decisions.

A fourth form in which the problem of equity presents itself to policy makers is the question of what priority should be given to the interests of consumers, as against those of producers. In one sense, this is a false dilemma, since most members of society play roles both as consumers and as producers, and what will help them in one capacity may hurt them in the other. Nonetheless, the problem arises in this form when governments are deciding what to do about such questions as controlling the price of foodstuffs. From the standpoint of the low-income consumer, equity suggests that these prices should be held down; but from the standpoint of the low-income agricultural producer, a policy of price supports appears more likely to promote an increase in output. Frequently this dilemma becomes a special case of the urban-rural problem, since the producers of foodstuffs live in the countryside, while the most politically vocal consumers are likely to be urban populations.

A fifth form in which issues of equity arise has to do with competing claims or shares of the national product among the different functional groups in the population. Should special consideration be given in governmental policy to wage earners represented by unions, to farmers, to small entrepreneurs, to civil servants, to teachers and professional groups? One of the difficulties here is that the political influence of special functional groups may not be closely correlated with either their numbers or their real importance to the economy.

A special problem of equity of particular importance in many underdeveloped countries is created by a large volume of unemployment. In the developed countries, the standard remedy for large-scale unemployment is to increase the aggregate level of economic activity to whatever degree is necessary to reduce unemployment to a tolerable minimum. This is usually a feasible policy because the other items required for economic expansion, like capital and raw materials, are usually available in the developed world in sufficient quantity to absorb virtually the whole of the labor force. In the underdeveloped countries, the ceilings on output are set, not by the labor force, but rather by the availability of capital, foreign exchange, managerial talents, and the like, and the economy may therefore be operating at the full capacity set by these ceilings while there are still large numbers of unemployed workers. In these circumstances, more employment may be obtainable only by sharply reducing the efficiency of production and thus the total national income; and yet the inequities created by large-scale unemployment can be peculiarly destructive.

Finally, the tug of war between equity and productivity may take the form of conflicts over the problem of what things are to be produced in a developing society. Equity may call for a heavy expenditure on housing, social services, health, and education. These things are all expensive in resources. They all undoubtedly make a contribution to productivity, but per dollar of expenditure, that contribution may be very much less than an equivalent investment in plant and equipment of a more directly productive kind. An underdeveloped country that sets itself the immediate goal of providing what, by some standards, would be described as decent housing for its entire population would almost certainly have no capital resources left over to do anything else.

Having outlined a few of the many dimensions of the problem of social justice in the development context, it is appropriate to ask how far and in what circumstances pursuit of any of these sorts of equity is complementary with maximizing the rate of growth of productivity and how far it is competitive. It is important at the outset to underline one point with particular emphasis. This is that without substantial development, in the sense of a rapid increase in the economic productivity of the economy, no real improvement in the lot of the underprivileged is possible. The pie is so small in all the underdeveloped countries that the welfare of any substantial underprivileged group cannot be significantly advanced by mere redistribution to them from the more fortunate. This is not a matter of opinion, but is demonstrable from a little rough arithmetic. The average per capita income figure for a country indicates what the income of each citizen would be if incomes were distributed absolutely equally to every member of the society. A comparison of this figure with the estimated income of the less fortunate will give some indication of the maximum amount by which their welfare could be advanced by the most extreme measures of redistribution that could be adopted. For most underdeveloped countries, this gap is fairly small. Thus, the basic hope of improvement in the lot of the less fortunate lies in increasing the size of the pie rather than changing the way it is cut.

One implication of this proposition is that wherever one finds situations in which what appears to be the equitable thing to do is clearly and demonstrably in conflict with increasing productivity, the increase in productivity must take precedence. In other words, the pursuit of equity without reference to or in conflict with productivity is very likely to prove self-defeating.

To set the stage for a discussion of some of the possible areas of conflict, let me first give some examples of situations in which considerations of equity and productivity, rather than competing, complement and reinforce each other. Firstly, with respect to the urban-rural or the industry-agriculture dimension, economists, after engaging in numerous fruitless polemics as to whether urban-based industry should have priority over rural-based agriculture, have now generally concluded that in most countries each is necessary to the other and that a lag in the development of either can inhibit or stall the growth of the other. There are almost no cases on record of sustained agricultural development without some industrial development, and a common index of the rate of modernization is the decline in the proportion of the labor force in agriculture. On the other hand, recent experience throughout most of the underdeveloped world has underlined the conclusion that urban industrial development depends, both for markets for its products and for supplies of food and clothing for its labor force, on a prosperous and expanding agriculture. There are some conflicts in specific areas of policy to which we shall come presently between urban–rural equity and the productivity of both sectors; but, broadly speaking, it is clear that promotional effort by government must be divided between them reasonably equitably, if national productivity is to advance.

Again, broadly speaking, the taxation necessary to finance the development efforts of governments in the underdeveloped world must fall ultimately on virtually all classes in the society, because with the exception of a few special cases like the oil-producing countries, there is no single group or activity capable of providing enough resources to finance the kind of effort that is needed to launch self-sustaining economic growth. Again, at the margin, there are some conflicts between equity and productivity to which we shall return presently; but, in the large, the arithmetic of governmental need dictates that all sectors shall make a contribution.

Now let us turn to a number of the stickier problems of conflict between equity and productivity. The first of these relates to the basic question of who is to pay for the substantial volume of government expenditure that is necessary for growth in virtually all underdeveloped countries. The basic problem here is that it is necessary to design the tax system with two purposes in mind. The first purpose is to restrict the consumption expenditures of the community to the extent required to release productive resources for purposes of public and private investment and for expenditures on at least minimal quantities of social services like education and public health. The second purpose is to design the tax structure in such a way as to maintain at a high level the incentives for saving and productive investment in the private sector. If taxation is designed simply to divert resources from private, productive investment into public investment or services, leaving consumption essentially unchanged, the goal of higher national economic productivity cannot be reached. In developed countries, heavy reliance is placed today on the progressive income tax. The higher levels of income are sufficiently great here and profit prospects sufficiently attractive so that a large part of the required government financing can come from the middle- and upper-income groups without creating a seriously depressing effect on private incentives. In many underdeveloped countries, the basic arithmetic is different, and the adoption of similar techniques of taxation at rates high enough to yield the necessary revenues is very likely to inhibit private investment and bring development to a halt. Another problem in underdeveloped countries is that the effective administration of a progressive income tax requires a level of statistical sophistication and administrative competence in tax collection that is beyond the capabilities of most underdeveloped countries.

Accordingly, it has been increasingly recognized in recent years that underdeveloped countries must rely much more heavily than developed ones on sales and excise taxes. These are less equitable because they are less progressive than income and corporation taxes; but this simply reflects the hard fact that when average incomes are low, the reduction of consumption essential to development is inevitably going to hurt more people and create more short-run inequity than in countries at higher levels of development. One can attempt to design excises so that their incidence is least on the essential goods necessary to survival, but if a poor country wishes to raise itself from poverty by its own bootstraps, there is no other way than by imposing some burden on the poorer sections of the community.

A second area in which some inescapable conflicts between equity and productivity arise is that of regional concentration vs. dispersion. A great deal of attention has been paid in the development literature to the concept of take-off, or the theory of the big push. The central notion here is that the rate of development is not strictly proportional to the effort put into it, but that for many reasons there is a certain minimum scale or threshold of effort required before a country has any prospect of moving into self-sustaining growth. Part of the reason for this is that a wide variety of economic activities are dependent on each other and that when they are all present together, they mutually reinforce and strengthen each other; but when a few elements are missing, the whole enterprise is stalled on dead center. Thus, an industrial complex requires transport, power, repair facilities, credit institutions, industries to supply raw materials and parts, other industries to take the product and provide processing and merchandising facilities, and so on.

This argument applies not only to whole countries but to regions of countries and even to metropolitan complexes. It is cited as one of the reasons why the history of development in the presently developed countries has not been one of balanced growth throughout the whole economy, but rather one of spurts of growth in growing points centered in particular cities or parts of the country that have moved ahead rapidly, leaving other regions behind to catch up later, sometimes much later. This is a problem that is now beginning to plague a good many underdeveloped countries, which confront the dilemma of whether to concentrate their very scarce resources in a few areas, in the hope of getting them over the threshold of mutually reinforcing activities necessary to sustained expansion, or to spread their resources more evenly, giving everyone a little and running the risk that more or less everywhere this little will be too small to have any permanent effect.

There are standard economic difficulties on this course, such as the interdependence of large numbers of economic activities and the fact that for technical reasons in many cases larger units are more efficient (and therefore have lower cost per unit) than smaller ones. To these must be added another factor peculiar to the underdeveloped world. This is that the scarcest resource in many underdeveloped countries—scarcer than capital or foreign exchange or tax capacity—is the supply of administrative and managerial talent capable of giving guidance and direction to an economic development effort. The pool of administrative talent is likewise subject to thresholds of effectiveness and can produce much more significant results if it is concentrated on a few areas and on a few problems than if it is spread thinly over the whole economy. It is increasingly coming to be recognized that an underdeveloped country will have much better chances of success in its development efforts if it concentrates both regionally and by sector, rather than by trying to do a little bit of everything. This inevitably creates problems of equity, which are rendered more severe by the fact that such concentration is likely to be more productive if it is focused on regions and sectors that are already doing significantly better than average. In other words, it exaggerates the natural disparities that would occur in any case.

This problem of concentration occurs not only in the aggregate, as between broad geographic regions, but perhaps even more acutely within individual sectors. In agriculture, for instance, the issue poses itself as one of whether to attempt to help all farmers in a given region with a little fertilizer, extension advice, access to credit, and improved seeds or to concentrate initially on the 5 or 10 per cent of the farmers who have demonstrated the most energy, willingness to innovate, and capacity to adopt new ideas. Recent experience suggests that from the standpoint of productivity, the most effective procedure is the so-called package approach, in which a relatively small number of farmers are supplied with everything they need to make a major effort at modernization of agricultural technology, in the hope that this can later be extended to a larger and larger fraction of the farming community.

Within industry, similar problems arise, but for somewhat different reasons. There is great attraction in the idea of attempting in each industrial field to support the efforts of a substantial number of relatively small producers to expand simultaneously and thus to develop a highly competitive situation in the early stages of industrial growth, training through experience a large number of entrepreneurs, of whom the best will ultimately develop into managers of large-scale enterprises. The difficulty with this approach is that it postpones, perhaps too long, the benefits of the great economies that large-scale units can achieve in a number of fields and thus keeps costs of the products being produced too high to encourage their utilization. Fertilizer is a good illustration of this. Recent technological advance has made it possible to reduce the costs of manufacture of fertilizers very substantially by increasing the scale of the individual producing unit. This may be critical to making the use of fertilizer sufficiently attractive economically to induce large numbers of farmers to adopt it. It does, however, conflict with the policy of providing equitable opportunity for the largest possible number of entrepreneurs to get into the fertilizer business. The evidence from a number of countries suggests that in many industries, government policy to date has led to too many producing units, each of which is of an uneconomically small size, with a consequent inhibition on the over-all growth of the economy.

In the long run, there is some evidence that the development of small-scale industry is complementary to, rather than competitive with, the emergence of large-scale units. In the developed economies, large enterprises like automobile firms, which expand the market for their product rapidly by taking advantage of the economies of scale, provide in turn a flourishing market for the products and services of a large number of small firms who supply them with specialized components, parts, repair facilities, and service opportunities that would not exist if the large enterprise were not present. Thus, what appears superficially to be a policy violating equity may in the long run produce a more hopeful environment for the little man than a restrictive policy designed explicitly for his benefit.

Another area in the industrial field where equity may superficially be in conflict with productivity has to do with governmental policy toward large profits. In the underdeveloped world, profits are widely regarded, for good historical reasons, as a type of income not closely related to social welfare, and governments are under strong political pressures to restrict profits by price controls, steeply progressive profits taxes, and other means. When applied, however, to the newer manufacturing and productive activities in which entrepreneurs are increasingly engaging in the underdeveloped countries, these measures may well inhibit investment by discouraging the flow of savings into such activities. It is possible to discourage nonproductive uses of profits in other ways, such as by high excise taxes on consumer goods, luxury housing, and the like, and these techniques are likely to be less inhibiting to industrial expansion than direct profit limitation.

The third area in which, during the past decade, politics in a number of underdeveloped countries has thrown up what looks like a conflict between equity and productivity has to do with the concerns of consumers as opposed to those of producers. The place where this conflict is most evident is in policies affecting what the economist calls the rural-urban terms of trade, which means the relative prices of foodstuffs and agricultural products, on the one hand, as compared with manufactured goods on the other. In countries like India, the government has been under great pressure to keep the prices of foodstuffs low, especially to urban consumers, by a variety of means, including price controls. On the other hand, the most accessible markets for manufactured consumer goods are in the middle- and upper-income brackets in the metropolitan areas, and therefore there has been little incentive for the industrial community to concentrate on the production of really cheap manufactured necessities for the low-income rural market. The result has been that the relation between the prices farmers could get for their products and the prices they have had to pay both for agricultural inputs like fertilizers, tools, pumps, and the like and for manufactured consumer goods has been very unfavorable to the farmer and has prevented economic incentives for the modernization of agriculture from operating effectively.

There are several paradoxes in this situation. The first is that the political influence of different underprivileged groups has been inversely proportional to their numbers. In most underdeveloped countries, there are many more farmers than low-income city dwellers, and yet the politically effective pressures for the kind of price policies that have been pursued have been exerted in behalf of equity to a small minority group which has, in fact, been unfair to the rural majority. It is only in countries like the United

States, where farmers are less than 10 per cent of the labor force, that they have been able to achieve special economic treatment on grounds of equity.

The second paradox is that these policies have had the consequence of seriously inhibiting the production of precisely those items of the national product most urgently needed by the poorest sector of the population, namely, food and simple clothing. What we have here is not a real substantive conflict between equity and productivity, but a conflict between one group, representing a minority of the population, and the national welfare, which has been cast in symbolic equity terms. In fact, holding down the prices of food not only inhibits production but also depresses the incomes of the agricultural sector in which the majority of the population in all these countries lives.

There are several ways out of the dilemma. The first, which should be pushed much more vigorously than it has been, is the improvement of storage, marketing, and distribution, so as to reduce sharply the margin between what the farmer receives for his produce and what the city dweller pays for his food. If successful, this would have the effect of raising both incomes and incentives for the farmer without penalizing the urban consuming groups. Similarly, on the other side of the coin, improvement in marketing and distribution in rural areas of both agricultural inputs and the manufactured consumer goods available to farmers could reduce the cost of these things to the rural buyer without limiting the incentives to the manufacturer of a satisfactory price for his product. Economists have been negligent in studying ways of reducing marketing margins for both agricultural products and manufactured goods delivered to rural areas. Accordingly, we do not know how far the conflict between equity to consumers and productivity to producers can be resolved by improving marketing efficiency. My suspicion is that it cannot be wholly resolved in this fashion and that some programs of subsidy may be necessary to ensure equity to low-income consumers and still retain the necessary production incentives. This has been tried in a few places with such items as fertilizer with very promising results, but it needs much more thoroughgoing study. In any case, one conclusion we can draw with some certainty is that efforts to maintain equity to consumers by holding final prices down are very likely to be self-defeating because of their negative effects on productivity.

Finally, a word about an area of conflict relating to employment. Here the problem arises from the fact that many of the key activities involved in industrial development take the lion's share of a developing country's limited capital funds, but do not create many jobs. There has been much talk about the urgency of seeking a new labor-intensive technology in industries which in the West require very large amounts of capital per employee, but nobody has yet come up with ways of generating power, pumping and refining oil, or making steel which use lots of labor and very little capital. The experience of many underdeveloped countries provides ample evidence that the forces of the market, left to themselves, will not stimulate types of economic activity that will provide full employment for the rapidly growing labor force being created by the population explosion. The very real pressures of the growing army of unemployed have led some countries to adopt legislative measures intended to protect employment and generate more, even where this reduces the efficiency of production and thus slows down the rate of growth. This is the wrong solution. There are ways of utilizing the surplus labor resources of the underdeveloped countries in activities that require very little capital, but can make an important positive contribution to the output and productivity of the economy. These include such things as rural public works programs, the building of roads, the construction of irrigation and drainage facilities, the clearing and preparation of land for more effective agriculture, and the like. These are kinds of activities that are not likely to be stimulated by market forces and require very high levels of organizational and administrative attention, which can probably come only from government. They are, however, one of the important ways of trying to solve the socially and politically serious injustices of massive unemployment without conflicting seriously with the goal of economic growth.

In conclusion, in examining a number of apparent conflicts between equity and productivity in development policy, we have concluded, first, that some of these conflicts are more symbolic than real and require mainly a change in the language in which things are described. Others are subject to resolution by pushing forward vigorously with solutions that avoid the dilemma. A few are real and perhaps unavoidable. In these cases, to yield to the demands of equity at the expense of productivity in the short run is likely to be self-defeating in the long run. The only ultimate solution for the problems of the underprivileged in the underdeveloped countries is to generate more rapid economic growth, out of the fruits of which, once achieved, social justice can be realized.

Chapter 24

Breakdowns
in Modernization

Joseph J. Spengler

Modernization has numerous dimensions, of which only some are economic. These dimensions are interrelated, but not in a hard and fast fashion.

We may think of increase in modernization as representing broadening in man's range of choice. Economic progress extends —though it never completely removes—the physical limits thereto. Modernization, of course, brings in its wake additional constraints on man's freedom of choice, but far fewer than it eliminates; these constraints are associated mainly with changes in noneconomic dimensions of modernization.

Interruption of the forward movement of societies is not new. Many instances are to be found in ancient and premodern times and even in recent times, before modernization as we understand it had got under way. Of greater current concern is the persistent depression of the rate of economic growth and modernization in relatively advanced countries as well as threats to incipient modernization in formerly colonial or nonautonomous countries.

Premodern Interruptions

Premodern societies differed from modern societies. First, they were based mainly on muscle power, whereas modern societies really began to flourish only with the advent of widely used mechanical power, which in turn is now being strongly complemented and sometimes superseded by brain power. Second, premodern societies tended to be smaller than modern societies, though a number of large land-borne empires did come into existence, of which only the Chinese and the Russian survive as entities. Third, premodern societies, especially the large ones, were much less tightly knit than modern societies. In premodern societies, the sinews that bind men together in modern societies—common language, effective means of communication, and a good transport system—were quite imperfectly developed; hence the empires that men formed, being unstable systems, tended to fragment into the more stable and tightly knit subsystems of which they were composed. Premodern societies thus were more vulnerable than modern societies to internal and external disruptive forces. Moreover, they were less effectively equipped with stabilizing politicoeconomic institutions that responded somewhat homeostatically to threats of internal or external origin. Finally, average output was very small, and the standard of life of the vast majority must have been extremely low and not generally expected to improve appreciably. They were not equipped with built-in fomenters of economic change. Indeed, until the advent of modern times, the pace of improvement must have been very slow, and periods of economic stagnation, if not also of economic retrogression, must have been quite common.

Many instances of stagnation and decline are reasonably well documented. Mention may be made of classical Greek and later Italian and other medieval city-states, of Roman Italy, of such great Western agrarian empires as the late Roman and the Byzantine, and even of periods in the histories of Bulgaria, France, Greece, Holland, and Portugal, among others. While decline was often set in motion by military defeat or descendancy, it was frequently accompanied by simple inability to meet the growing competition of newly emerging competitors. Among the economic changes sometimes accompanying decline, one finds diminution in population and economic aggregates, disruption of external and internal trade, increase in regional self-sufficiency and tax inequity, and monetary disorder. Even so, had these societies been equipped with the growth potential of modern societies, the immediate causes of their economic decline would not have halted their progress for long.

MODERNIZATION: ITS BEGINNINGS

The modernization of the Western world may be said to have begun little more than a century and a half ago when the very low rate of growth of per capita national product began to accelerate somewhat in the wake of the economic and technological revolutions already under way. Even so, at that time, the countries of northern and western Europe were economically much better off than most of today's emerging lands. They were much less densely populated, as a rule, and their rates of natural increase were still quite low and subject to further reduction through emigration. Their per capita incomes, which had long been increasing, albeit very slowly, were several or more times those found in present-day emerging nations. Their governments were based largely and increasingly on the application of empirical science.

Of perhaps even greater importance, these countries had already undergone something of an agricultural revolution. In some, the proportion of the labor force in agriculture was already below the three-fifths or more still so engaged in many underdeveloped countries. Furthermore, agriculturalists in these Western countries were already extricating themselves from that unpromising stationary condition of Malthusian trap in which the rural populations of many emerging lands still find themselves. The state of their agricultural arts was undergoing improvement, though not in a measure at all comparable to that experienced in a number of relatively advanced countries in the past several decades. It was possible for some operators of farms to save and form capital, a portion of which was plowed back into agriculture and

ment in the agricultural sector. Indeed, modernization and economic development long proceeded most slowly in those parts of Europe in which agriculture was least progressive. Representative is the Mediterranean world, long handicapped, as today is south Asia in even greater measure, by a social structure unconducive if not inimical to the improvement of agriculture through investment and technical progress. Modernization proceeded rapidly, on the other hand, in those parts of western Europe in which agriculture was progressive and the supply of foodstuffs and agricultural raw materials, especially cotton, was elastic, in part as a result of importation from abroad where European investment (mainly British) had facilitated the opening up of virgin lands. Meanwhile coal was displacing wood, directly as fuel and the source of energy, and indirectly as a means to the cheapening of brick and the production of iron and later steel and hence the provision of a much more elastic supply of construction materials. In sum, with the addition of inorganic materials to those of organic origin and the eventual ascendancy of inorganic over organic materials in relative importance, modernization and economic development became relatively free of the inelasticities that constrained agricultural expansion in and before the nineteenth century.

The beneficial role of a flexible price system was already clearly perceived in the eighteenth century, and measures designed to reduce this flexibility were strongly opposed. With improvements in transport and communication, moreover, and the enlargement of markets and their interconnections, the price system became increasingly effective in the performance of its various allocative functions. These same improvements served to complement sea-borne commerce and enlarge the trading area, thus generating the large-scale demands so significant for economic development in the West, the lack of which must have contributed importantly to the failure of industrialization to progress in India and China.

Where Modernization Was Interrupted

It is evident, from what has been said, that modernization could not emerge in the absence of capital formation, scientific and technical progress, adequacy of education, and a sufficiency of produce and raw materials. Primitive societies, in which little or no modernization is manifest except for negligible influences of foreign origin, are characterized by the deficiencies named; in them the standard of life becomes virtually stationary at a level compatible with a very low level of equipment, technical knowledge, education, and flow of produce and utilizable raw materials.

It is also evident that modernization can continue only so long as the sources of modernization and the constituents of development—capital, scientific and applied technical knowledge, education, produce, and raw materials—continue to grow appreciably faster than the population.

Instances of interrupted development in recent centuries are China and Japan. Three and one-half centuries ago, average output in these countries probably did not differ markedly from that in western Europe, for only later and mainly in and after the late eighteenth century did average output in western Europe begin to pull significantly away from that in advanced Asian countries. In these countries, traditional agriculture and handicraft industry were incapable of rapid expansion, and little attention was given to modifying the technological base of their economies. Nor could capital formation have been very high. Japan and, in lesser measure, China remained quite unreceptive to influence from Western nations, then beginning to modernize. In China, however, the role of the merchant, or businessman, often an important initiator of progressive activities, was quite restricted, whereas in Tokugawa, Japan, it was not prevented from growing in importance. It was not until these lands believed themselves threatened by Western powers, however, that they gave consideration to the selective absorption of Western technology and methods. This response proved ineffective in China, handicapped as it was by a weak government, poor means of transport and communication, and a system of thought and bureaucratic procedure inimical to change;

hence, only in quite recent decades could modernization really begin. In Japan, on the contrary, an able government, with the widespread support of important elements in the population, was able in the eighteen-sixties to initiate modernization of the country, a task facilitated by the considerable groundwork in education, enterprise, and so forth developed prior to the Meiji restoration. Under the aegis of this government, Japan gradually erected pillars of modernization until today, despite a residual dualism in its economy, it is included among the small number of modern states. In the past several decades, of course, the rate of economic development and modernization has risen notably in China, though not yet in all sectors.

India supplies still another example of arrested development. It differs from China and Japan, however, in that it fell partly under foreign rule with the Moslem conquests and eventually passed into colonial status under British rule after having experienced more than a century of decline. British rule brought with it the seeds of modernization, but they did not take root widely and flourish in the interval between 1850 and 1950, although some industrial undertakings were initiated already in the eighteen-fifties. There was aggregate growth, of course, but little if any more than enough to match the growth of population. Thus, average income grew between 1900 and 1920, only to become stationary until in the nineteen-fifties. While various circumstances contributed to this retardation—shortage of capital, attitudes and values of many Indian businessmen, cultural obstacles—operation under alien government may have been the major handicap, for British interests did not entirely coincide with what would have been India's interests, were she autonomous. Moreover, the British government in India was unwilling to undertake in the public sector sufficient investments essential to the development of the private sector or to depend, as it might have done, on Indian industry for sufficient purchases of equipment to stimulate that industry's expansion. Not until independence, therefore, did the interests of government and society become roughly identical. Although modernization is now effectively under way, its pace is conditioned by the rate of detraditionalization of its agriculture, the degree to which its formation of capital and skilled personnel can be stepped up, and, as in China, the measure in which its population growth can be brought under effective control.

Where Modernization Was Temporarily Interrupted

The countries of the world are divisible into those capable of self-sustaining economic growth and modernization and those in which this capability has not yet been attained. This capability is of relatively recent historical origin and manifest in only a small number of countries; yet they have been responsible for most of the modernization, development, and income growth taking place in the past century and one-half, and they have been the principal source of such modernization as is manifesting itself in lands in which full capability has not yet been attained.

The preconditions of this capability have already been identified. What is really of utmost significance, however, is the institutionalization of these preconditions. A variety of institutional arrangements have been developed to ensure that requisite amounts of physical capital are formed each year, that there are sufficient outlays on education and scientific progress, and that, through invention and innovation, additions to the stock of nonobsolete knowledge are put to work. Upon the institutionalization of these arrangements, they are carried out automatically; then men need no longer continually choose whether to save, invest, and modernize, but only to decide into which channels to introduce increments in capital, man power, resources, and science. Capability for self-sustaining modernization and growth is attained when appropriate ways of doing have become internalized in men's minds, supported by external sanctions, and built into a society's public repositories of information.

Capability for self-sustaining modernization and growth does not imply immunity against forces that may slow down and even temporarily interrupt modernization and growth. Illustrative of such interruption in advanced countries is the trade cycle that decelerates growth and can even stop it altogether, though only for short periods until regenerative forces have become ascendant. Illustrative of growth-decelerating influences are whatever changes reduce the rates at which capital is formed and provision is made for investment in science and education or prevent the expansion of internal and external demand commensurately with the modernization of economies and growth in their capacity to produce.

With the exception of the impact of trade cycles and of policies that have slowed down economic development, there seems to have been only one fairly widespread deceleration of progress since countries began to acquire a capability for sustained modernization and growth. It had its origin principally in the two world wars that involved many countries, though in varying degrees, undermined international connections (for example, international monetary institutions), accentuated trade-cycle influences, and destroyed large amounts of the constituents of economic development as well as prevented their formation. Had the wars been confined to a small number of countries, there would have been deceleration in these; yet growth rates would have been quickly restored through assistance from those not materially affected. Indeed, recovery after World War I and particularly after World War II was greatly speeded by the fact that there remained countries which, though involved, had escaped the main ravages of conflict.

Between 1870 and 1913, output per head was advancing over 1 per cent per year in most of the advanced countries in Europe, though there seems to have been some slowing down in the eighteen-nineties—"the climacteric of the eighteen-nineties"—associated with partial exhaustion of improvement potentials in steam and steel without their replacement as yet by the potentials present in electricity, the internal combustion engine, and industrial chemistry. During the succeeding period, 1913–1950, output per head continued to advance as before in only one or two countries. In the others, it proceeded at a somewhat lower rate, especially in countries heavily affected by war. By 1950, however, productive capacity was restored. Since then, modernization and economic growth in developed countries have generally proceeded at rates 25–100 per cent above those attained in 1870–1913, for accumulating potentials in these countries are being effectively exploited, investment and education are at unusually high levels, demand has been allowed to expand freely, and various international barriers to economic development have been lowered.

Deceleration, if not actual reversal, of modernization assumes a different form in dualistic economies, of which there are many, in the underdeveloped world. Such an economy consists of two rather distinct sectors, one in which traditional methods predominate and the other centered in one or more cities and around modern primary industrial undertakings. Most of these economies were colonial or at least nonautonomous in status until recently; and the forces making for their modernization and the gradual displacement of traditional by modern ways came largely from outside. With the advent of independence, however, this situation changed, sometimes and perhaps often with the result that the rate of economic growth and modernization slowed down.

The responsible changes assume two principal forms: a diminution in means and alteration in the major objectives pursued. The loss of skilled foreign personnel has been common. The inflow of foreign capital may decline. Domestic capital, even if undiminished in supply, may be less efficiently used, as when industrialization is made to take excessive precedence over agriculture, with the result that dearth of food prevents orderly growth. Expansion of private enterprise may be retarded by governmental planners, given the usual shortage of competent bureaucrats and a frequent animus toward enterprise in general as well as toward successful ethnic minorities. Civil disorder may accentuate some of these difficulties by checking specialization and interregional commerce. Even when there is order, governmental propaganda may be used to hide failures and thereby weaken feedback mechanisms that normally produce corrective reaction.

Redirection of a society's objectives from emphasis on modernization to emphasis on other ends is much more unfavorable to modernization than diminution of means. After all, in time, the supply of means can be stepped up. But this will not take place unless the values of a society's leaders dictate that it shall take place, for traditionalist ideologies can become more powerful in the wake of independence. Group value differences can emerge, with the result that leaders divert resources from economic growth to the achievement of greater cultural unity. Or, as in Indonesia, appeal may be made to the political emotions of a people, rather than to their economic interests, with the result that such ends as economic autarchy are sought, even at the expense of a reduced standard of life.

LESSON FOR THE FUTURE

Three lessons emerge. First, until a country attains the capability for self-sustaining modernization and development, its progress is quite susceptible of interruption, resulting in stagnation and even decline. Second, even having attained such capability, a country remains susceptible to decelerative influences, if only because any and every potential source of progress is subject to exhaustion. Third, a country still in process of attaining this capability will fail if it ceases to emphasize the objective of growth or if it slackens unduly in its efforts to supply the means.

SELECTED BIBLIOGRAPHY

PHELPS-BROWN, E. H. *with* HANDFIELD-JONES, S. J. "The Climacteric of the 1890's: A Study in the Expanding Economy," *Oxford Economic Papers*, IV (October 1952), 266–307.

KIRBY, E. STUART. *Introduction to the Economic History of China*. London: Oxford University Press, 1954.

KUZNETS, SIMON. "Quantitative Aspects of the Growth of Nations. I. Levels and Variability of Rates of Growth," *Economic Development and Cultural Change*, V (October 1956), 5–94.

MADDISON, ANGUS. *Economic Growth in the West*. New York: Twentieth Century Press, 1964.

MALENBAUM, WILFRED. *Prospects for Indian Development*. Glencoe, Ill.: The Free Press, 1962.

NEF, JOHN U. *The Conquest of the Material World*. Chicago: University of Chicago Press, 1964.

PAUKER, G. J. "Indonesia in 1964: Toward A 'People's Democracy'?," *Asian Survey*, V (February 1965), 88–97.

ROSTOW, W. W., ed. *The Economics of Take-Off into Sustained Growth*. New York: St. Martin's, 1963.

SCHULTZ, THEODORE W. *Transforming Traditional Agriculture.* New Haven: Yale University Press, 1964.

SVENNILSON, INGVAR. *Growth and Stagnation in the European Economy.* Geneva, 1954.

WRIGLEY, E. A. "The Supply of Raw Materials in the Industrial Revolution," *Economic History Review,* XV (August 1962), 1–16.

V

CONCLUSION

Chapter 25

The International Gap

Lucian W. Pye

When the United Nations declared this "the decade of development," the overriding hope of all the officials involved was that through a massive effort it would be possible by the end of the decade to have reduced to some degree the gap between developed countries and the less-developed ones. No one assumed that in a scant ten years the emerging nations would have been able to achieve all that the developed ones have over many decades, and indeed centuries. The hope was, however, that a significant start could be made toward constructive development so that the distance between the rich countries and the poor would seem less great.

The record to date does not bear out the optimistic hope with which the United Nations initiated this effort. Each year, as the figures for economic growth have been reported from Asia, Latin America, and Africa, there is the disturbing realization that instead of reducing the gap, the trend in many cases has been in the opposite direction. The economies of the developed countries have been growing at an even more rapid rate; and even where many of the less-developed countries have shown successes in comparison with their past performances, they have not been able to keep pace in a relative sense.

Before we draw any gloomy conclusions from this record and

decide that the gap between rich and poor is going to increase over the years, we should first ask some questions about the proper ways of judging development within the less-developed areas of the world. What rates of growth should one expect in countries that are still finding themselves and only beginning to establish their new senses of identity? How much economic development can be expected in societies still seeking to achieve national integration? Are there any realistic criteria or standards of performance that we can use in measuring the progress of countries that are at the early stages of industrial life and organization?

Above all, in speaking about standards of judgment with respect to the problem of the gap between the developed and the less-developed, we must remember that we are treating only economic performance. There are, of course, numerous other ways in which human societies can be evaluated; and, needless to say, according to many of these, the difference between the "developed" and the "less-developed" disappears, and, indeed, in some categories it is precisely the latter that excel.

At the same time, there is the sobering reflection that, although in discussing the so-called gap we presume that we are treating economic matters only, there is considerable evidence that economic performance is, in fact, closely linked with a broad range of human life. Economic achievement is, for example, directly tied to the spirit of industry and entrepreneurship of a people and the nature and policies of their government; more indirectly, it is related to the ability to organize education, the capacity to generate and transmit knowledge, and the sophistication in relating scientific imagination to technological innovations. Clearly, the rate of economic growth of a society reflects something more than just economic reality, but exactly what the "more" is remains hard to tell.

Our uncertainty on this matter dramatizes the extent to which our knowledge about the developmental process is inadequate to provide us with either scientific theories to guide policies or a solid perspective for predicting probable patterns of development. Indeed, we must confess that in spite of all the attention that the problems of development have been given since the end of World War II, we are still in a position where intellectually it is very difficult to arrive at realistic forecasts about the prospects of development. And, of course, as long as we lack tested theories and proved methods for forecasting, it is impossible to establish any definitive standards for judging relative performance in national development.

There are several reasons for these intellectual deficiencies. The most important is that the process of development is inherently an extraordinarily complex one, involving such a range of factors that it is impossible as yet to treat the whole process systematically. Usually we can deal only with bits and parts, and although we have been accumulating a great deal of knowledge over the last few years, we cannot as yet fit it all together to make a general theory of development.

Under these conditions, it is all too easy to let hope, sentiment, and desire color the forecasts we make. Political leaders in the new countries should, and indeed have to, hold out the vision of rapid development as a realistic possibility, for they must inspire their peoples to ever greater efforts. The result, however, is that slogans often become confused with hard realistic predictions.

Even if we narrow down the problem of forecasting to technical considerations of economic development, the problem is still exceedingly difficult. For example, over the last few years, some of the countries that seemed to be in a good position to move ahead rather rapidly have run into difficulty, either of their own doing or as a result of factors beyond their control. On the other hand, there have been some countries that only a few years ago appeared to be in a stagnant condition with little prospect for advancement, but have dramatically changed and are now moving more rapidly ahead. There have been not only differences in the actual performances of countries but also changes in what specialists look for in making their judgments about the prospects for development. We have, for example, learned to place far less stress on some of the more spectacular features of economic development. A few years ago, many countries felt that if they could have certain symbols of development such as steel mills, industrial plants, new airports, and the like, they might be able to create the environment necessary for broader and more rapid growth. We now recognize that this is not the way to achieve significant development. We have learned that planning economic development is a very complex art and that it is not enough for a government simply to declare its intentions and to establish a planning commission. There is wise planning and foolish planning; there is flexible planning to adjust to changing realities and rigid planning that wastes scarce resources.

As we have increased our understanding of the prospects of development and as we have learned of ways in which eventually it may be possible to reduce the international gap, one conclusion has become unmistakably clear. This is that agriculture is going to be a most crucial area for the development of most of the newly emerging countries. Very few of them will be able to raise their standard of living without significant improvement in this area. This is in part because the vast majority of people in these countries depend on agriculture for their life. It is also true because agriculture provides the only possibility for obtaining the savings necessary to carry on industrial development.

At the same time, we have learned, unfortunately, that agriculture is an extremely complex form of economic activity, and it may not be easy to achieve significant improvements in this sector of life. This is true for several reasons. First, in most of the less-developed countries, agriculture does not have a high degree of prestige, and as a result it does not attract the attention and the energies of the more dynamic elements of the population. The bright young people who have the greatest potential to be the innovators in the society are not attracted to agriculture, in spite of its importance for national development.

Second, the problems of agriculture cannot be generalized; so it is impossible to adopt the practices and procedures that work in one area and apply them universally. Each area has its own peculiar problems that must be worked out within the context of the local setting. This is true not only in terms of transferring knowledge and learning from one country to another but even within a country. Indeed, one of the reasons for the failure of the Chinese Communists in their Great Leap Forward was that they tried to apply a single formula to the whole country. The Chinese have discovered that what works in one mountain or valley may not work in even a neighboring area. It is certainly impossible to follow a single plan for the entire country. Unfortunately, some of the non-Communist nations have not learned this lesson yet and are still trying to find single solutions for their entire countryside.

A third reason why it is hard to plan for rapid agricultural development is that it is peculiarly difficult to transfer technologies from the advanced agricultural countries to less-developed areas. In fields other than agriculture, such as the processing of steel, it is appropriate to construct the same type of plant and apply the same technology from one place in the world to another. When it comes to agriculture, however, there is a need to develop new kinds of technology for each type of agriculture. The kind of power tools that work in one environment will not be effective in another. This is particularly true, for example, with respect to the industrialization of rice production. Much of Western agricultural technology was developed in response to a basic shortage of man power in relation to land. In the countries of Asia and Africa, the opposite problem exists, and therefore quite different technological innovations are necessary.

A fourth reason why agriculture is such a difficult area for planning is that it involves such a complex of factors in the production and marketing of the product. Agriculture depends on large numbers of producers. Thus, there is the need to affect the attitudes, calculations, and expectations of a significant part of the population if there is to be impressive change. This is not so much the case with industrial development, where the process depends on the decisions of a far smaller number of people.

All of this suggests that rapid agricultural development will have to depend on new research and new creative work in each of the developing countries. This is the type of activity that calls for the collaboration of people from all over the world. Above all, there is the need for people within each country to contribute. Indeed, it would be impossible to overstress the importance of innovation and creativity in the whole developmental process. It is quite clear from an analysis of the problem of agriculture that change and growth are going to be closely tied to imaginative innovations in technology and social organization. Growth cannot come from just looking at the practices of the currently more de-

veloped countries. And what is true for agriculture is equally true
for all other aspects of development.

After all that has been said of the difficulties of getting rapid
agricultural development, we must recognize that there have been
some success stories in this area. Possibly the most dramatic example at the moment is that of East Pakistan. During the five years
from 1955 to 1960, agriculture here was in a state of stagnation.
The population was growing far more rapidly than output. Since
1960, however, there has been a profound change. During the five
years from 1960 to 1965, production has increased at a rate of 3.5
per cent—a rate that exceeds population growth. Indeed, at the
present time, planners are making the forecast that it may be possible for East Pakistan in the next five years to increase agricultural production at the rate of 6 to 7 per cent. These changes in East
Pakistan have altered the whole prospect of Pakistan's total economic growth. Pakistan has now moved into a category of being
one of the more promising of the less-developed countries with
respect to its planning goals. There have been some very fundamental structural changes in the pattern of relations between government and people in East Pakistan, encouraging far greater initiative on the part of the population. All of this augurs well for the
future.

I cannot dwell here on the other examples of successful development. Nor can I go into the setbacks and failures in some
countries. The important point is that in viewing the larger problem of the future of the less-developed countries, we must recognize that the story is likely to be a very uneven one marked by
successes in some areas and failures in others. This means that it is
not entirely appropriate to talk about all the underdeveloped
countries as though they had the same set of problems and shared
a common future.

In the last decade, it has been common to speak of the situation in just this way, for only when we pose the problem in such
an aggregate form can we talk about the gap between the rich
and the poor countries as though there were just two sides to the
story. However, as we look to the future, it is most reasonable to
expect that we shall see a world in which some countries achieve

great successes in overcoming their problems, while others do not. "Gaps" will thus begin to appear among the currently less-developed countries. Some will find that they are comfortably fitting into the modern picture, and their citizens will feel as much citizens of the world as are the people of developed countries. In other countries where even minimum development does not take place, there will be frustration and hostile feelings against all who seem more fortunate.

Since we cannot, even now, speak of all the less-developed countries as being at the same stage of development—and this will be even less likely in the future—it is not appropriate to paraphrase Lincoln's statement about freedom and suggest that "a world cannot long endure which is half rich and half poor." The truth is that in all countries there is a difference between rich areas and poor areas, and this difference is likely to continue for a long time to come. Indeed, during the last few years, the general concern with the problems of development have made some of the industrial countries more aware of their own backward areas. In the United States, for example, we have become quite sensitive to the problems of Appalachia. In Europe, there is a greater interest in the question of uneven economic development within all countries. The Soviet Union is concerned with enlarging economic development in some of its backward areas.

In short, domestic economic inequalities challenge all governments in varying measures; no land is without problems of poverty and growth.

The fact that we cannot at the present foresee the possibility of creating a world of uniform standards of economic life should not be taken to mean that there is not a great urgency to the whole problem of development. Indeed, the United Nations, in calling this "the decade of development," was pointing to the very serious fact that during this decade we may be advancing beyond the time in history when it will be possible for countries to develop. The note of urgency comes from the inescapable pressures of population and the shocking growth in the numbers of the world's people.

Any discussion of the future prospects of development must

treat seriously the discouraging fact that increasing population growth rates can easily soak up all the achievements to date and leave us with a world in which per capita standards of living are even lower than before. We must face the problem of population squarely and honestly. In many ways, it is a most depressing subject, for there is a great element of truth in Malthus' thesis that population grows at a geometrical rate, while economic growth can proceed only arithmetically.

It should be noted that the problem of population is not just a question of the ratio of man to land. True, in some parts of the world, the population situation is one in which there is a staggering number of mouths to be fed on very limited land. In other areas, however, where the man–land ratio is not as yet overwhelming, there may still be a serious hidden problem, owing to a very youthful population in which there are more consumers than people who are able to produce for the economy. For example, in West Africa over half the population is under fifteen years of age. The total population in terms of resources may not be so severe as it is in parts of Asia, but a majority are not productive. By the time they grow to the age of being productive, they are already beginning to reproduce more mouths and more consumers, so that the balance remains against greater savings and production. The result is that we shall probably see even a growing ratio of consumers to producers in Africa.

We are all familiar with the frightening projections of the world population growth. It is sobering to reflect that it took all of recorded time—at least a million years—for the world to reach its present population level of 3,300,000,000 people. Yet the second three billion people will be reached in only thirty-five years, and if the prohibitive 2 per cent yearly rate of increase is maintained, we shall find that the world population will be doubling every thirty-five years.

What this means with respect to some of the underdeveloped areas is truly staggering. India, the second most populous country in the world, has been struggling for the last ten years to raise its standard of living, and yet its population growth has been proceeding at so rapid a rate that the rise in per capita income has been meager. India, with more than 450 million people, will have 187 million more in fifteen years, according to the most reliable projections we have. This means that in the next fifteen years, India will have to find a way of feeding an increase in population that is about equivalent to the present population of the United States. The seriousness of this problem is underlined by the fact that last year one in every fifteen Indians was fed by imported surplus American grain.

If—and it is a very big if—we are able to achieve some check on the rate of population increase, then it does appear that at the current rate at which we are improving our technology and our understanding of the problems of development, it should be possible in much of the world to achieve at least certain minimal standards of well-being. For this goal to be achieved, however, a high degree of co-operation will be necessary. The people in the developing areas will have to collaborate with each other and with their governments to carry through the most effective planning possible. Industrial countries and the developing countries must help, too.

To speak of co-operation is to speak of political stability. Indeed, the whole prospect of economic development rests, in the end, on the possibility for political development.

During the last few years, there have been far too many glib generalizations about political development. In many cases, it is thought of as simply the political conditions necessary for economic development. At other times, we use the term to refer to political stability or political effectiveness. Some people also treat political development as being the same thing as democratic development.

I should like in these concluding remarks to point up the confusion that arises when we use such broad and undefined terms as "democracy" and "authoritarianism" in forecasting the prospects of national development. Some people argue that there are certain inherent advantages in authoritarian methods as compared with the democratic approach in speeding national development and reducing the international gap. Others justify poor performance in national development on the grounds of their commitment to democracy. In its most perverse form, this argument becomes one of pointing to governmental inefficiencies and even corruption as evidence of democracy.

What needs to be noted is that there have been a host of authoritarian societies that have not had great successes in national development. Indeed, there is quite as much evidence to suggest that authoritarian ways can impede rather than speed up modernization. There are, in short, both efficient and inefficient authoritarian systems, just as there are efficient and inefficient democracies.

Also it is important to observe that the characterization of "democratic" and "authoritarian" is much too general a label to describe usefully total approaches to political development. Authority is necessary in all political systems. Some institutions and processes, if properly conducted, must always reflect the spirit of authority appropriate to the society. Similarly, democratic institutions and practices must have their orderly dimension.

In practice, societies will differ in the ways in which they create a mix between authoritarian and democratic, between disciplined and fluid, between restricted and popular, practices and institutions. Some societies seem to be more comfortable if they are professing democratic ideals, while in many sectors of their life they adhere to highly rigid and even authoritarian procedures. In other societies, there may be less regard for the popular ideals of democracy and yet a remarkable degree of permissiveness in many aspects of public life.

What is important is for each society to achieve the mix that is constant with its cultural spirit and will make steady progress possible. Once a society feels at home with itself and senses that it has found its own national style, it can focus on achieving modernization in its own unique way.

Indeed, once a people has achieved the dual goals of expressing its uniqueness and realizing progress in becoming a part of the modern world, the question of relative position in a pluralistic community of nations will no longer seem so important. More particularly, if individuals are able to find themselves in some of the modern professions and then become fully competent teachers, doctors, lawyers, soldiers, or administrators, they can

stand in a spirit of equality with their professional peers everywhere. The fact that the aggregate economic statistics for their
homeland are not so high as those for another will have no more
significance than the fact that within any developed country there
are similar regional inequalities.

Index

349